ELIXIR

A Journey into Ancestral Alchemology

GISELLA ROSE

ELIXIR: A Journey into Ancestral Alchemology

First Edition

ISBN: 979-8-9987155-0-1

Printed in the United States of America

Published by **Sangetta Star Arts & Publishing LLC**

www.somamagical.com

Cover Design: Kam Bains https://www.kamthedesigner.com/

Interior Artwork, Editing & Formatting: Gisella Rose https://www.somamagical.com/

Legal Disclaimer

This book is intended for educational and inspirational purposes only. The information within is not meant to replace medical, psychological, or therapeutic care. Always consult a qualified professional before beginning any new health, movement, or spiritual practice.

The author and publisher disclaim any liability for loss, injury, or damage resulting from the use or application of any information presented in this work.

For the woman who birthed me,

my Mother

For the child I have birthed,

my Son

For my Ancestors

For my Father

For my Family

For the Stars

For the Moon

For Earth

For our Remembering

A NOTE FROM THE AUTHOR

This book shares practices, reflections, and insights intended to support your journey. This is not medical advice and should not be used as a replacement for therapeutic care.

ELIXIR is rooted in lived experience, shaped through ancestral research, astrological exploration, and transformational work within my own lineage and with others. While this work has been informed by years of study across mystical, somatic, and spiritual traditions, what you'll find here is my synthesis, an intuitive body of work developed through practice, experimentation, and deep listening.

It reflects the essence of **Ancestral Alchemology**: a grounded, creative method of connecting with your roots through ritual, astrology, embodiment, and sacred remembrance.

If you feel called to explore more deeply, you can connect with me at:

www.somamagical.com

Gisella Rose

TABLE OF CONTENT INGREDIENTS

Part Five
WE ARE THE ANCESTORS OF THE FUTURE

INTRODUCTION

At the age of three, I experienced a moment that would forever shape my relationship with life, death, and the unseen. I was on the verge of drowning in a swimming pool. My heart stopped. My consciousness began to drift. As darkness enveloped me, I saw my Mother, pregnant with my sister, reaching out her hand to rescue me. Time slowed. That moment, suspended between two worlds, remains etched in the deepest layers of my being.

Since that day, I have felt tethered to more than this life alone. I walk within the liminal, a mysterious in-between space that has colored how I love, create, and seek meaning. I am a dancer. An artist. A genealogist. An astrologer. A mystic. A mother. A daughter. These aspects of self intertwine like threads in a ritual cloth, guiding and shaping the path I walk.

My work lives in the spaces that connect the living with the dead, the past with the present. In tracing family trees, I act as a bridge, linking generations and carrying the echoes of those who came before into the lives of those who follow.

That near-death experience was more than a moment of survival, it was an awakening. It marked the beginning of my life's calling.

Genealogy, for me, is not simply the study of ancestry. It is a sacred act. To construct a family tree is to build a temple of memory. To uncover forgotten names and hidden stories is to light candles in the dark. This is reverence. This is ritual. This is remembering.

Through this work, I discovered a radiant thread that connects genealogy with astrology—a place where the mystical and the tangible meet. That discovery became a doorway into a new path: the creation of **Ancestral Alchemology**.

Elixir is the culmination of that journey.

It is a guide into our hidden histories, the ancestral gifts and griefs that live within us, and the healing power of remembrance. This book invites us to recognize that while we are rooted in the stories of our ancestors, we are also part of a vast and interconnected mystery. We are not separate, we are part of a grand and luminous design. A sacred web woven across time, spirit, and breath.

Part One

ANCESTRAL ALCHEMOLOGY

What is
Ancestral Alchemology?

Ancestral Alchemology is a *transformational* practice that connects us deeply with our family *lineage* and the *essence* of our *ancestors*. It is a *sacred* journey of **alchemical** discovery, where we become **vessels** capable of *transmuting* inherited energies into something **powerful** and **intentional**. This practice integrates *genealogy*, *astrology*, and the *elemental* energies of **Fire, Water, Earth,** and **Air,** revealing the patterns woven into the fabric of our family histories. Through this *exploration*, we uncover the hidden *mysteries* of our family trees— insights shaped by *Alchemical Ancestral* energies and *elemental essences* that have been present through *generations* into the present day.

Imagine yourself as a *vessel*, akin to a bottle crafted by the **Earth** and filled with the **Waters** of your *lineage*. These **Waters** carry emotions, wisdom, and experiences passed down through generations. The interplay of the elements - **Fire, Water, Earth,** and **Air** - affects the energy flow within your own life and your family's *lineage*.

At its core, Ancestral Alchemology strengthens our bond with those who came before us, the natural world, and the cosmic magic that permeates all life.

This *Alchemical* process reveals how the **Fire** within us ignites *transformation*, burning away stagnation and catalyzing growth. The **Waters** within us **must be stirred and filtered**, often carrying *treasures* and *sediment*. These *sediments* - **traumas, struggles,** and **unresolved patterns** - settle at the bottom of our being, but through intentional practice, they can be transformed into clarity and understanding. The breath of **Air** inspires and expands our perspective, while **Earth** provides grounding and stability, offering the structure necessary for true healing and integration.

A key aspect of *Ancestral Alchemology* is the creation of *MoonTree Charts*. These charts are **alchemical blueprints** that map out the *elemental* and *astrological* influences within your family tree. Unlike natal charts, which analyze *astrological* influences for an individual, *MoonTree Charts* simplify this information into an elemental framework specific to your *lineage*, focusing on the ***Sun, Moon,*** and ***Venus.*** These charts reveal the *astrological elemental* patterns that flow through *generations*, showcasing the shared energies that shape family dynamics.

- For instance, a *lineage* strong in **Water, Earth,** and **Fire** may carry emotional depth, resilience, and creative passion, qualities that ripple through *generations* like the currents of a river. By understanding these ***elemental patterns***, we can identify the hidden strengths within our *lineage* and the inherited challenges and opportunities for growth.

Combining *Genealogy, Astrology,* and *Elemental Magic* into this unique *method* of exploring family histories. *Ancestral Alchemology* reveals the energetic flows and hidden dynamics, it offers *valuable* insights into the *interconnected* nature of our lives. This journey entails not only observing surface traits but also delving into the deeper layers of *elemental energy and astrological patterns within our lineage.*

THE ELEMENTS - *FIRE, WATER, EARTH,* AND *AIR* - BECOME TOOLS FOR UNDERSTANDING THESE ENERGIES:

- **Fire**: ignites passion and transformation, providing the heat necessary to purify and reshape.
- **Water**: carries emotional depth, acting as the menstruum that holds ancestral wisdom and nurtures intuitive flow.
- **Earth**: provides stability and grounding, serving as the vessel that keeps us steady throughout this process.

- **Air**: brings inspiration, clarity, and expansion into our work, helping us envision and create new possibilities.

This *alchemical* process encourages a deep exploration of our inner selves, unearthing past traumas and challenges. This process offers a chance to **recognize, rework,** and **release** these burdens, thus paving the path toward transformational healing. This *sacred* work both re-establishes our connection to **life's** natural *cycles* and grounds us in the vast **cosmic** order. Understanding our *lineage's* inherent strengths allows us to mend *Ancestral* wounds, appreciate *Ancestral* gifts, and cultivate a deeper relationship with our surroundings. *Ancestral Alchemology's* illuminating insights unlock *Ancestral mysteries*, bridging past and present, and it unites the wisdom of our ancestors with the infinite possibilities of tomorrow. Through **experiencing, cultivating, embodiment** of and **creating** with this *alchemical* process, we not only reconnect with our origins and embrace our *lineage* but also move forward with **purpose, spirit,** and **love**. As we *root* down, we send more *love* into the collective - the web that connects all living beings.

*Ancestral Alchemology
is a Practice that
Connects the Living & the Dead*

———•———

Elemental forces and *celestial* rhythms, the same ones affecting us today, shaped our ancestors' lives. Whether through *astrology, genealogy,* or the symbolism of **Earth, Air, Fire,** and **Water,** *Ancestral Alchemology* offers a curious lens through which we can view our lives as part of a continuum, a flowing narrative *embued* by the **decisions, triumphs,** and **lessons** of those who came before us. This practice **isn't static; it's dynamic,** like a river carving its path through time. **Decoding** *Ancestral* patterns reveals our deep connection to the natural *cycles* of ***growth, decay,*** and ***renewal.*** It invites us to reflect on our place in this larger story and consider how we can carry it forward with intention. *Ancestral Alchemology* involves both letting go and holding on. Through this practice, we honor our *ancestors* not by clinging to their burdens but by *transforming* them. This **act** of release is a profound *alchemy* that turns pain into *wisdom* and *limitations* into possibilities. It's a journey filled with hope and **inspiration**, demonstrating that *transformation* is always attainable. The process of release requires **compassion** for ourselves, our *ancestors*, and the complex histories intertwined within us. It invites us to approach these **stories** with **empathy**, acknowledging the struggles of those who came before while freeing ourselves from **patterns** that no longer serve us. This emphasis on **compassion** fosters understanding and kindness in our *healing* journey.

———•———

*Letting go does not erase the past.
It transforms it into fertile
ground for new growth*

CULTIVATING HEALING FOR THE COLLECTIVE

Cultivating healing for the *collective* involves exploring connections between **ancestry,** our **bodies,** and the **cosmos** to align with a greater *rhythm.* This journey is both personal and communal, as we delve into the depths of our *lineage* and *roots.* Healing our *Ancestral lineage* and *roots* contributes to a collective ***Ancestral* garden,** blooming with resilience, understanding, and compassion. By becoming *stewards* of our heritage, we ensure that the energy we transmit forward is positive and in tune with *love,* kindness, and future possibilities. Through this *transformational* process, we *venerate* and pay tribute to *Ancestral* strengths, break free from inherited patterns, and sow the **seeds** of a ***living and loving legacy*** that will continue to *nurture* and inspire future *generations.*

An Invitation to Begin

This *book* serves as your guide to the world of *Ancestral Alchemology.* Whether you are just starting to explore your *roots* or are already well-versed in **genealogy** and **astrology**, this practice provides tools to uncover the hidden treasures within your *lineage.* You don't need to know every detail of your family tree or have all the answers before you start. This *journey* is about discovery, *listening, reflecting,* and moving forward with *intention.* Each step brings you closer to understanding and recognizing the **gifts** you inherit from those who came before you.

Ancestral Alchemology teaches us that *healing* is not about perfection, but about **connection**. It provides room for growth, respects life cycles, and enables the wisdom of the past to shine a light on the present. You are invited to let this ***method become a practice,*** *integrate* it into your established practices, create *rituals,* and allow it to guide you as you delve into the *mysteries* of your *lineage,* the *rhythms* of the *cosmos,* and the wisdom within yourself. Delve into the beauty of *transformation,* merging the **past** and **present** to shape a **future** grounded in *clarity*, *balance*, and *purpose*.

> *"The alchemist's way of regarding things is not only one of the oldest but also one of the most fundamental and one of the most truly empirical."*

— CARL JUNG

COSMIC FLOWERS

Honoring Our Earth Mother

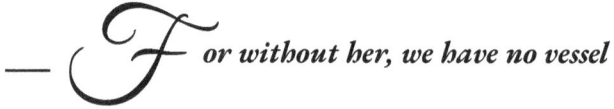

— or without her, we have no vessel

WE ARE NOT JUST PART OF **Nature**; we are **Nature** itself. This profound connection shapes our feelings, experiences, and relationships, presenting challenges and growth opportunities. The rhythms of the **Earth**, which mirror our own, guide us through cycles of growth, loss, and renewal. By immersing ourselves in the elements - **Earth, Water, Air,** and **Fire** - we tap into their wisdom and re-establish our connection with the universe.

Cosmic Flowers

The *Sun, Moon*, and *Venus* movements resonate with the elemental rhythms crucial to *Ancestral Alchemology*. The *Sun* and *Moon*, acting as our cosmic parents, profoundly influence our lives. The *Sun* symbolizes energy and purpose, while the *Moon* represents feelings and intuition. Together, they shape our existence through the subtle energy channels in our bodies. *Venus*, embodying love and harmony, bridges the celestial and Earthly, providing the nurturing guidance of our cosmic parents. The union of the *Sun* and *Moon* creates life, grounding their children in these elemental forces. *Ancestral Alchemology* centers on the *Sun, Moon,* and *Venus*, recognizing their roles as cosmic parents connecting us to our *Ancestral* lines through **life, death,** and **rebirth** *cycles*. Our inherited *energetic* and *somatic* **patterns**, as well as the energies that shape us, are reflected in these *elements*.

———

Other planets, like *Saturn*, which imbues **discipline**, and *Jupiter*, which cultivates **expansion**, enhance this understanding by offering additional insights into the energies we receive from our ancestors. However, in *Ancestral Alchemology,* the main focus remains on the ***Sun, Moon,*** and ***Venus***, helping us uncover the hidden **patterns** of our *lineage* and the wisdom and ***magic*** that are etched into our *bones*.

The Elements like Wind, Rain, and Sun teach us about resilience and impermanence.

- **Earth** provides *stability* and *grounding*, teaching us resilience and the importance of building sound foundations to navigate life's obstacles.
- **Water** signifies *emotional* adaptability and the ability to *let go*, encouraging us to release what no longer serves us and to *heal* openly.
- **Air** promotes *creativity* and clear thinking, *planting* new ideas and possibilities.
- **Fire** represents courage and transformation, *clearing* away the past and *motivating* us to pursue our goals.

———

Through these *elements* and their *cosmic* influences, *Ancestral Alchemology* helps us appreciate our *connection* to life's *cycles*, the wisdom of the **Earth**, and the *cosmic* forces connected to our existence.

Our Cosmic Parents - Sun & Moon

The SUN & Moon

THE *Sun* AND *Moon* ARE MORE THAN JUST CELESTIAL BODIES in the sky; they profoundly shape our daily lives and influence our emotions. The *Sun* brings energy and encourages us to be creative and purposeful. In contrast, with its gentle glow, the *Moon* helps us look inward by providing emotional insight and the strength to adapt to change. Together, they *embody* the balance between our external actions and internal thoughts, light and darkness, activity and rest. These *cosmic parents* remind us that life has its ups and downs. Like them, we *experience* times of renewal and letting go. The *Sun* encourages us to be brave and take action, while the *Moon* invites us to pause and reflect. Their *relationship* mirrors the dualities we encounter in our desire to push forward, our need to recharge, and our strengths and weaknesses. **Connecting** with their *cycles* allows us to find balance within ourselves and the universe. With each breath, we tap into both the *Earth* and the *sky*. The *Sun* energizes us to act and create, while the *Moon* brings calmness, facilitating reflection and understanding of our emotions. Our *ancestors* recognized this connection, using the *Moon's* phases to plan farming, celebrating the *Sun* during critical times of the year, and looking to the *cosmos* for wisdom. These *rhythms* are not just historical; they guide us today.

WE CAN RECONNECT WITH THESE *ANCIENT ENERGIES* BY focusing on the *Sun*, *Moon*, and *Venus*. The *Sun* fuels our creative spirit; the *Moon* deepens our emotional understanding. *Venus* encourages us to seek beauty, harmony, and genuine *connections*. Together, these forces help us live in alignment with Nature, balancing our actions, *reflections*, and *relationships*. The *Sun*, *Moon*, and *Venus* each symbolize key aspects of both our inner and outer lives, imparting unique lessons. The **Sun** inspires us to be **confident**, focus on our **strengths**, and share our *gifts* with others, inspiring *creativity* and *action*. The **Moon** reminds us of the importance of *cycles*, **growing**, letting go, and **renewing**, helping us reflect on our *feelings* and work with the *shadows* of our subconscious through honoring the *lunation*. **Venus** invites us to *cultivate* and plant strong *connections*, to appreciate the surrounding *beauty* of *life*, and to enjoy the harmony in our relationships. and lead a life with **heart**.

ECHOES OF ANCESTRAL WISDOM

The **Sun**, **Moon**, and **Venus** also connect us to the wisdom of our ancestors. Ancient cultures observed their cycles for survival and guidance, incorporating them into *rituals* and everyday life. People revered the **Sun** as the source of **life**, using its **rising** and **setting** to track the passage of time. The **Moon** served as a guide for change, with its phases aligning with Nature's pace and life's cycles. **Venus** inspires *creativity*, love, and appreciation for the connections that support us. By engaging with these **celestial patterns** today, we honor this *Ancestral* wisdom. They remind us that life is *cyclical* and interconnected, bridging the **past**, **present**, and **future**. Aligning ourselves with these *rhythms* gives us *strength, clarity,* and *purpose*.

The Moon's enchanting light reveals the wisdom of our ancestors. while the Water reflects the stories of our past. connecting us to the present

THE FOUR PILLARS OF ANCESTRAL ALCHEMOLOGY

Genealogy, Astrology, Alchemy and Elemental Magic

his method revolves around four *core* elements: ***Genealogy, Astrology, Alchemy,*** and ***Elemental Magic,*** which together establish the basis of *Ancestral Alchemology*. By blending *ancient* traditions with *modern* perspectives, *Ancestral Alchemology* provides a distinctive approach to delving into our *ancestry* and *relationship* with the *cosmos*.

Discovering Our Roots

1. Genealogy

Genealogy connects us to the stories of our *ancestors*, forming the basis of who we are. By using *family records, oral histories*, and today's DNA testing, we discover the people that came before us and the wisdom *woven* through our family lines. In *Ancestral Alchemology*, *genealogy* goes beyond collecting names and dates; it's about venerating and exploring the lives and legacies of our *ancestors*. Discovering *birth dates* and places of birth is essential to *decoding* patterns and energies within your *Ancestral* family tree. All types of *lineage*, **biological**, **chosen**, or **adoptive**, hold significant meaning, and we collect and research the lineages and lines we are called to explore first, and in their own time, our *Ancestors* by blood, chosen, and of place connect and *spiral* back in. Through exploring our *roots*, we connect with the wisdom of our **past** while paving a *healthy* and *magical* path forward. *Genealogical research* is a meaningful act of *connection* that honors the legacy shaping us and *plants* our place in the larger story of life.

2. Astrology   *Mapping Celestial Connections*

Astrology helps us understand the *cosmic* influences impacting our lives and *lineage*, particularly in *Ancestral Alchemology*, where we focus on the **Sun**, **Moon**, and **Venus** as central aspects of this **decoding** method. These placements in *natal charts* reveal emotional, creative, and spiritual patterns inherited from our families. In *Ancestral Alchemology*, the *MoonTree Chart* serves as a visual representation of *astrological* and *elemental* themes shared within a family. For example, recurring **Water** placements might indicate a *lineage* rich in *emotional* depth, while dominant **Earth** influences could point to a legacy of *stability*. This *method* allows us to uncover unseen *Ancestral* patterns, linking the personal and *cosmic* realms. Ultimately, *astrology* transforms our family tree into a collection of shared energies, providing insights that deepen our understanding of ourselves and our connection to the universe and our *lineage*.

3. Alchemy   *Transforming Inherited Patterns*

Alchemy is about *transformation*, turning base materials into something valuable. *Ancestral Alchemology* symbolizes our ability to change *inherited* challenges into strengths, encouraging us to engage with our *lineage's* **gifts** and *shadows*. By recognizing *inherited* traits and letting go of what no longer serves us, we create space for *renewal* and growth. *Alchemy* teaches that *transformation* involves reshaping the **past** into something **meaningful** and **empowering**, aligning us with natural *cycles* of change and *renewal*. This practice and method explore the journeys of our *ancestors* while embracing our full potential.

4. Elemental Magic

Aligning with Nature's Forces

With the final pillar, *Elemental Magic,* we *align* ourselves with the primary forces of **Earth**, **Air**, **Fire**, and **Water**. Each of these *elements* **embodies** unique *energies*. **Earth** provides *stability*, **Air** nurtures *creativity* and *clarity*, **Fire** sparks *passion* and *courage*, and **Water** promotes *adaptability* and *emotional* flow.

———————

IN THIS PRACTICE, WE CREATE ENERGETIC ***ANCESTRAL Alchemical Potions*** infused with *elemental* and *astrological* energies from the *Moon Tree Chart*. These ***potions*** are tools for healing, transformation, cultivating intuition, and tapping into our unique magic. *Elemental magic* is part of our daily lives, for example, walking barefoot on the **Earth**, breathing deeply outdoors to feel the **Air**, lighting a candle to connect with **Fire**, or bathing in **Water**. When we notice these daily *elemental rituals* and move through them with intention, we create a deeper *connection* with ourselves, with *Nature,* our *ancestors,* and the *cosmos.*

———————

We embody the stories of our Ancestors, carrying their wisdom as we move with the rhythms of existence

THE BIRTH OF THIS BOOK

My Story

I created this book to share *Ancestral Alchemology* and with the purpose of providing a simple way for everyone to connect with their *ancestors*, establishing a personal and meaningful link to our *heritage*. Through this *connection*, we can honor the **past** while embracing the **present**. Each of us harbors the *elemental* forces of **Fire**, **Earth**, **Water**, and **Air**, and comprehending these elements *empowers* us to derive strength from our *lineage*. The concept of *Ancestral Alchemology* stemmed from a significant near-death experience in my youth, profoundly influencing my **life** and understanding of the elements. **Water**, in particular, holds great significance for me, as it was the element that nearly claimed my life before ultimately restoring me. As a child, I had a close brush with drowning, slipping into unconsciousness as my *heart* ceased to beat. Just before I lost consciousness, I saw my *Mother* pregnant with my unborn *sister*, reaching towards me, to save me. **Water**, symbolizing the essence of the *Mother*, embodies nurturing qualities, is life-affirming, and is deeply associated with emotions and transformation. *Astrologically*, this connection permeates through my *lineage*, with my *Mother's* **Moon** being in *Scorpio*, a **Water** sign. My *astrological* makeup — *Pisces* **Sun**, *Cancer* **Moon**, and *Scorpio* Rising — is rooted in the **Water** element. This *elemental* resonance has been a defining aspect of my **life**, influencing how I navigate the world and connect with my *lineage*. This influence even manifested during my *birth*, as I was born **en caul**, still enclosed in the amniotic sac, a rare occurrence known as a *"mermaid birth."*

The Motherline and the Elemental Ties of Water

MY STORY

Stardust Elixir & Roses - My Story

I AM HONORED TO CARRY MY **MATERNAL** *GRANDMOTHER'S* name, a legacy that has always held special meaning for me. I was born ten months after her passing, yet I have always felt a deep *connection* with her that transcends both *time* and *space*. Even at the young age of three, I *instinctively* understood the importance of the **Mother-line**, the thread of **wisdom, love, nurture**, and **resilience** that runs through *generations*. **Water**, with its fluid nature, mirrors the *essence* of **life** - the capacity to **carry, purify**, and **rejuvenate**. It has taught me to respect the *cyclical* rhythm of existence, navigate through and tap into profound emotions and intuition, and draw *strength* from surrendering and *flowing* with **life's** currents. This personal *journey*, enriched by the *alchemy* of the elements, led to the development of *Ancestral Alchemology*. This practice intertwines the **tangible** with the **mystical**, enabling us to comprehend how the *elemental* forces of **Fire, Earth, Water**, and **Air** influence our *lineage* and paths. The book I present to you is a tool to *support* you in *exploring* your *elemental* bonds, honoring your *Ancestral* threads, and **crafting** a personal *ritual* that nurtures *connection* and growth.

My Introduction to Astrology and the Elements

Despite our small size, my family was far from ordinary. **Mysticism** was intertwined with our daily lives, making *astrology* a natural topic of conversation. This early exposure ignited a lifelong *journey* of discovery, influencing my understanding of my **family, myself**, and the **elements** that impact us all. At the age of eight, my *Mother* and *Uncle* introduced me to *astrology*, linking each sign to the **four elements: Water** for *Pisces*, **Earth** for *Virgo*, **Fire** for *Sagittarius*, and so on. They illustrated how these elements interact, showcasing their *dynamic* relationships. They taught me that an excess of **Fire** can dry things out, while an abundance of **Water** can extinguish **Fire** or muddy the **Earth**. These lessons felt like revelations, *unveiling* a deeper comprehension of how the natural world mirrors our *inner* lives. The way these *elemental* forces combined to form something new, like *relationships* between individuals, intrigued me. For instance, the *interplay* of **Sun Signs** could influence our *connections* and experiences, offering insights into the unique dynamics within families and friendships. This concept fascinated me, and I eagerly *absorbed* all I could, immersing myself in *Linda Goodman's* books and analyzing the *elemental* **patterns** within myself and others. *Astrology* unfolded from a mere curiosity into a full-fledged *passion*. As I delved *deeper*, I learned that our **Moon Signs** reflect our emotional core and *subconscious* nature. My rudimentary understanding of *astrology* expanded, revealing the *layers* beneath the external identity of **Sun Signs**. The **Moon Sign** dictates how we **feel**, **react**, and **navigate** our *inner world*. By the time I was ten or eleven, I routinely asked people if they knew their **Moon Sign**. If they were unsure, I would assist them in *calculating* it using the planetary charts from a book I always had in my backpack. For me, it wasn't just *enjoyable*—it was a means to connect with others and share the **enchantment** of *astrology*.

My early interest in *astrology* eventually led me to discover its *connection* to *genealogy*, which laid the foundation for *Ancestral Alchemology*. *Astrology* not only provides insights into individual traits, but when paired with family tree research, it brings our family history to life as a vibrant library of *Ancestral* stories. Viewing a family tree through an *astrological* lens reveals more than just names and dates; it unveils the **lives**, **patterns**, and **energies** of our *ancestors*. Each *ancestor* emerges as a distinct presence, their characteristics *illuminated* by the *celestial* alignments at the time of their *birth*. For instance, a *grandparent* with prominent **Water** placements may have left a legacy of **emotional** depth, **intuition**, or **adaptability**. By merging *astrology* with *genealogy*, we deepen our *connection* to our *ancestors*, transforming dry records into **narratives** that *echo* the *cosmic* influences in their lives and ours. Exploring the *elemental* and *astrological* **patterns** within our *lineage* creates a link between the **past** and **present**, showing how *celestial* forces shaped our *ancestors'* experiences and how those energies continue to flow through us. Just as the *elements* of **Fire**, **Water**, **Earth**, and **Air** interact in a natal chart, they also influence the energies within our *lineage*. This fusion of *genealogy* and *astrology* lies at the core of *Ancestral Alchemology*, breathing **life** and depth into our family history while grounding *astrology* in the tangible experiences of our *ancestors*. Together, they offer a comprehensive framework for understanding the forces that mold our lives and *lineage*. This **fusion** of *mysticism* and family heritage *embodies* the *essence* of *Ancestral Alchemology*, a method that honors the *interconnectedness* of **elements**, **stars**, and **ancestors**. It serves as a reminder of our role in a profound *narrative* shaped by those who came before us and one that we, in turn, will shape for those who follow.

Grief, Astrology, and the Bridge Between Generations

Following my *Mother's* unexpected passing, **grief** took on a dual role in my **life**. It served as both a *devastating* force and a *transformative* **gift** that reshaped my *connection* to family history. Her loss marked a life-altering moment that *shattered* my world. Even before her passing, I had looked into my family's *genealogy*. However, her **death** *intensified* my interest, turning it into an obsession, almost for a time. *Genealogy* became a **bridge** between the **living** and the **dead**, a way to *preserve* her **memory** while uncovering the ties of our shared *lineage*. I delved deeply into her *astrological* signs, meticulously researching even the *lunar phase* during her passing. This exploration **grounded** me, offering insights and *solace* as I unraveled not only her *story* but also the broader *narrative* of our family. It led me to delve into my ***grandmother's*** *astrology* and older generations, expanding the *magical* web of our family history. Just like a growing **tree**, our family *stories* continued to deepen and expand with each new piece of knowledge gained. Initially, I integrated *astrological* details, specifically **Moon Signs**, into my genealogical research, a practice I called **GeneaLunagy,** which later grew into **Ancestral Alchemology**. The ***Moon***, with its intimate *connection* to **emotions** and **intuition**, emerged as a pivotal element in deciphering the emotional undercurrents within my lineage and what I like to call the "**Shadow Thread**". Recognizing these **patterns** was not just enlightening, but also crucial in navigating and processing my *grief*. Throughout my life's journey, I have developed a *powerful* belief in **reincarnation**. I perceive our lives as *intertwined* through time, repeatedly connecting us to our *ancestors*. The *roots* of our **past** influence our **present** and extend into the **future**.

WE ARE THE *ANCESTORS* OF THE FUTURE, AND THE *HEALING* we partake in today resonates through *generations* both before and after us. This belief binds us to a **collective** *Ancestral* wellspring, a reservoir of shared *wisdom* and energy that binds all individuals across time. This **exploration** has been meaningful in my process of *grief*. With my *Moon* in *Cancer*, a sign that embodies nurturing and protection, I deeply resonate with my relationship with my Mother. Her passing created a void that compelled me to investigate the *Moon Signs* of my family members. Starting with her, I delved into the *Moon Signs* of her *parents* and *grandparents*, tracing the emotional and intuitive threads of our lineage. For relatives whose exact birth times were unknown, I gathered whatever information was available, piecing together their planetary alignments with the resources at my disposal.

THE PRACTICE OF ANCESTRAL ALCHEMOLOGY BECAME AN invaluable tool in this endeavor. Even without precise birth times, I could determine the Sun, Moon, and planetary positions based on birth dates, years, and locations. With this discovered information, I could map out the celestial patterns that influenced their lives and even uncover the lunar phase under which they were born - Waxing, Waning, or Full. These **patterns** unveiled remarkable insights. For instance, recurring lunar phases or prevailing elemental themes surfaced, linking one generation to the next. These revelations provided a profound outlook, aiding me in processing my grief and recognizing the continuum between the past, present, and future. This journey of grief and exploration has enabled me to pay tribute to my ancestors, uncovering their stories while finding meaning and solace in my own. By delving into their planetary alignments and elemental influences, I have realized how their energy flows within me and shapes the world around me. We serve as **vessels** of inherited energy, carrying the essence of those who came before us. The elements - **Fire**, **Earth**, **Water**, and **Air** - live within us, reflecting the dynamics of our lineage. Similar to how the *Moon's* phases mirror *cycles* of growth and release, our lives follow patterns influenced by cosmic forces and *Ancestral wisdom*. This endeavor has revealed to me that **grief** is not a conclusion but a **gateway**, an opportunity to forge deeper *connections* with the **past** and carry its *wisdom* into the future. By embracing the narratives of my *ancestors*, I have discovered healing in their teachings and resilience in their journeys. This practice acts as a *sacred* bridge that enables us to pay homage, heal, and strengthen ourselves and the forthcoming generations, imbuing *lineages* with understanding, veneration, and **love**.

OUR ALCHEMICAL ELIXIR

The Elixir
of
Ancestral Alchemology

ANCESTRAL ELIXIR

his is a *sacred* journey into *essence* - a remembrance of who we are through the intricate threads of *ancestry*, the living *elements* of Nature, and the guiding energies of the *cosmos*. Like an

Alchemical potion, this practice invites us to become the **vessel**, holding within us the *raw materials* of our *lineage*. Through the process of the *Ancestral Alchemology* method of *Ancestral* exploration, we awaken the *mysticism* embedded in our *lineage*, transmuting the **past** and opening space for both personal and collective *transformation*. At its **heart** is the recognition that we are the *living bottle* of this sacred *elixir*, our bodies the container, our lives the medium. The **Waters** of our *lineage* swirl within us as the *menstruum*, the sacred *solvent* of change. The **Fire** within ignites *transformation*, bringing warmth and *illumination* to inherited experiences. **Air** moves through us like breath, *expanding* awareness, carrying clarity, and sparking *insight*. **Earth** anchors and *steadies* us, offering a grounded container for this **sacred** work. Even the **sediments**, the *traumas*, *griefs*, and *unresolved* stories are vital **ingredients**. They hold the *raw material* for healing, refinement, and growth. This *alchemical* process is not only a journey through **Earth** and *body*, but it is also a *magical* dialogue with the *cosmos*. The **Sun** lends vitality and *courage*. The **Moon** illuminates *intuition* and emotional truth. **Venus** brings harmony, beauty, and connection. **Earth** offers *grounding* and presence. Together, these **celestial** forces weave with the *elements*, aligning us with universal *rhythms* while anchoring us in the *Ancestral* stories that live within us. Through this *sacred* alchemy, we begin to **distill** the unique *potions* of our becoming, transforming the raw inheritance of our *ancestry* into an *elixir* of **resilience**, **remembrance**, and **embodied** *wisdom*. *Ancestral Alchemology* invites us to harmonize with the *rhythms* of **Nature**, attune to *cosmic* guidance, and become **vessels** of **lineage magic**, allowing its **mysticism** to move through us and into the world.

The Art of Spiritual Wildcrafting

Life is a living **garden** woven with hidden *treasures*. Emotions, experiences, and insights waiting to be unearthed. *Spiritual Wildcrafting* is the **art** of tending this inner terrain, gathering what arises, and *transforming* even the most unexpected **moments** into *medicine*. It invites us to turn challenges into tools for growth and to uncover the *extraordinary* hidden within the ordinary. By approaching each moment with **presence, curiosity,** and **love,** we elevate *experience* into meaning. With *reflection* and *courage,* obstacles become **invitations,** pathways to *resilience, transformation,* and deeper **self-discovery.** *Spiritual Wildcrafting* is not separate from daily life; it moves through it, quietly and powerfully. Each step, conversation, and moment of stillness becomes part of the *sacred* tending of the **garden** that we are. When we nurture this **garden** with *intention,* we **cultivate** harmony within *ourselves,* in relationship with *others,* and with the **Earth** itself. This practice allows our truest *essence* to rise and be expressed, fully and **authentically,** *rooted* in **presence** and alive with **purpose.**

Alchemizing, Extracting, and Transforming

Alchemy is more than an **ancient** science, it is a *sacred* metaphor for personal and spiritual *transformation.* It invites us to recognize the untapped potential hidden within life's *raw materials* and engage in a *conscious* process of *shadow work, healing,* and *growth.* When we learn to **extract** meaning from experience, we **transmute** pain into understanding and adversity into **embodied** *wisdom.* This **alchemical** path is one of *integration.* It asks us to meet both **light** and **shadow** with *honesty,* allowing the full spectrum of our being to reveal itself. Through this union, we uncover our *essence,* the truth of who we are, and the *magic* we carry in our bones. The process is not *linear,* but **fluid,** like the metaphorical **Waters** that live within us, *deep, emotional,* and *Ancestral.* These **Waters** are *sacred* reservoirs of *intuition,* memory, and emotion, passed down through *generations.* They carry the **joys** and insights of those who came before, as well as the **sediments**—the unresolved *griefs* and **patterns** that *settled* over time. By entering into a *relationship* with these **Waters,** we open ourselves to the emotional *wisdom* of our *lineage* and begin to move it through us with *reverence.* The *Ancestral* **Waters** remind us that we are part of a greater, flowing narrative, one where the **past** moves with us, molding the **present** and laying the groundwork for what is yet to come in the **future**.

Crafting the
Ancestral Alchemical Potion

At the heart of *Ancestral Alchemology* is the **Ancestral Alchemical Potion**, a symbolic elixir that embodies the sacred interplay of genealogy, astrological wisdom, and elemental magic. This **potion** is not a physical **brew**, but a living metaphor, a vibrational *blend* that reflects the profound *interconnectedness* of **life**. It honors the legacies **encoded** within us by our *ancestors*, while attuning to the *celestial* forces that continue to guide our path.

———

THE **POTION** BEGINS WITH THE **WATERS OF OUR LINEAGE**, our emotional and *intuitive* inheritance and is **activated** by the *elements*:

- **Fire** provides the heat of transformation, igniting courage, passion, and renewal
- **Earth** grounds and stabilizes, offering structure, support, and balance
- **Air** breathes inspiration and clarity, expanding perception and awareness
- **Water** flows through the entire process, connecting us to intuition, feeling, and ancestral memory

Even the **sediments** - the *griefs*, *traumas*, and inherited *struggles* - are *ingredients*. They present us with *raw material* for healing and reflection. Through this *sacred* **alchemical** process, we blend *Ancestral mysticism*, *elemental* forces, and **celestial** *insight*, revealing the *essence* of who we are and *illuminating* the **path** forward.

Gathering
the Ingredients

THE *CREATION* OF YOUR **ANCESTRAL ALCHEMICAL POTION** begins with *intention*, an *embodied* choice to connect with your *lineage* and enter into *sacred* **exploration**. This step includes **researching** your *family tree*, exploring documented genealogical *history*. Begin by gathering **names**, **dates**, locations of birth, and *Ancestral* **stories** where available. Calculate each ancestor's *Sun, Moon, and Venus* placements at the time of their **birth**, and if choosing to, also the Lunar phases at birth/death if available for discovery. This *foundational* work reveals the *raw material* of your *elixir*, the **elements**, **signs**, and **planetary** energies that are your **Ancestral Elemental Blueprint**. Through *genealogical* research, *Ancestral* conversations, and intuitive gathering, this *spiritual wildcrafting* is part of the *sacred* act of **remembering**. It deepens your *awareness* of the energies you're working with and prepares the **vessel** for **alchemical** *transformation*.

BREWING THE POTION

This **Elixir** is woven, not rushed.

- **Combine the Elements** – Blend the energies of your **Sun, Moon, and Venus** placements with the *elemental* forces present in your *lineage*. These are the base *ingredients* of your *Ancestral Elemental Blueprint*.
- **Set Intentions** – Clarify your desires for *healing, growth*, or *renewal*. Let these *intentions* shape the flavor and direction of your *elixir*.
- **Engage in Rituals** – *Activate* the *alchemical* current through *Ancestral* ceremony. This may include lighting candles, offering flowers or herbs, speaking names aloud, or reciting words of *remembrance* and gratitude.

Becoming Stewards of Our Lineage

The **Ancestral Alchemical Potion** is crafted through the *sacred* fusion of *alchemy* and *spiritual Wildcrafting*. In this *process*, we step into our role as **stewards** of the *lineage*, conscious collaborators in creating a more *balanced* and *intentional* legacy. Through *transformation*, we learn to **harmonize** with the *elements*, the cosmos, and the deeper *truth* of who we are. By transmuting the *raw materials* of our *heritage*, both the **gifts** and the **griefs**, we convert *Ancestral* inheritance into *tools* for **healing**, **resilience**, and **love**. This *alchemical wildcraft* nurtures not only our own *equilibrium* and *compassion* but also sows **seeds** of healing for future *generations*. It is a living *offering*, crafted in **veneration**, and carried forward with **love**.

ANCESTRAL SEDIMENTS

Body Memories

*O*ur *bodies* hold *memories* that shape our reactions to the world, triggering physical and emotional responses based on past experiences. For example, a **Fire** survivor may react to the *smell of smoke,* while an abuse survivor may flinch at sudden *movements*, showing how these *memories* influence our interactions. Alongside these memories, our *bodies* also store **strength** and **wisdom**. By tuning into our *bodily sensations,* we can identify stored experiences and release tension, a **healing** process that reminds us of our resilience and *wisdom*. Techniques like *meditation, breathwork*, and *mindfulness* can help us ground ourselves and process *trauma*. **Creativity** is a *powerful* tool to *express* what words cannot. Through physical *movement* and *art*, we can release and **give** form to our *feelings*, transforming *pain* into something understandable. This *creative* power inspires new ways of healing and self-expression. Through these processes, we can break free from the *stories* that once held us back. We **enter** a *new* phase, carrying the lessons of our **past** and embracing the strength we've *cultivated*. Once weighed down by *pain*, our *bodies* become symbols of **resilience** and **rebirth**, a testament to the healing process and the journey toward *wholeness*. *Trauma* can significantly affect families, leaving lasting marks that influence future *generations*. These effects can be **subtle** but deeply *impactful*, shaping how individuals approach *relationships, emotions*, and **life**.

Ancestral Trauma

When *unresolved* **emotions** from **past** hardships stick around a family, they become part of that family's **story**. For *example*, a family that went through war might *unconsciously* start avoiding *conflict* to protect themselves from more **pain**. These *survival* strategies can become so *routine* that they affect how family members *communicate* and cope with

emotions. The impact of *Ancestral trauma* may be hard to see, but it's *widespread*. Families that have faced *significant* challenges often deal with increased **anxiety**, **hypervigilance**, or a **reluctance** to confront issues. These *behaviors*, which were once *necessary* for **survival**, can *linger* long after the *trauma*, affecting family *dynamics* and individual well-being.

Generational Trauma

When *trauma* lasts over time, it can create *cycles* of insecurity and emotional *struggles* within families. Take the *children* of parents who experienced *severe* poverty; they might carry a *fear* of not having *enough*, even when they're doing well. This *anxiety* can affect their **relationships**, **choices**, and overall sense of **stability**. *Generational trauma* often shows up in *emotional* and *behavioral* **patterns**. Parents who have been through tough times might struggle with regulating their emotions or forming close attachments, which can *unintentionally* affect their children. As a result, issues like **anxiety**, **depression**, or trouble forming **secure** bonds can pass through *generations*, continuing the *cycle*.

Intergenerational Trauma

The effects of *trauma* extend beyond *immediate* family members; they can reach across many *generations*, shaping **fears**, **behaviors**, and **identities**. For example, a family that has faced *displacement* might develop a deep fear of being *abandoned*. Even future *generations* who didn't experience the original events directly may struggle with trust and stable relationships. *Intergenerational trauma* highlights how **historical** events can impact **present** lives. Families affected by **displacement**, **genocide**, or systemic **oppression** often carry *emotional* wounds that get passed down through *stories*, *behaviors*, and *fears*. These matters are **potent** reminders of how much history can *influence* our lives.

Exploring Epigenetic Changes

Research shows that *trauma* can affect how *genes* function without changing **DNA**. These *epigenetic* modifications can make people more *vulnerable* to stress and may even be passed down to future *generations*. Our *ancestors'* struggles can impact their *descendants'* health and well-being. **Epigenetics** examines how factors like stress and *trauma* leave molecular "**marks**" on **DNA** that change gene activity. While these marks *don't* alter the **genetic code**, they influence whether specific *genes* are *activated* or *turned off*. This process can affect how individuals respond to *stress* and can be handed down through *generations*, leaving a mark on **past** experiences. Our **circumstances** and **behaviors** also influence how *genes* behave, impacting *essential* brain functions such as adaptability, learning, and emotional management. For instance, ongoing trauma can modify the brain's stress response, mainly how **cortisol**, the *stress hormone,* is regulated. These changes can make future *generations* more **sensitive** to stress, potentially affecting their *emotional* and *psychological* strength.

EPIGENETIC CHANGES ALSO AFFECT *NEUROTRANSMITTERS* like **serotonin** and **dopamine**, which are crucial for *regulating* mood, cognitive abilities, and emotional well-being. Disruptions in these chemicals are often connected to mental health issues, including *anxiety* and *depression*. For example, *trauma*-related changes can lower **serotonin** production, which is *vital* for *emotional* balance. Decreased *serotonin* levels can raise the risk of mood disorders, highlighting the link between **inherited trauma**, *gene activity,* and *mental health*. Addressing inherited *trauma* involves exploring *personal* and *collective* **histories**. The **patterns** inherited from our *ancestors* can bring pain, but also provide **resilience** and **wisdom**. By exploring the experiences of our *predecessors*, we learn how they **faced** and **overcame** *challenges*. This knowledge allows us to *recognize* detrimental **patterns** and learn how to replace them with **healthier** *behaviors*. It fosters a sense of *connection* and enlightenment, bridging the gap between our **past** and **present**.

ANCESTRAL HEALING WORK ENCOURAGES US TO

- Acknowledge the pain our *ancestors* experienced.
- Honor their strength in *overcoming* difficulties.
- *Transform* inherited struggles into *wisdom* through understanding and *compassion*.
- *Rewrite* cycles that are not serving the family tree and the collective.
- Infuse our *roots* with *Love*.

This *process* enables us to break harmful *cycles*, *heal* **past** wounds, and promote *personal* and *generational* **growth**. By integrating the **wisdom** of our *ancestors* into our lives, we establish a legacy of *resilience* and emotional *liberation* for future *generations*. **Generational trauma** underscores the profound link between our *history* and current circumstances, shaping our way of **life**. Viewing these ingrained patterns through the lens of *Ancestral Alchemology* offers opportunities to *transform* suffering into knowledge and fortitude. By acknowledging the experiences of our *ancestors* and implementing their *teachings*, we facilitate **healing** and development, setting the stage for a future **flourishing** in *awareness* and fresh *possibilities*.

THE MOONTREE CHART

Decoding
Ancestral Energies

*T*he *MoonTree Chart* offers a practical **exploration** of the *Ancestral Alchemology* method, **decoding** the **celestial** influences embedded in your *lineage*. **Weaving** together *astrology, genealogy,* and *elemental alchemy,* this chart provides a unique way to connect with *inherited* **patterns,** strengths, and *Ancestral* **wisdom.** The *MoonTree Chart* maps the collective **celestial** story of your *lineage* by tracing the *Sun, Moon,* and *Venus* placements of your *ancestors,* revealing the **elemental** energies flowing through it. This illuminates *generational* themes, inherited emotional **blueprints,** and the *unseen* threads connecting you to your *ancestors.* Ultimately, the chart serves as both a reflection and a tool, guiding you toward understanding the **cosmically coded** elemental influences in your family history and unlocking the wisdom of your *Ancestral Alchemical Elixir.*

⋅⋅⋅

THE *MOONTREE CHART* REVEALS **PATTERNS** RELATED TO *Zodiac* **Signs,** like *Scorpio Moon* placements, showing emotional intensity and transformation. It shows the prevalent *elements* - **Earth, Air, Fire, Water** - and how they affect the *alchemical* **Elixir.** It also highlights *Venus, Sun,* and *Moon* placements, both *collectively* and *individually,* for each *ancestor.*

MoonTree - Ancestral Alchemology

How to Create Your MoonTree Chart

THE MOONTREE CHART IS THE ANCHOR OF THE **ANCESTRAL Alchemology** method, a sacred spiral of astrology, elemental resonance, and inherited energy.

STEP 1: GATHER ANCESTRAL INFORMATION

Begin by collecting as much ancestral detail as you can. This is the foundation of your *MoonTree Chart*.

- Names of ancestors
- Birth dates
- Birth locations

Tips for Gathering Lineage Threads:

1. **Start with stories** - Speak to parents, grandparents, or anyone who holds memories. Their words often contain gold.
2. **Explore documents** - Use birth, death, marriage certificates, immigration papers, and census records.
3. **Consider DNA testing** - It may offer clarity or connections when paper trails run thin.
4. **Include chosen family** - Adoption and chosen lineage hold energetic weight and spiritual presence.

STEP 2: CHART CELESTIAL SIGNATURES

With birth data in hand, begin charting the ***Sun, Moon***, and ***Venus*** signs for each ancestor in your chosen *lineage*. You can focus on one line, either the **mother-line** or **father-line**, or explore both simultaneously, using astrology software, ephemerides, or online astrology chart calculators.

- **Sun Sign**: Vital force, inherited essence, core identity
- **Moon Sign**: Emotional memory, intuition, inner tides
- **Venus Sign**: Love languages, relational legacy, artistic inheritance
- **Lunar Phase**: Timing of *Ancestral* births and deaths, cyclical imprints

STEP 3: TRANSLATE TO ELEMENTAL LANGUAGE

Each *zodiac* sign aligns with one of the four classical elements - **Fire**, **Water**, **Earth**, or **Air**. For every *Sun*, *Moon*, and *Venus* placement, note its *elemental* correspondence.

FIRE	EARTH	AIR	WATER
Aries	Taurus	Gemini	Cancer
Leo	Virgo	Libra	Scorpio
Sagittarius	Capricorn	Aquarius	Pisces

Zodiac Sign Corresponding Elements

- **Example:** A great-grandmother with a Leo *Sun* (**Fire**), Scorpio *Moon* (**Water**), and Taurus *Venus* (**Earth**) would carry a **Fire–Water–Earth** *elemental* signature. This trio *weaves* passion, emotional depth, and grounded sensuality.

- Begin tracking **patterns** across *ancestors*. Which elements appear most often? Are certain combinations repeating?

STEP 4: CONNECT TO THE SOMATIC ZODIAC

Each zodiac sign governs a part of the body. These correspondences reveal *Ancestral* **patterns** in physical expression, health tendencies, and embodied energies. Refer to the *MoonTree Chart* **Body Map** and note the corresponding **somatic regions** for each sign. These body areas may hold tension, memory, or *Ancestral* gifts.

STEP 5: DISCOVER THE ELEMENTAL ARCHETYPE

Once you've charted the **Sun, Moon,** and **Venus** *elements* for each *ancestor*, identify the **Ancestral Elemental Archetype** for those who stand out to you, or for the overall *lineage* pattern. This archetype is formed through the **trio of elements**—a unique blend that carries *Ancestral* frequency, **memory**, and **medicine**. In *ELIXIR*, you'll find guidance for each archetype based on elemental trios.

STEP 6: CALCULATE ELEMENTAL ESSENCES

When working with multiple *ancestors*, a deeper **pattern** often emerges. Sometimes, one element dominates. Other times, a **secondary element** consistently appears, forming a blended alchemical essence.

- If one element dominates the entire chart, it becomes your **Core Element**
- If two elements appear repeatedly, they may form a **Dual Essence** (e.g., Fire + Water = *Steam*)

EXAMPLE

In my **Mother-line** *MoonTree Chart*, **Water** flowed strongest, with **Earth** grounding it as a close second. Together, they formed **Mud**, an element of sensuality, fertility, and emotional rootedness.

- You'll find a full list of **Dual Elemental Essences** in the corresponding chapter on **page 197.** These offer another layer of mystical insight.

STEP 7: REFLECT, INTEGRATE, REMEMBER

1. What emotional or relational patterns repeat through your lineage?
2. What zodiac signs, elements, or archetypes appear most often?

3. Where do you sense energy moving in your own body that corresponds to Ancestral placements?

These reflections are for *listening* to your body and connecting to your ancestors and the message they have for you. Your *Moon Tree Chart* is a **map of memory and elemental ancestral essence**. It bridges the **star** with **dust**, the **chart** with **body**, and **ancestry** with **embodiment**.

Mapping your Ancestral Celestial Imprint

USE THESE TEMPLATES TO RECORD AND ANALYZE THE *astrological* and *elemental* influences in your lineage. Fill in the details for each *ancestor* to create your personalized *Moon Tree Chart*.

STEP 1: GATHER ANCESTRAL INFORMATION

ANCESTOR	BIRTH DATE	NAME	BIRTH LOCATION
SELF			
Parent 1			
Parent 2			
Grandparent 1			
Grandparent 2			
Great-Grandparent 1			
Great-Grandparent 2			
2x Great-Grandparent			
3x Great-Grandparent			
4x Great-Grandparent			
5x Great-Grandparent			

Step 1: Moon Tree Chart - *Gather Ancestral Information*

STEP 2: CHART CELESTIAL SIGNATURES

Record the **Sun, Moon, and Venus** signs for each ancestor.

ANCESTOR	SUN Sign & Element	MOON Sign & Element	VENUS Sign & Element
SELF			
Parent 1			
Parent 2			
Grandparent 1			
Grandparent 2			
Great-Grandparent 1			
Great-Grandparent 2			
2x Great-Grandparent			
3x Great-Grandparent			
4x Great-Grandparent			
5x Great-Grandparent			

Step 2: MoonTree Chart - *Chart Celestial Signatures*

STEP 3: TRANSLATE TO ELEMENTAL LANGUAGE

Analyze the elemental distribution of **Sun, Moon, and Venus** placements to identify dominant energies.

ELEMENT	SUN Placements	MOON Placements	VENUS Placements	TOTAL
FIRE				
EARTH				
AIR				
WATER				

Step 3: MoonTree Chart - *Translate to Elemental Language*

STEP 4: CONNECT TO THE SOMATIC ZODIAC

Refer to the Zodiac Body Map and note the corresponding **somatic regions** for each sign.

ANCESTOR	Lunar Phase at Birth	Zodiac Sign (Sun)	Zodiac Body Area (Somatic)
SELF			
Parent 1			
Parent 2			
Grandparent 1			
Grandparent 2			
Great-Grandparent 1			
Great-Grandparent 2			
2x Great-Grandparent			
3x Great-Grandparent			
4x Great-Grandparent			
5x Great-Grandparent			

Step 4: Moon Tree Chart - Connect to the Somatic Zodiac

STEP 5: DISCOVER THE ELEMENTAL ARCHETYPE

Combine the **Sun, Moon, and Venus** elemental influences for each ancestor to create a **Triple Elemental.**

ANCESTOR	TRIPLE ELEMENTAL PROFILE (Sun + Moon + Venus)
SELF	
Parent 1	
Parent 2	
Grandparent 1	
Grandparent 2	
Great-Grandparent 1	
Great-Grandparent 2	
2x Great-Grandparent	
3x Great-Grandparent	
4x Great-Grandparent	
5x Great-Grandparent	

Step 5: Moon Tree Chart - Discover the Elemental Archetype

DETERMINE THE KEY ANCESTRAL ELEMENTAL ARCHETYPE

Identify the most recurring or dominant archetype/s within your lineage. As well as the secondary, if any.

YOUR ANCESTRAL ELEMENTAL ARCHETYPE

KEY Ancestral Elemental Archetype	SECONDARY Ancestral Elemental Archetype

Step 6: Moon Tree Chart - Ancestral Elemental Archetype results

STEP 6: CALCULATE ELEMENTAL ESSENCES (IF PRESENT)

If a **secondary element** emerges consistently alongside the dominant element, it may combine to form a dual *elemental essence*.

PRIMARY Element	SECONDARY Element (if present)	Resulting Elemental Essence (if secondary is present)

Step 7: Moon Tree Chart - Calculate Elemental Essences

- *Example:* If **Water** is the dominant element and **Fire** is the secondary, their interaction forms **Steam**, an energy representing *transformation*, *fluidity*, and *resilience*.

STEP 7: REFLECT, INTEGRATE, REMEMBER

Refer back to **pages 58 - 59** for *Moon Tree Chart* reflection questions.

Patterns Provide Guidance

CELESTIAL ANCESTRAL IMPRINTS OF MY MOTHER LINE

My MoonTree Chart

Exploring My Maternal Lineage

*A*s I delved into my *family* history, what started as a simple search for names and origins transformed into an amazing journey of *Ancestral* discovery. By exploring my ancestors' **Sun**, **Moon**, and **Venus** placements, I unearthed **patterns** that *wove* through *generations*, revealing a deep connection between my *lineage* and the cosmos. The *MoonTree Chart* became my roadmap, *illuminating* recurring themes and *celestial* influences that shaped my maternal line. Unlike standard *astrology*, this process was about understanding not just individual charts but how my family's *celestial* **patterns** intersected, influencing inherited strengths, challenges, and *wisdom*. For this chart, I focused on my **maternal** *lineage*, tracing back to my **seventh great-grandmother.** To keep living relatives' information private, I included their birth months instead of specific names or dates on the chart example I provided in this book. Using the methods outlined in this book, I mapped each ancestor's **Sun**, **Moon**, and **Venus** signs, uncovering our *astrological* connections. As I worked, clear **patterns** emerged. The *elements*, themes, and *archetypes* showed the unique energy of my *family* line. For my **maternal** *lineage*, the chart highlights two triple *elemental* combinations:

1. **Water-Water-Water**
2. **Water-Water-Air**

These *energies* reflect emotional depth, *intuitive* understanding, and a thirst for knowledge. **Water** represents the emotional support and *nurturing* presence passed down through *generations*. **Air** symbolizes the pursuit of knowledge and the ability to connect ideas, encouraging *creativity* and *adaptability*. This mix resonates strongly, not just in the lives of my *ancestors* but also in my own experiences. Their influence shapes my emotions, creative projects, and intellectual interests. My **exploration** of this *lineage* pauses with my **seventh great-grand-mother.** In *genealogical* research, when records stop, it's often called a "*brick wall.*" While this can feel limiting, I believe in the value of this process. If my search ends here, my *ancestors* want me to take a break. This is the chapter they've chosen to share, trusting that what is *unveiled* is what is meant to be known, and as this work is ever-changing and *cyclical*, in time, more will be revealed.

MOONTREE CHART OF MY MOTHERLINE

ANCESTOR	SUN Sign & Element	MOON Sign & Element	VENUS Sign & Element
SELF	Pisces (Water)	Cancer (Water)	Aquarius (Air)
Mother	Virgo (Earth)	Scorpio (Water)	Cancer (Water)
Grandmother	Aquarius (Air)	Sagittarius (Fire)	Capricorn (Earth)
Great-Grandmother	Capricorn (Earth)	Sagittarius (Fire)	Capricorn (Earth)
2 x Great Grandmother	Scorpio (Water)	Pisces (Water)	Sagittarius (Fire)
3 x Great Grandmother	Virgo (Earth)	Capricorn (Earth)	Libra (Air)
4 x Great Grandmother	Aries (Fire)	Pisces (Water)	Aries (Fire)
5 x Great Grandmother	Pisces (Water)	Taurus (Earth)	Aquarius (Air)
6 x Great Grandmother	Scorpio (Water)	Pisces (Water)	Scorpio (Water)
7 x Great Grandmother	Sagittarius (Fire)	Cancer (Water)	Scorpio (Water)

MoonTree Chart of My Motherline

THE MOONTREE CHART'S CORE ASTROLOGICAL INFLUENCES

The ***Sun*** symbolizes creativity and self-expression passed down through the family. The ***Moon*** affects emotions and intuition, revealing how ancestors cared for themselves and others. ***Venus*** represents *connection*, harmony, love, beauty, and relationships. Incorporating **lunar** phases added more meaning to the chart. The ***Moon's*** cycles deepened the story of my **maternal** *lineage*. Creating the chart felt like a personal link to my ancestors. Their struggles and successes are reflected within me, showing how their energy still melds into my life. Making the chart connected me with *Ancestral wisdom*. It honored their influence and tied me to cosmic forces guiding us. The *MoonTree Chart* isn't just a tool; it illustrates the enduring connections between **Earth**, the *cosmos*, and the **human/spirit.**

DECODING MY MATERNAL LINEAGE'S KEY ELEMENTS:

Through the *MoonTree Chart*, I identified the elemental dominance across my maternal lineage:

ELEMENT	SUN Placements	MOON Placements	VENUS Placements	TOTAL
FIRE	2 (1 x Aries, 1 x Sagittarius)	2 (2 x Sagittarius)	2 (1 x Aries, 1 x Sagittarius)	6
EARTH	3 (2 x Virgo, 1 x Capricorn)	2 (1 x Taurus, 1 x Capricorn)	2 (2 x Capricorn)	7
AIR	1 (1 x Aquarius)	0	2 (1 x Aquarius, 1 x Libra)	3
WATER	4 (2 x Pisces, 2 x Scorpio)	6 (2 x Cancer, 3 x Pisces, 1 x Scorpio)	3 (2 x Scorpio, 1 x Cancer)	13

My Maternal Lineage's Key Elements

The predominant elements in my Motherline are **Water** and **Earth**, symbolizing deep emotional wisdom, grounding, and ancestral resilience. **Water** represents inherited emotional intelligence, healing, and intuition, while **Earth** embodies stability, nurture, and the strength to create and sustain.

THE UNDERLYING ELEMENTAL ESSENCE: MUD

Although **Earth** does not appear in the primary *Ancestral Elemental Archetypes*, its presence as the second-most dominant element creates an underlying energetic force within my *Motherline*. When **Water** and **Earth** come together, they form **Mud**, an essence of nourishment, depth, and transformation through rooted connection. This *Mud Essence* represents the grounding force of my lineage, blending the deep emotional flow of **Water** with the stabilizing strength of **Earth**. *Mud* holds, shapes, and nurtures, offering a foundation for growth and renewal, just as the wisdom of my ancestors provides a steady presence in my life. This recognition honors the enduring, fertile energy inherited alongside the emotional and intuitive gifts of my lineage, reflecting the profound balance of creation and connection within my *Motherline*.

ANCESTRAL ELEMENTAL ARCHETYPES

From this elemental blueprint, two key *Ancestral Elemental Archetypes* emerged:

- **The Psychic Weaver (Water-Water-Water)** – A lineage deeply tied to intuition, emotional depth, and ancestral mysticism. This archetype reflects a strong connection to unseen realms, dreams, and inner knowing.

- **The Inventive Oracle (Water-Water-Air)** – A legacy of visionaries, healers, and messengers. This blend of elements represents fluidity in communication, heightened perception, and the ability to channel ancestral guidance.

BODY AREAS GOVERNED BY DOMINANT ASTROLOGICAL SIGNS

The dominant astrological signs in my Motherline also reveal key somatic correspondences, reflecting inherited energies through the body:

Astrological Sign	BODY AREA connection
Pisces	Lymphatic system, feet, pineal gland
Scorpio	Reproductive system, pelvis, urinary tract
Virgo	Digestive system, spleen, intestines
Aquarius	Ankles, circulatory system
Capricorn	Knees, bones, teeth, skin

My MoonTree Chart: Zodiac Sign and Body Area

LUNAR PHASES AT THE TIME OF BIRTH

ANCESTOR	Lunar Phase at Birth	Total
SELF	Waxing Gibbous	
Mother	Waxing Crescent	
Grandmother	Waning Crescent	
Great-Grandmother	Waning Crescent	
2 x Great-Grandmother	Waxing Gibbous	
3 x Great-Grandmother	Waning Gibbous	
4 x Great-Grandmother	Waning Crescent	
5 x Great-Grandmother	Waxing Crescent	
6 x Great-Grandmother	Waning Crescent	
7 x Great-Grandmother	Waxing Gibbous	
	Waxing Gibbous	3
	Waxing Crescent	2
	Waning Crescent	4
	Waning Gibbous	1
Dominant Lunar Phase	WANING CRESCENT	

My MoonTree Chart: Lunar Phase at Birth

REFLECTIONS & PERSONAL CONNECTION

This journey began in the wake of my Mother's passing. In the depths of grief, I turned to her *astrological* placements and wove them into our family's *MoonTree Chart*. This practice became a source of comfort, a way to find stability amid the loss and clarity in the midst of pain. The chart reflected the profound connection I shared with her, affirming our bond through the *elemental* and *astrological* **patterns** that flow through our *lineage*. Through this exploration, I've come to see how the *wisdom* and struggles of my *ancestors* live within me. This process has deepened my connection to them, reminding me of the importance of honoring, embodying, and transforming their legacy. This *connection* feels deeply personal. I am a *Pisces* with a *Scorpio* Rising, and I have always felt a strong pull to my *Motherline*. Seeing the emphasis on the **Water** element in my family's *MoonTree Chart* brings everything together in a way that feels both magical and affirming. My *Mother*, with her *Sun* in *Virgo-Pisces'* opposite on the zodiac wheel, adds another layer of *synchronicity* and connection.

FROM THE *MOONTREE CHARTS*, THREE DECODED ELEMENTS create the *Ancestral Elemental Archetype*. For my *lineage*, the results reveal two archetypes: **Water-Water-Water** and **Water-Water-Air**. Reflecting on these *archetypes* resonates deeply with some significant life experiences. My *near-death* drowning as a child connects directly to these *elements*. I lost my breath (**Air**) in the depths of **Water**, and since that moment, I've lived with a sense of walking with one foot in this world and one foot in the other.

THE INSIGHTS FROM THIS PRACTICE HAVE REVEALED A predominant *essence* in my **maternal** *lineage*, stretching as far back as my **7th Great-Grandmother.** The *Pisces* and *Scorpio astrological* energies, along with the **Water** element, create a recurring theme that affirms the archetypal **patterns** uncovered. This realization not only ties my family's energies into the archetypes but also reinforces the profound *connection* to the *Motherline* and its influence on my path in life. My chart reveals a link to *Pisces*, a sign associated with the feet. As mentioned already, my Sun Sign is Pisces, and also being a *dancer (feet)*, this connection holds a special significance, highlighting qualities like **movement** and a *mystical* nature. Every layer of my *chart* explains why these *astrological connections* resonate with me. The **stars** reveal the links we share with our *ancestors* and the **patterns** that influence our lives, creating a deep sense of **belonging** and **continuity**. My sister's *Moon-Tree Chart* is an interesting example of how uniquely our individual *Ancestral* Elixirs can differ. Her *elemental* makeup contrasts with mine because her **Sun** and **Moon** signs are of the **Fire** element: *Aries* and *Sagittarius*. We share the same *Venus sign*, but our **Sun** and **Moon** signs differ. My sister's *Ancestral Archetype* is the *Ethereal Shapeshifter*, which mixes **Water**, **Fire**, and **Air** *elements*, while mine consists primarily of **Water**. Even though we come from the same *maternal line*, her birth placements give her a different result in her *MoonTree Chart*, showing that our *essences* and *imprints* are all unique.

CRAFTING MY *ANCESTRAL ELIXIR*

So this is my Ancestral Alchemology imprint, pattern, recipe. I can now create my Ancestral Elixir using the identified archetypes and the Mud Essence that is prevalent in the elemental pattern.

- **The Psychic Weaver** (*Water-Water-Water*) → See **page 267** for its *Alchemical Recipe*.
- **The Inventive Oracle** (*Water-Water-Air*) → See **page 257** for its *Alchemical Recipe*.
- **Mud Essence** (Water + Earth) → See **page 224** for its *Elemental Integration*
- **Lunar Phase at Birth** → *Waning Crescent*

Exploring my MoonTree Chart has helped me Recognize the emotional and intuitive gifts passed down through my lineage and learn how my ancestors' experiences are reflected in my body and life

In this work, I realized that the energies of our *ancestors* are still **present**. They *flow* through us as an *Essence* of memories, wisdom, a unique familial mysticism, and in the very **celestial cosmic blueprint we were born with.**

Holding Lightness Amid Shadows

Our hearts carry both the weight and the wonder, experiences, emotions, and inherited stories. By exploring our *ancestors'* **Sun, Moon,** and **Venus** signs, we begin to understand the **energetic** influences that shaped their lives. This isn't about excusing their actions, but about **witnessing** the deeper motivations, the *elemental imprints* present at **birth**, and the **patterns** they were trying to **live with**, **live through**, and perhaps never fully *resolve*. Recognizing the burdens, challenges, or painful experiences passed through your *lineage* is a powerful beginning. It's the first step in **pattern** disruption and *healing*. Through the lens of *Ancestral Alchemology*, we can explore these stories with **compassion**, creating space to understand without being consumed by the pain.

An Invitation to Explore

Your *lineage* holds gifts - *quiet*, *potent*, and waiting to be *remembered*. Within the **sediments** and **strengths** of your *family tree* lies wisdom that can guide you toward **healing**, **connection**, and **love**. These are not distant relics of the **past**, but living energies, *Ancestral* threads you can weave into your daily **life**. In doing so, you deepen your understanding of who you are and how you are influenced and **connected** by those who came before you.

Part Two

THE ZODIAC

The Zodiac in Ancestral Alchemology

The Zodiac - Ancestral Alchemology

In *Ancestral Alchemology*, the **Zodiac** helps us discover *astrological* and *elemental* energies in **three** ways:

1. DECODING ELEMENTAL ESSENCES

The **Zodiac** helps us identify the *Elemental Essences* on the *MoonTree chart*, which maps the positions of the **Sun**, **Moon**, and **Venus** in our *ancestors'* natal charts. By recording these positions, each associated with one of the four elements - Fire, Earth, Air, or Water - we can begin *calculating* the **archetypes** and *essences* that are found in our family **patterns**.

2. SOMATIC CONNECTION THROUGH ASTROLOGICAL SIGNS

Ancestral Alchemology reveals the dominant **zodiac** signs in a *lineage*. These signs connect to parts of our *body* that they influence and govern. For instance, **rituals** and exercises focusing on the feet (governed by the *astrological* sign *Pisces*) or the head (*Aries*) help us *establish* a personal connection to the *Ancestral* energies associated with these signs. This *connection* strengthens our bond with both our *lineage* and ourselves, making the exploration process more **engaging** and **tangible**.

3. CONNECTING THROUGH ANCESTRAL PLACEMENTS

Identifying our *ancestors'* **Sun, Moon,** and **Venus** signs gives us valuable insights into their core **energies**, **emotions**, and **relationships**. These signs reveal unique aspects of their *essence*. Creating a deep sense of unity and **continuity**, *rooting* us in our shared family essences, our *Ancestral Elixirs*. Cultivating and *spiritually* **wildcrafting** a deep sense of belonging and strengthening family *roots* with **love**.

THE ASTROLOGICAL SIGNS

Astrological Essences

ARIES

*T*he prominent position of *Aries* in the *Ancestral* chart signifies *bravery*, *uniqueness*, and *lively* energy. Being a cardinal **Fire** sign, *Aries* symbolizes daring, beginnings, and perseverance, mirroring a family history of guidance and strength. When found in the **Sun**, **Moon**, or **Venus** placements, it underscores a heritage *characterized* by **drive**, **goals**, and an **innovative** mindset.

ARIES MOON - EMOTIONAL AND INTUITIVE LEGACY

A **Moon** in *Aries* indicates *ancestors* who felt emotions *intensely* and *immediately*, often facing challenges with bravery and decisiveness. However, they may have *found* patience and emotional balance challenging. **Descendants** may inherit this energy, feeling *compelled* to confront emotional obstacles head-on and seeing challenges as chances for growth. Nonetheless, this energy can also lead to *restlessness* or *impulsivity*, calling for thoughtful reflection.

ARIES SUN - CORE ESSENCE AND VITALITY

Ancestors born under an *Aries **Sun*** were known for their *leadership* and *initiative*, often **blazing** new trails for the family. Their vibrant *energy* manifested through **daring** deeds, **creative** ideas, and a **passion** for **life**. This *heritage* instills *confidence*, *drive*, and the *bravery* to embark on fresh starts. Future *generations* might be inspired to embrace their **uniqueness** and make *bold* decisions.

ARIES VENUS - LOVE AND RELATIONAL DYNAMICS

A ***Venus*** in *Aries* suggests a *lineage* that viewed love and relationships with **passion** and **spontaneity**. Relationships were likely marked by **intensity**, **enthusiasm**, and a focus on the **present** moment. This placement encourages a *bold* and direct approach to relationships, urging descendants to value *authenticity* and *passion*. However, it also emphasizes the importance of **patience** and the emotional depth of *love*.

When *Aries* appears as a dominant sign in the *MoonTree chart*, it amplifies themes of **strength**, **initiative**, and **determination** throughout the family's legacy.

THIS MIGHT INDICATE:

- A lineage of leaders and trailblazers.
- Ancestral strengths include courage, ambition, and resilience.
- Patterns of impulsivity or emotional intensity that require balance and reflection.
- A call for descendants to honor their fiery determination and drive while cultivating patience and mindfulness.

TAURUS

♉

When *Taurus* assumes a prominent position in the ancestral chart, it emphasizes qualities like enduring strength, stability, and sensuality. Being a fixed **Earth** sign, *Taurus* represents grounded-ness, patience, and a profound connection to the material and natural realms. Whether it appears in the ***Sun, Moon,*** or ***Venus*** placement, it signifies a lineage marked by resilience, practicality, and an appreciation for *beauty* and comfort, offering a feeling of security and steadiness.

TAURUS MOON - EMOTIONAL AND INTUITIVE LEGACY

A ***Moon*** in *Taurus* shows ancestors who valued emotional stability and nurtured their relationships with steadfast care. They likely expressed their feelings through acts of service, ensuring the well-being of their families in consistent and tangible ways, fostering a sense of being cherished and supported. *Descendants* may feel this legacy as a desire for emotional security and an appreciation for sensory delights such as food, art, and nature. This influence encourages them to balance comfort and growth, fostering adaptability while staying *rooted*, offering a feeling of luxury and contentment.

TAURUS SUN - CORE ESSENCE AND VITALITY

Ancestors born under a *Taurus* ***Sun*** embodied traits like patience, determination, and a passion for creation. They probably found *joy* in constructing and nurturing aspects of their lives, whether it was family, career, or artistic pursuits. Their energy shone through their dedication to achieving long-term objectives and their admiration for the beauty of life. The energy passed down from them encourages a steadfast attitude towards life, urging their *descendants* to cherish persistence and live in the present moment. It underscores the significance of building a stable base while enjoying life's simple pleasures.

TAURUS VENUS - LOVE AND RELATIONAL DYNAMICS

A **Venus** in *Taurus* suggests a family history characterized by *love* and relationships based on loyalty and harmony. Ancestors with this placement probably showed affection through physical presence, caring actions, and an appreciation for the beauty of relationships. This inheritance promotes a strong regard for stability and emotional connections in love, inspiring future generations to cultivate deep and long-lasting relationships. It emphasizes the importance of patience and the rewards of nurturing bonds.

WHEN *TAURUS* APPEARS AS A DOMINANT SIGN IN THE *MoonTree Chart*, it amplifies themes of **grounding**, **persistence**, and **connection** to the natural world throughout the family's *lineage*.

THIS MIGHT INDICATE:

- A lineage of caretakers, builders, and individuals who created beauty and stability in their lives.
- Ancestral strengths in resilience, patience, and practicality.
- Patterns of stubbornness or resistance to change call for reflection and flexibility.
- A call for descendants to embrace their ability to nurture and sustain while balancing the need for growth and adaptability.

GEMINI

♊

GEMINI'S PROMINENT POSITION IN THE ANCESTRAL CHART emphasizes themes of curiosity, adaptability, and intellectual exploration. Being a mutable **Air** sign, *Gemini* symbolizes communication, learning, and a lively approach to life. When it appears in the **Sun, Moon**, or **Venus** placement, it underscores a family history characterized by curiosity, versatility, and a talent for forming connections.

GEMINI MOON - EMOTIONAL AND INTUITIVE LEGACY

A **Moon** in *Gemini* shows ancestors who likely dealt with emotions by thinking and talking about them. They probably tried to find answers and solutions through *communication* and intellectual pursuits, but may have found it challenging to connect deeply on an emotional level. *Descendants* may inherit a tendency to analyze their feelings openly, which can benefit adaptability and clarity, but also emphasizes the importance of balancing emotional expression with forming meaningful *connections*.

GEMINI SUN - CORE ESSENCE AND VITALITY

Ancestors born under a *Gemini* **Sun** naturally radiated intellectual curiosity and versatility. They flourished in settings that encouraged learning, exploration, and exchange of ideas. Their vibrant energy showcased their talent for adapting, innovating, and communicating effectively, motivating their descendants to embody these qualities. This **Sun** placement motivates *descendants* to embrace their curiosity, versatility, and passion for learning. It underlines the significance of honing clear communication skills, embracing various viewpoints, and managing distractions to maintain focus.

GEMINI VENUS - LOVE AND RELATIONAL DYNAMICS

A **Venus** in *Gemini* suggests a family history in which intellectual rapport and energetic interaction characterized relationships. Ancestors who likely prized humor, *communication*, and mutual curiosity in their relationships, even though they may have faced challenges with staying dedicated or consistent. This position nurtures a preference for mental stimulation and vibrant interactions in relationships. Future generations are urged to welcome their desire for diversity and intellectual connection, all while understanding the significance of fostering stability and emotional depth in their relationships.

When *Gemini* appears as a dominant sign in the *MoonTree Chart*, it amplifies themes of communication, adaptability, and curiosity throughout the family's lineage.

THIS MIGHT INDICATE:

- A lineage of storytellers, teachers, and individuals with a gift for language and connection.
- Ancestral strengths in intellectual adaptability, networking, and creative thinking.
- Patterns of restlessness or difficulty with emotional grounding that call for balance and self-awareness.
- A call for descendants to honor their intellectual gifts while cultivating deeper emotional connections and focus.

CANCER

When *Cancer* is prominent in the *MoonTree Chart,* it highlights themes of **emotional** depth, **nurturing**, and a strong **connection** to **home** and family. Being a cardinal **Water** sign, *Cancer* represents care, intuition, and sensitivity, reflecting an ancestral heritage that values compassion and the importance of family ties. Whether in the *Sun*, *Moon*, or *Venus* placement, Cancer *signifies* a *lineage* characterized by emotional strength, protection, and a deep attachment to tradition, providing a feeling of security and support to future generations.

CANCER MOON - EMOTIONAL AND INTUITIVE LEGACY

Ancestors with a *Moon* in *Cancer* showed great sensitivity to their own emotions and the emotions of others. They probably showed care and nurturing, though they may have faced emotional vulnerability or times of self-sacrifice. Descendants might experience this as a deep bond with family and tradition and a talent for offering emotional support. This energy encourages empathy and intuition, emphasizing the importance of balancing caregiving with self-care and emotional boundaries. This empowers descendants to manage their emotional well-being effectively.

CANCER SUN - CORE ESSENCE AND VITALITY

Ancestors born under a *Cancer Sun* possessed a nurturing and emotionally wise nature. They probably thrived in establishing and preserving safe spaces, prioritizing family, and fostering emotional bonds. This position encourages *descendants* to tap into their caregiving instincts, develop emotional intelligence (the capacity to comprehend and regulate one's emotions as well as empathize with others), and cherish their ties to **home** and heritage.

CANCER VENUS - LOVE AND RELATIONAL DYNAMICS

A *Venus* in *Cancer* suggests a family history characterized by expressions of love through nurturing, loyalty, and emotional closeness. Ancestors with this placement likely prioritized security and dedication in their relationships, although they may have shown tendencies towards emotional dependence or overprotectiveness. This energy encourages a loving and nurturing approach to relationships, highlighting the importance of emotional connection and commitment. Future generations are advised to embrace their ability to care for others while also developing independence and mutual respect in their connections.

WHEN *CANCER* APPEARS AS A DOMINANT SIGN IN THE *Moon Tree chart*, it amplifies themes of **nurturing**, e**motional wisdom**, and fa**milial connection** throughout the family's lineage.

THIS MIGHT INDICATE:

- A lineage of caregivers, healers, and individuals deeply connected to family and home.
- Ancestral strengths in empathy, intuition, and the ability to create emotional security.
- Patterns of emotional sensitivity or self-sacrifice that require boundaries and self-care.
- An encouragement for descendants to honor their emotional depth while cultivating resilience and independence.

LEO

WHEN *Leo* TAKES A PROMINENT POSITION IN THE *MoonTree* *chart*, it *illuminates* themes of **creativity**, **courage**, and **self-expression**. *Leo*, as a zodiac sign, embodies warmth, leadership, and passion. Being a fixed Fire sign, it mirrors an ancestral heritage of charisma and vitality. When present in the ***Sun***, ***Moon***, or ***Venus*** placement, it underscores a *lineage* characterized by **confidence**, **generosity**, and the **motivation** to motivate others.

LEO MOON - EMOTIONAL AND INTUITIVE LEGACY

A ***Moon*** in *Leo* could suggest that *ancestors* were sociable and enjoyed entertaining others. They likely sought *attention* and *strived* to bring **joy** to their families, although they may have struggled with pride and sensitivity to criticism. This energy may inspire descendants to express their feelings openly, inspiring others with their emotional **strength**. It promotes creativity and self-confidence while also teaching the importance of balancing self-*expression* with humility and attentive listening, guiding personal growth.

LEO SUN - CORE ESSENCE AND VITALITY

Ancestors born under a Leo Sun were known for their creativity and leadership, often standing out in their communities or families. They thrived on showcasing their special talents and motivating others with their vision and deeds. This trait inspires future generations to embrace their own uniqueness, value their skills, and lead with bravery and genuineness. It also underlines the importance of balancing ambition with self-awareness and teamwork.

LEO VENUS - LOVE AND RELATIONAL DYNAMICS

A *Venus* in *Leo* suggests a *lineage* that expressed love with grandeur, loyalty, and **affection**. *Ancestors* in this line probably cherished **romantic** gestures, admiration, and deep connections, though they may have sought validation through *relationships*. This placement encourages a **passionate** and **generous** attitude towards *relationships*, prompting descendants to view **love** as a source of **creativity** and **joy**. It also highlights the significance of balancing the desire for admiration with mutual respect and emotional **authenticity**, emphasizing the importance of healthy boundaries and open **communication** in *relationships*.

WHEN *LEO* APPEARS AS A DOMINANT SIGN IN THE *MOONTREE chart*, it amplifies themes of self-expression, courage, and creativity throughout the family's legacy.

THIS MIGHT INDICATE:

1. A lineage of leaders, performers, or visionaries who inspired others with their talents and charisma.
2. Ancestral strengths include creativity, confidence, and the ability to unite people.
3. Patterns of pride or a need for external validation that require self-reflection and inner grounding in Shadow work.
4. A call for descendants to honor their gifts and lead authentically, balancing ambition with humility.

VIRGO

Virgo's prominent position in the *MoonTree chart* brings to light the key themes of precision, service, and a down-to-earth attitude towards life. Being a mutable **Earth** sign, *Virgo* represents **practicality**, **analytical** reasoning, and a strong sense of **commitment**, reflecting a family heritage *rooted* in diligence and thoughtful *consideration*. When found in the *Sun*, *Moon*, or *Venus* placements, *Virgo* underscores a *lineage* characterized by a dedication to *progress, meticulousness*, and a deep sense of mission in aiding others, *encouraging* us to walk in their admirable footsteps.

VIRGO MOON - EMOTIONAL AND INTUITIVE LEGACY

A *Moon* in *Virgo* indicates *ancestors* who tended to deal with emotions in a **practical** and **discerning** manner. They might have been hesitant in showing their feelings, choosing to concentrate on finding solutions and assisting others, although they could have faced difficulties with *self-criticism* or striving for *perfection*. This influence could lead descendants to approach emotions carefully, relying on *intuition* and analysis to handle obstacles. While this trait promotes dependability and understanding, it also underscores the significance of *self-kindness* and, notably, emotional vulnerability, urging us to openly express our feelings without holding back.

VIRGO SUN - CORE ESSENCE AND VITALITY

Ancestors with a *Virgo Sun* carried an *essence* of humility. They often dedicated themselves to work, family, or community. Their vitality was expressed through a *commitment* to growth and efficiency, ensuring their efforts benefited those around them. This placement encourages *descendants* to embrace their **practicality**, develop skills with precision, and seek fulfillment through meaningful contributions. It also highlights the need to *balance* striving for excellence with self-acceptance and *flexibility*, providing a more nuanced understanding of the *Ancestral* influences.

VIRGO VENUS - LOVE AND RELATIONAL DYNAMICS

A **Venus** in *Virgo* indicates a *lineage* where love and *connection* are expressed through acts of service, loyalty, and attention to detail. These *ancestors* may have demonstrated **love** through practical gestures rather than grand displays, sometimes becoming overly critical in their quest for perfection. This placement fosters a thoughtful and dependable approach to relationships, encouraging *descendants* to show care through meaningful actions. It also highlights the importance of balancing high standards with kindness and appreciation for imperfections in **love**.

WHEN *VIRGO* APPEARS AS A DOMINANT SIGN IN THE *MoonTree chart*, it amplifies themes of service, precision, and practicality throughout the lineage.

THIS MIGHT INDICATE:

1. A *lineage* of *caregivers*, & problem-solvers dedicated to improving their surroundings.
2. *Ancestral* strengths in organization, critical thinking, and *perseverance*.
3. Patterns of self-criticism or an overemphasis on perfection require *self-love* and a focus on balance.
4. A call for *descendants* to honor their skills & contributions, and embrace the beauty of *imperfection*.

LIBRA

When *LIBRA* holds a prominent position in the *Ancestral* chart, it underscores themes of harmony, balance, and relational dynamics. Being a cardinal **Air** sign, *Libra* represents diplomacy, fairness, and a profound admiration for beauty, which mirrors a family *lineage* centered on connection and balance. Whether it appears in the *Sun*, *Moon*, or *Venus* placement, it signifies a *lineage* characterized by teamwork, artistic creativity, and a pursuit of justice.

LIBRA MOON - EMOTIONAL AND INTUITIVE LEGACY

A *Moon* in *Libra* indicates *ancestors* who prioritized emotional balance and harmony, valuing relationships and striving for **peace** and **fairness**. They may have faced challenges with indecision or avoiding conflict. This influence can be felt by *descendants* as a tendency to nurture relationships and handle emotions carefully. The graceful and diplomatic *energy* of this placement brings beauty into **life** and emphasizes the importance of addressing emotional needs while *maintaining* a **balanced** approach to relationships, without overly focusing on external *harmony*.

LIBRA SUN - CORE ESSENCE AND VITALITY

Ancestors born under a *Libra* **Sun** radiated a sense of partnership and justice. They thrived in roles that valued fairness, teamwork, and aesthetic elegance. Their vibrant energy manifested in creating harmony and bringing people together. This influence encourages their descendants to appreciate their collaborative spirit, strive for balance in various aspects of life, and embrace beauty and fairness. It also highlights the significance of asserting one's individuality while engaging in partnerships, guiding them to understand the delicate equilibrium between personal desires and harmonious relationships.

LIBRA VENUS - LOVE AND RELATIONAL DYNAMICS

A **Venus** in *Libra* suggests a family history characterized by mutual respect, shared values, and a profound appreciation for aesthetics shaping the concepts of **love** and relationships. *Ancestors* with this placement likely prioritized harmony in relationships but may have faced challenges in setting boundaries or making decisions. This positioning promotes a sophisticated and fair-minded attitude towards love, urging future generations to prioritize cooperation and justice in their relationships. It also emphasizes the significance of balancing individual needs with the goal of fostering harmony in relationships.

WHEN LIBRA IS THE DOMINANT SIGN IN THE *MOONTREE chart*, it enhances themes of balance, connection, and diplomacy across the family's legacy.

THIS MIGHT INDICATE:

1. A *lineage* of mediators, *artists*, or individuals devoted to justice and fairness.
2. *Ancestral* strengths in building relationships, *cultivating* peace, and appreciating *beauty*.
3. *Patterns* of indecision or over-accommodation that require the cultivation of *assertiveness* and *clarity*.
4. A call for *descendants* to honor their ability to bring *harmony* and *beauty* into the world while maintaining *authenticity* and self-assurance.

SCORPIO

SCORPIOS' SIGNIFICANT PLACEMENT IN THE *MOONTREE chart* highlights themes of *transformation* and depth. It serves as a strong *connection* to your *Ancestral* legacy. Being a fixed **Water** sign, *Scorpio* is known for its intensity, emotional **power**, and ability to **regenerate**. This reflects an *Ancestral* heritage characterized by great **strength** and **healing**. Whether it appears in the *Sun, Moon,* or *Venus* placement, *Scorpio* emphasizes a *lineage* filled with **mystery**, emotional depth, and *transformative* experiences. This connection links you to a rich history marked by *resilience* and intense **passion,** and *depth*.

SCORPIO MOON - EMOTIONAL AND INTUITIVE LEGACY

A **Moon** in *Scorpio* indicates *ancestors* who frequently delved deep into their inner worlds, experiencing **intense** emotions. They likely faced significant emotional hurdles, which helped them build resilience and *wisdom*. However, issues with trust and *vulnerability* may have been a challenge for them. Their descendants may sense a profound emotional depth and a strong desire to uncover **hidden** truths within themselves. While this *energy* encourages **intuition** and **healing**, it also underscores the significance of embracing *vulnerability* and letting go of emotional control and tendencies to lean into *jealousy*.

SCORPIO SUN - CORE ESSENCE AND VITALITY

Ancestors born under a *Scorpio* **Sun** possessed a *transformative* and powerful *essence*, serving as a source of **inspiration** and **motivation** for you. They were often viewed as **magnetic** and **mysterious** individuals, unafraid to confront life's *darker* aspects and capable of **creating** significant changes. This *transformative* energy has become a part of your family legacy, urging you to tap into your inner strength, seek personal growth, and respect the *cycles* of **life**, **death**, and **rebirth**. This *alignment* encourages their *descendants* to embrace their resilience, pursue their **passions**, and honor the natural *cycles* of **life**.

SCORPIO VENUS - LOVE AND RELATIONAL DYNAMICS

A ***Venus*** in *Scorpio* suggests a family history where **love** and relationships are marked by **passion**, **loyalty**, and **deep** *emotions*. *Ancestors* with this placement may have experienced intense and sometimes challenging connections, as they sought deep bonds while dealing with *possessiveness* and **secrecy**. This placement encourages a strong and devoted attitude towards **love**, inspiring *descendants* to pursue meaningful and *intense* relationships. It also highlights the need to **balance** emotional depth with openness and trust, offering a supportive foundation for navigating relationships with bravery and openness.

WHEN *SCORPIO* IS THE DOMINANT SIGN IN THE *MOONTREE chart*, it enhances themes of **transformation**, emotional **depth**, and **resilience** within the family's legacy.

THIS MIGHT INDICATE:

1. A *lineage* of *healers*, *mystics*, or individuals adept at navigating life's challenges with strength and insight.
2. *Ancestral* strengths in transformation, loyalty, and emotional *power*.
3. *Patterns* of *secrecy*, emotional control, or resistance to vulnerability that require healing and balance.
4. A call for *descendants* to honor their intuitive gifts and embrace change as a path to growth and empowerment.

SAGITTARIUS

WHEN SAGITTARIUS ASSUMES A PROMINENT POSITION IN THE *Moon Tree chart*, it brings attention to the themes of **exploration, wisdom**, and **freedom**. Being a mutable **Fire** sign, *Sagittarius* represents the quest for knowledge, adventure, and expansive growth, mirroring a heritage of curiosity and *optimism*. Its influence in the *Sun, Moon*, or *Venus* placements underscores a *lineage* characterized by open-mindedness, **philosophical** exploration, and a desire for **life's** profound truths.

SAGITTARIUS MOON - EMOTIONAL AND INTUITIVE LEGACY

A *Moon* in *Sagittarius* indicates *ancestors* who viewed emotions with optimism and a sense of **adventure**. They valued *freedom* and *independence* in their emotional journey, avoiding *stagnation* despite possibly facing challenges such as restlessness or emotional detachment. This influence may lead *descendants* to seek emotional fulfillment through exploration and new encounters. While it *encourages* a positive perspective, it also highlights the importance of **balancing** freedom with emotional *connection* and **grounding**.

SAGITTARIUS SUN - CORE ESSENCE AND VITALITY

Ancestors who had a *Sagittarius* **Sun** embodied a *spirit* of **adventure** and **expansion**. They were probably **adventurous** and forward-thinking, finding purpose in **travel, learning**, or **philosophical** *quests*. This influence motivates their descendants to tap into their own curiosity, seek wisdom, and approach life with openness. It fosters a drive for personal development and a strong bond with the world at large.

SAGITTARIUS VENUS - LOVE AND RELATIONAL DYNAMICS

A **Venus** in *Sagittarius* suggests a family history where love and relationships were embraced with **enthusiasm**, a sense of **adventure**, and a thirst for personal development. These *ancestors* probably cherished freedom and thrills in their relationships but might have found it challenging to maintain *consistency* or *commitment*. This position promotes a lively and daring attitude towards **love**, urging future *generations* to seek companions who stimulate personal growth and have a **passion** for discovery. It also emphasizes the significance of maintaining a **balance** between *independence* and emotional *closeness*, offering valuable insights into relationship *dynamics*.

<hr />

WHEN *SAGITTARIUS* IS THE DOMINANT SIGN IN THE *Moon Tree chart*, it enhances themes of wisdom, freedom, and expansion within the family's legacy.

THIS MIGHT INDICATE:

1. A *lineage* of *philosophers*, *educators*, or *adventurers* driven by curiosity and a *love* for learning.
2. *Ancestral* strengths in optimism, adaptability, and the pursuit of broader perspectives.
3. *Patterns* of *restlessness*, avoidance of deeper emotions, or fear of limitations that require *grounding* and *reflection*.
4. A call for *descendants* to honor their *adventurous* spirit while *cultivating* balance, *commitment*, and emotional depth.

CAPRICORN

WHEN *CAPRICORN* IS IN A PROMINENT POSITION IN THE *Moon Tree chart*, it brings attention to themes of **structure, persever-ance**, and **responsibility**. Being a cardinal **Earth** sign, *Capricorn* repre-sents **discipline, ambition**, and **resilience**, showcasing an *Ancestral* heritage of unwavering resolve and determination. Whether it appears in the ***Sun***, ***Moon***, or ***Venus*** placement, it underscores a *lineage* character-ized by practical *wisdom*, leadership, and dedication to achieving long-term objectives.

CAPRICORN MOON - EMOTIONAL AND INTUITIVE LEGACY

A ***Moon*** in Capricorn indicates that *ancestors* perceived emotions from a perspective of **responsibility** and **practicality**. They likely prioritized emotional control and independence, which could have made them struggle with *vulnerability* or *expressing* emotions openly. The *descen-dants* might sense a strong sense of duty in their emotional *experiences*. This sense of duty can *cultivate* **resilience** and stability, but it requires a careful **equilibrium** between being practical and expressing emotions, along with practicing **self-compassion.**

CAPRICORN SUN - CORE ESSENCE AND VITALITY

Ancestors born under a *Capricorn **Sun*** possessed qualities of **ambition** and **perseverance**. They were probably diligent individuals who valued stability and structure, often assuming leadership positions within their family or community. This trait not only encourages their descendants to tap into their leadership potential but also motivates them to focus on their goals and establish a reputation based on integrity and hard work. Furthermore, it promotes a balanced approach to ambition, self-care, and joy, offering inspiration and empowerment to future generations.

CAPRICORN VENUS - LOVE AND RELATIONAL DYNAMICS

A *Venus* in *Capricorn* suggests a family history where **love** and relationships were valued for their loyalty, seriousness, and emphasis on long-term stability. Ancestors with this placement likely prioritized commitment and responsibility in their relationships, although they may have found it challenging to be emotionally vulnerable. This placement encourages a grounded and purposeful view of love, urging future generations to seek partners who align with their values and goals. It emphasizes the significance of nurturing emotional closeness alongside practical harmony in relationships, underscoring the importance of emotional bonds.

⊷⸺⸱⸺•

WHEN CAPRICORN IS THE DOMINANT SIGN IN THE MoonTree chart, it enhances themes of ambition, discipline, and resilience across the family's legacy.

THIS MIGHT INDICATE:

1. A *lineage* of *leaders, builders,* or *caretakers* who prioritized *stability* and long-term success.
2. *Ancestral* strengths in *responsibility*, *perseverance*, and creating a solid foundation for future *generations*.
3. *Patterns* of emotional restraint, workaholism, or fear of vulnerability that require *mindful* balance and healing.
4. A call for *descendants* to honor their drive and *ambition* while embracing emotional depth and the joys of *life*.

AQUARIUS

AQUARIUS OFFERS A UNIQUE PERSPECTIVE IN THE *MOONTREE chart*, delving into themes of **innovation, independence**, and **collective vision**. Being a fixed **Air** sign, *Aquarius* represents originality, intellectual curiosity, and a strong sense of **humanitarianism**, reflecting an *Ancestral* heritage of forward-thinking ideas and individuality. When *Aquarius* appears in the **Sun**, **Moon**, or **Venus** placement, it highlights a *lineage* defined by progressive values, *unconventional* methods, and a profound bond with the **community**.

AQUARIUS MOON - EMOTIONAL AND INTUITIVE LEGACY

A **Moon** in *Aquarius* indicates *ancestors* who viewed emotions with intellectual detachment and objectivity. They likely cherished freedom and individuality, placing importance on the collective over personal feelings. Their descendants may inherit a tendency to approach emotional situations with innovative thinking and embrace unconventional viewpoints and relationships. It encourages a delicate balance, urging them to merge intellectual autonomy with emotional openness and connection, creating a potent and motivating blend.

AQUARIUS SUN CORE ESSENCE AND VITALITY

Ancestors born under the *Aquarius* **Sun** were known for their originality and forward-thinking mindset. They were often **innovators, visionaries**, or champions of social **change**, motivated by a desire to make a positive impact on their **community** or the world. This aspect serves as an *inspiration* for their descendants to celebrate their uniqueness and challenge conventional norms. It motivates them to follow their interests while recognizing their role in advancing collective growth.

AQUARIUS VENUS - LOVE AND RELATIONAL DYNAMICS

A *Venus* in *Aquarius* suggests a family history *characterized* by an **open** and **curious** approach to **love** and relationships. *Ancestors* with this placement may have prioritized intellectual *connections* over conventional *romantic* standards, nurturing distinct and **unconventional** relationship dynamics. This positioning encourages a **creative** and *independent* attitude towards **love**, urging future generations to pursue relationships that celebrate individuality and common values. It emphasizes the *significance* of *authenticity* and mutual respect in relationships, valuing and honoring each person's distinct viewpoint.

⁕

WHEN AQUARIUS IS THE DOMINANT SIGN IN THE *MOONTREE* *chart,* which is a unique astrological tool that illustrates the emotional and relational dynamics within a family, it enhances themes of innovation, independence, and humanitarianism across the family's history.

THIS MIGHT INDICATE:

1. A *lineage* of *visionaries* and *philosophers* who valued *freedom* and *progress.*
2. *Patterns* of emotional detachment or resistance to conformity that require *balance* and *self-awareness.*
3. A call for *descendants* to honor their unique *perspectives* while cultivating deeper emotional *connections* and collective harmony.

PISCES

The prominent position of *Pisces* in the MoonTree chart sheds light on a lineage characterized by artistic beauty, compassion, creativity, and spiritual connections. Being a mutable **Water** sign, *Pisces* represents emotional depth, intuitive wisdom, and a strong sense of empathy, reflecting a heritage of **healing**, **imagination**, and **mysticism**. When *Pisces* appears in the Sun, Moon, or Venus placement, it underscores a lineage enriched with artistic talents, emotional understanding, and spiritual journeys.

PISCES MOON - EMOTIONAL AND INTUITIVE LEGACY

A *Moon* in *Pisces* indicates *ancestors* who felt emotions deeply with great *sensitivity* and intuitive awareness. They may have been **healers**, **dreamers**, or **visionaries**, highly attuned to the hidden aspects of life, but possibly susceptible to emotional overwhelm or **escapism**. Their descendants may sense this as a strong link to their intuition, creativity, and emotional understanding. Nonetheless, it is important to incorporate grounding techniques to maintain a balance of sensitivity and prevent emotional exhaustion.

PISCES SUN - CORE ESSENCE AND VITALITY

Ancestors born under the *Pisces* **Sun** possessed a nurturing *essence* characterized by compassion, imagination, and spiritual wisdom. They often channeled this energy through **art**, **healing**, or **mystical** *pursuits*, embodying a selfless and caring attitude that still influences their *descendants*. This aspect motivates later generations to embrace their **artistic** and **empathetic** tendencies, drawing power from vulnerability and human *connection*. It also prompts them to seek spiritual development and use their creative talents in a purposeful way.

PISCES VENUS LOVE AND RELATIONAL DYNAMICS

A **Venus** in *Pisces* indicates a family background marked by deeply emotional, idealistic, and spiritually or creatively oriented **love** and relationships. *Ancestors* with this placement might have seen **love** as a strong force, yet faced challenges with idealization and establishing boundaries. This placement promotes a romantic and **compassionate** perspective on relationships for future *generations*, motivating them to seek meaningful and soulful connections. It emphasizes the importance of striking a balance between **idealism**, **boundaries**, and **self-care**, enabling individuals to *effectively* navigate their relationships.

WHEN *PISCES* IS THE DOMINANT SIGN IN THE *MOONTREE chart,* it enhances themes of **sensitivity**, **creativity**, and **spirituality** across the family's legacy.

THIS MIGHT INDICATE:

1. A *lineage* of mystics, artists, healers, or deeply empathetic individuals.
2. Ancestral strengths in intuitive understanding, emotional connection, and artistic expression.
3. Patterns of emotional vulnerability or escapism that require grounding and self-awareness.
4. A call for descendants to honor their sensitivity and creativity while cultivating resilience and emotional balance.

SUN. MOON. VENUS.

The SUN

*O*ur Cosmic Vitality:

The *Sun* represents **life** force, individuality, and **creative** vitality. It is the source of our *inner light*, fueling the drive to express ourselves authentically and contribute meaningfully to the world. The *Sun* not only embodies purpose and confidence but also serves as a **catalyst** for personal growth, *inspiring* us to embrace our unique *essence* and journey. In *Ancestral Alchemology*, the *Sun* symbolizes the core vitality passed through *generations*. It serves as a powerful link, reflecting the creative *essence* and resilience of our *ancestors*, showing how their individuality and strength continue to influence the stories we carry. The *Sun* inspires us to shine boldly, honoring the legacy of **creativity**, **courage**, and **self-expression** embedded in our lineage. As the center of the solar system, the *Sun* is a cosmic anchor, uniting all *planetary* energies with its radiant light. Across cultures, the *Sun* has been revered as a symbol of renewal, power, and the life cycle. The *Sun* connects us to the universal *rhythm* of vitality and purpose. It encourages us to celebrate our individuality while recognizing the shared humanity that binds us, reminding us that we are all part of a larger, *interconnected* whole. Through the *Sun*, we find the balance between self-expression and the greater collective, aligning our journey with the cosmic flow.

FIRE - THE FLAME OF CREATION

The *Sun's* association with **Fire** embodies its *transformative* and creative force. **Fire** symbolizes passion, courage, and the ability to illuminate darkness. As the flame of creation, the *Sun* sparks innovation, drive, and renewal. In *Ancestral Alchemology*, the *Sun's* **fiery** *energy* highlights the vitality and determination of our ancestors. It encourages us to embrace our inner light, using it to navigate life's challenges and fuel personal growth. The *Sun* reminds us that, like **Fire**, our *creative* power must be nurtured and directed with intention.

The Sun - Ancestral Alchemology

THE *SUN* SYMBOLIZES THE *ESSENCE* AND INFLUENCES OF OUR ancestors on our lives, revealing *vitality* and purpose passed down through *generations*. It offers insights into our inherited **strengths** and

gifts, while also teaching us lessons in resilience and growth beyond individuality. By examining *Sun Signs* in our *Moon Tree Chart*, we can discover the creative vitality that flows through our *lineage*, prompting us to reflect on our ancestors' purpose, spirit, and light. This reflection guides us to cultivate these traits within ourselves, helping us to embrace the ***Sun's*** qualities and radiate authenticity and confidence in our lives. This process honors our ancestors' creative legacy and sets us on our unique path forward. In *Ancestral Alchemology*, the ***Sun*** represents renewal and strength, guiding us to harness our creative vitality and align with our purpose. It emphasizes that *endurance* is both a gift and a responsibility. By aligning with the ***Sun's*** energy, we awaken our inner light, *illuminating* our path and inspiring future generations.

The MOON

OUR COSMIC INTUITION:

The *Moon*, a celestial guide to self-reflection, governs intuition, emotion, and the *rhythms* of inner life. It *nurtures* our capacity for empathy, adaptability, and emotional depth, embodying growth, release, and renewal cycles that mirror our spirit's journey. In *Ancestral Alchemology*, the *Moon* symbolizes the emotional and intuitive patterns passed down through *generations*. It reveals how our ancestors nurtured, adapted, and connected to their inner worlds, weaving their emotional wisdom into the fabric of our lives. The *Moon* invites us to honor our inner cycles and embrace the flow of change as a natural part of life. The *Moon's* phases reflect the constant **beginnings**, **endings**, and **renewal** cycle. As it *waxes* and *wanes*, the *Moon* mirrors the rhythms of human experience, reminding us that all things are *interconnected* and ever-changing. The *Moon*, a bridge between the past and the present, connects us to the *unseen* world of intuition and subconscious memory. It's light, though borrowed from the *Sun*, *illuminates* the *shadows* of our psyche, guiding us to integrate and heal. This connection to the *unseen* world sparks our curiosity and invites us to explore the depths of our emotional and spiritual growth.

—·—

THE *Moon's* ASSOCIATION WITH **WATER** EMBODIES ITS nurturing and intuitive nature. **Water** symbolizes flow, adaptability, and emotional depth, mirroring the *Moon's* influence on tides, feelings, and inner transformation. The *Moon's Watery* energy reflects the emotional currents of our *lineage*. It highlights how our ancestors navigated their feelings, formed connections, and weathered life's storms. The *Moon* teaches us to honor these emotional legacies, using them as a source of strength and insight.

The Moon - Ancestral Alchemology

In *Ancestral Alchemology,* the **Moon** plays a significant role by revealing the emotional truths and subconscious patterns of our family story. It symbolizes nurturing qualities and intuitive wisdom that are passed down through our *lineage.* By examining *Moon Signs* in our *Moon Tree chart,* we can uncover emotional *imprints* left by our ancestors. This exploration guides us to delve into cycles of **emotion**, **intuition**, and **healing** within our family, helping us identify strengths and areas for real *transformation.* The **Moon** teaches us to view emotions as a source of power and resilience, inviting us to reflect on our ancestors' nurturing and intuitive gifts. By honoring their emotional journeys, we can *culti-vate* our growth. Through its guidance, the ***Moon*** serves as a beacon for emotional healing and connection in *Ancestral Alchemology*. Its wisdom enables us to navigate the *rhythms* of our inner world, aligning with life cycles and discovering deeper truths within ourselves. The ***Moon's*** presence assures us we are not alone, offering support and understanding along our journey. By embracing its energy, we acknowledge the *exquisite* gifts of intuition and emotion, allowing us to transmute inherited patterns for healing and growth. This connection calls us to embrace our emotional depth, *nurture our spirit*, and tap into the *Ancestral Mysticism* in the **sacred dance of rebirth.**

VENUS

Our Cosmic Heart Space:

Venus, the planet of connection, creativity, and harmony, plays a significant role in cultivating *love* and connections. It encourages us to appreciate everyday life's beauty and build uplifting relationships. More than just romantic *love*, *Venus* represents a universal *love*, an energy that heals and brings people together. *Venus* represents the beauty in connections. In *Ancestral Alchemology*, *Venus* unveils the legacy of *love* and relational values passed down through *generations*. It prompts us to consider our connections **with others, ourselves, and the world**, essential paths toward balance, joy, and personal growth. *Venus* teaches us that *love* is powerful, fostering healing and harmony in our lives and family histories. *Venus* connects the *sky* and the **Earth**, guiding harmony among different cultures and *generations*. Whether through *art*, *nature*, or relationships, *Venus* encourages us to value our connections, embrace creativity, and see *love* as timeless. As a unifying force, *Venus* urges us to balance our inner feelings with outside influences. It reveals how *love* shapes our family histories and the relationships we build and form, *planting seeds* to root further *generations*.

AIR - ESSENCE OF CONNECTION

Connected to the **Air** element, *Venus* symbolizes intellect, communication, and connection. **Air**, in the context of *Ancestral Alchemology*, represents the medium through which these intellectual and communicative aspects of *Venus* are expressed. It brings people together, sharing wisdom and understanding across *generations*. When the *heart* of *Venus* meets the clarity of **Air**, it helps us gain deeper insights into our relationships, values, and personal growth. This *combination* shows that *love* is both something we feel and a choice we make. It invites us to look at our ***ancestors' connection patterns***, encouraging *healing* and growth through open communication and thoughtful actions.

In *Ancestral Alchemology*, ***Venus*** helps us see our family stories' emotional and relational legacies. It highlights how *love*, values, and appreciation for beauty have been passed down, influencing who we are and how we connect with others. ***Venus*** teaches lessons beyond romance, including *empathy*, *balance*, and *communal joy*. Examining our ancestors' relationships and choices, we discover *emotional patterns* that guide our lives today. ***Venus*** allows us to honor our family *lineages* while rewriting negative patterns, creating harmony in ourselves and our *ancestry*.

Cultivating A Legacy Of Love

Venus, with her *transformational* **power**, encourages us to **infuse love** and care into our family stories. By fostering *compassionate* relationships and building *connections* that reflect and **inspire** our own **hearts**, we turn our family narratives into sources of beautiful wisdom. This *transformational* process strengthens the **love** that honors and threads the **past**, enriches our **present**, and encourages **future** *generations*. We create *magical ingredients* lovingly, as we **wildcraft our mystery.**

IN *ANCESTRAL ALCHEMOLOGY*, ***VENUS*** SYMBOLIZES ***LOVE'S*** lasting impact. Her guidance teaches us to appreciate *beauty*, foster connections, and recognize *love* as a powerful, creative force. ***Venus*** reminds us that we are both heirs and creators of **love**, integrating it into our lives. By embracing ***Venus'*** energy, which can be understood as the love, empathy, and balance she represents, we awaken our capacity for **love**. This involves practicing **understanding, forgiveness,** and **empathy** in our relationships. Bringing **joy, harmony,** and **renewal** to ourselves and future *generations* becomes possible when we **embody** these qualities in our daily lives.

LUNAR PHASES

Dancing with the Moon Cycles

*T*he **Moon** is a *sacred* rhythm keeper, a *celestial* mirror that reflects our inner tides while connecting us to the emotional *wisdom* of our *ancestors*. Its **luminous** presence has long witnessed *rituals*, *births*, *griefs*, and *transformations*, holding space for the dreams and resilience of those who came before. In *Ancestral Alchemology*, the **Moon** is not only a guide, it is an **activator**, a **catalyst**, a stirring force in the **alchemical** blend of *lineage, element,* and *self*.

Each *lunar* phase brings a unique energetic signature that enhances the crafting of your **Ancestral Alchemical Potion**. Like a *sacred* **solvent**, the **Moon's** cycles swirl through the **Waters** of your *lineage*, **dissolving** stagnation and awakening *insight*. As we align our practices with the *lunar* rhythm, we become *conscious* co-creators, heeding the same sky that once guided our *ancestors'* **rituals**, **communities**, **plantings**, and **magic**. The **Moon** invites us into a *spiral* of **reflection**, **release**, and **renewal**. It reminds us that healing is not **linear**, it is **cyclical**, *intuitive*, and deeply *personal*. As you attune to each phase, your *Ancestral elixir* is **stirred**, **activated**, and **refined**, phase by phase, drop by drop.

The Phases of the Moon

EACH *PHASE* OF THE *LUNAR* CYCLE BRINGS A DISTINCT *energetic* current for *Ancestral* exploration, *elixir* crafting, and *ritual* practice within the *Ancestral Alchemology* method.

A TIME OF *FERTILE* **VOID** SPACE and *potential*. The **cauldron** is empty; the **Waters** are *still*. This is where your **potion** begins: set your *intentions*, reflect in quiet, and call forward *Ancestral* guidance. Meditate, journal, or create vision boards infused with the strengths and **patterns** you wish to *transform* or continue.

NEW MOON
The Seed of Intention

Embodiment: Begin in stillness, seated or lying down. Place your hands over your *womb* space or lower belly and breathe deeply into your body. Let each breath feel like a whisper into the **void**. Move slowly in circles, *hips, shoulders,* or *spine*, inviting energy to gather in preparation. This is the body's *sacred* pause.

THE *SEEDS* ARE **STIRRING**. Momentum builds. This is the phase for **energizing** your *Ancestral elixir*, nourishing your *intentions*, and deepening your *lineage* connection. Visualize *Ancestral* resilience, explore family stories, and meditate on the pathways they've walked.

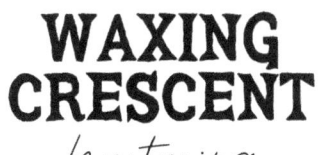

WAXING CRESCENT
Nurturing Growth

Embodiment: Rise slowly with the breath. Practice slow-flowing movements like *cat-cow, hip openers*, or gentle *spiraling dance* to encourage energy flow through the spine and hips. Light tapping on the chest and arms can awaken stored **memory** and help integrate intention into the body.

The **Fire** rises. Resistance meets movement. This phase *inspires* action and courage—confront inherited **patterns**, name emotional blocks, and draw on ancestral strength to transmute what surfaces. Your **potion** begins to *heat* and *change*.

Embodiment: Engage in *powerful*, structured movement, such as *Warrior poses, lunges,* or *stomping* movements onto the **Earth**, pulling energy up. Let sound *release* through the breath (e.g., "HA!" exhales). *Shake* out the limbs. Use movement to claim your space and **embody** *determination*.

FIRST QUARTER
Rising to the Challenge

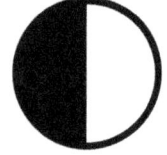

WAXING GIBBOUS
Refining the Brew

THE **MIXTURE** THICKENS; clarity sharpens. Use this phase to reassess and *refine*. Adjust your *rituals*, deepen your understanding of family *mysticism*, and prepare your **potion** for its next *transformation*. This is where *Ancestral* insight begins to **crystallize**.

Embodiment: Slow, *casting* movements, tai chi-*inspired* arm movements, *intention*-filled gestures, or *mirror* work. Use your hands "brushing" *energy* across your body and around you, shaping your **space**. You may also engage in slow, *rhythmic* walking or **spiral** dances to **embody** *recalibration*.

FULL MOON

The Illumination of Truth

THE *ELIXIR* **SHIMMERS**. *ILLUMI-nation* is complete. The Full *Moon* casts light into every corner of the *lineage*, celebrating what is whole and revealing what must be *released*. Engage in **moonlit** *rituals* of *gratitude*, *forgiveness*, and *Ancestral* **remembrance**. Burn old stories, offer flowers, or speak aloud what is ready to be let go.

Embodiment Practice: Move outside under the *Moon* if possible. **Dance** freely, *ecstatically*, or *circle* in **moonlight**. Open the chest and arms wide in *crescent* and heart-opening poses. *Chant, vocalize,* or *sing*. Allow breath and movement to *express* what is **overflowing**, offer it back to the sky, and *root* it into the **Earth**.

THE **BREW** SETTLES. NOW IS THE time to gather *insight* and give thanks. Reflect on the lessons your *lineage* has passed down and how they've shown up in your *journey*. Create *art, write* stories, or *share* your **reflections** to honor the *wisdom* now **integrated**.

Embodiment Practice: Practice slow, repetitive movements, *swaying, rocking,* or gentle *flowing* sequences that *mimic* gathering or cradling. Touch your **heart**, your *belly*, your *feet*, and thank your body for carrying so much. Incorporate *humming* to deepen the sense of *gratitude* and *connection* you are *cultivating*.

WANING GIBBOUS

Harvesting Wisdom

LAST QUARTER
Releasing and Realigning

THE *ELIXIR* **CLARIFIES**. RELEASE what no longer belongs in your system. This phase is for cleansing inherited beliefs, outdated roles, or burdens that have reached their end. *Grounding* practices, *salt baths*, or *Ancestral* smoke *rituals* are especially **potent** here.

Embodiment Practice: Use *deep squats, forward folds,* or *rooted* postures to draw *energy* downward and out. *Sweep* or *brush* the body with your hands as a cleansing gesture. Use your exhale intentionally, let it carry away *heaviness*. Walk *barefoot* on the **Earth** or press your hands into the *soil*.

THE **VESSEL** RESTS. THE **POTION** settles. This final phase is both the **Waning Crescent** and the **Dark Moon**, a threshold space of deep *release, stillness,* and *integration*. Here, we are invited to surrender fully, to enter the *fertile* darkness where everything **dissolves** before becoming new again. This is a phase of quiet *retreat*— a time to honor endings, **mourn** what has passed, and prepare the internal ground for the next *cycle* of *growth*. Reflect on the stories you've carried, the *rituals* you've moved through, and the *wisdom* now held within your *bones*.

WANING CRESCENT / DARK MOON
Rest and Integration

Embodiment Practice: Return to stillness. Let your body melt into restorative poses like supported fish pose or child's pose. Cover your eyes with an eye pillow to *connect* with the *unseen*. Breathe deeply into the *pelvis*, the *womb*, the *root*. This is a space of beautiful undoing, so that **rebirth** can happen. Let your breath slow. Let yourself be held. You may also **light** a single **dark** candle and speak the names of those whose *stories* you carry, letting the silence speak back. This is the *sacred* pause before the new *elixir* begins to stir again. In this fertile *void*, your *essence* is **distilled**.

> The Moon, like an ancient apothecary, stirs the elements within us-activating memory, intuition, and transformation. To dance with the Moon is to stir the elixir of your lineage with breath, emotion, and sacred intention. With each cycle, you distill your essence more clearly, becoming a vessel of ancestral wisdom shaped by both shadow and light

THE ANCESTRAL CONNECTION TO LUNAR PHASES

The ***Moon's*** cycles connect us to the deep, *rhythmic* intelligence of our *lineage*. By tracing the ***Moon*** phases present during *significant* family events, **births**, **deaths**, and turning points, we begin to reveal *energetic* **patterns** and emotional *themes* that echo through *generations*.

When a specific *lunar* phase recurs across your family's history, it speaks to the inherited *rhythms* your *ancestors* moved with, their emotional *imprints*, lessons, and ways of navigating **life.**

- **New Moon Dominance** - A *lineage* shaped by **beginnings**, **adaptability**, and the quiet courage to *plant* **seeds** in the fertile *void*.
- **Full Moon Presence** - A legacy of **emotional** visibility, **intuition**, and the power of **expression.**
- **Waning Moon Patterns** - Deep *gifts* of **reflection**, *sacred* **release**, and *transformation* through endings.

When we bring in the *elemental* layers - **Fire**, **Earth**, **Air**, and **Water** - we begin to sense how these *Ancestral* energies *swirl* through our lives as part of our unique *elixir* of being. The ***Moon's*** *cycles* **stir** these *elements* within us, *activating* different layers of **memory**, **instinct**, and *inherited* **emotion**.

The ***Moon's*** 29.5-day *lunation* is not just a **celestial** *rhythm*, it is a living inheritance, one our *ancestors* honored through *ritual*, *community*, *storytelling*, and the timing of birth and burial. To align with the ***Moon*** now is not merely to follow nature's *rhythm*, it is to remember. To stir the **Waters** of *lineage*. To *refine* the **potion** we carry within. Each phase becomes an opening, a chance to deepen our *embodiment*, reclaim *Ancestral wisdom,* and live with more *intention* as **vessels** of **love**, **healing,** and **remembrance**.

Lunar Phases

Sacred Lunar Essence

Sacred Lunar Essence - Ancestral Alchemology

Practical Ways to Connect with the Moon's Cycle in Ancestral Exploration

1. Create Rituals for Each Phase:

Design lunar rituals that attune to both the phase and your lineage. They may be simple or elaborate—what matters is intention.

Ritual Tip:
Include Ancestral elements: family herbs or recipes, traditional music, heirlooms,
or scents associated with your culture. Let the ritual be a bridge between timelines.

2. Honor Rhythms of Release and Growth:

Just as the Moon waxes and wanes, so too does ancestral energy flow in cycles of holding and letting go. Some patterns require nurturing; others call for sacred release. Reflect on how your ancestors may have followed these rhythms—planting by Moonlight, harvesting by phase.

Embodiment Tip:
Spend time outdoors under the Moon.
Let your body feel the difference between the expansive energy of the waxing Moon and the inward pull of the waning.

3. Journal with the Lunar Cycle:

Let each lunar phase guide your reflection.

Ritual Tip:
Use prompts such as:
"What ancestral strength wants to be reclaimed?"
"What am I ready to stop carrying for those who came before me?"

4. Create a Lunar Ancestral Altar:

A dedicated altar brings the practice into form. It becomes a living space where intention, lineage, and lunar energy meet.

• *Moon Symbols* – Silver objects, crescent shapes, water vessels, mirrors
• *Ancestral Items* – Photos, keepsakes, or handwritten names
• *Elemental Offerings* – Stones, shells, plants tied to family origins

Ritual Tip:
Refresh the altar each phase—flowers for growth, ashes or dark cloths for release,
moonstones or water for Full Moon illumination.

5. Dream Work with the Moon:

The Moon enhances intuition and dreamwork.

- Set intentions before sleep to receive messages from your ancestors.
- Journal dreams upon waking—note patterns, symbols, or Ancestral presences.
- Reflect on unresolved emotions or insights that emerge.

Ritual Tip:

Keep a moonstone or family heirloom beside your bed.
Use calming herbs like mugwort or lavender to deepen dreaming.

6. Moonlight Meditations:

Meditating under the Moon can strengthen the connection between body, spirit, and lineage.

• ***Full Moon:*** *Sit in the moonlight and visualize beams illuminating your ancestral lines.*
• ***New Moon:*** *Meditate in darkness—feel the mystery, listen inwardly, and invite Ancestral guidance.*
• ***All Phases:*** *Use breath to move energy—inhale lunar light, exhale inherited negative patterns.*

Meditation Tip:

Incorporate slow, flowing movement like breath-based swaying, lunar mudras,
or moon salutations to embody your connection.

7. Connecting with Feminine Lineage:

The Moon is deeply linked to the divine feminine, the cyclical body, and the Ancestral motherlines.

• *Honor women in your family through storytelling, cooking, or ritual acts of care*
• *Use the Waning Moon to release womb-based or maternal grief*
• *Reflect on the wisdom passed through your female ancestors—intuition, magic, and survival*

Note:

This work is for all genders. The Moon connects to everyone.
Men can also use lunar rhythms to connect to intuition, emotional lineage, and nurturing presence.

THE DARK MOON

Potent Ancestral Energy

Dark Moon

The **Dark Moon**, the final breath before the New Moon's renewal, is a sacred space for release, remembrance, and transformation. Shrouded in mystery, this phase marks the moment when the Moon disappears from the sky, inviting us into stillness, silence, and surrender. It is not merely an ending, but a potent moment of transition, a pause in the lunar alchemical process when the old sediments settle and the vessel is cleansed. For ancestral and grief work, the Dark Moon holds profound power. It offers a liminal space between worlds, where the veil is thin, the heart is open, and the soul is called inward. Here, we are invited to **empty**, to **shed**, and to **prepare the elixir for a new infusion of light**. In *Ancestral Alchemology*, this is a time to engage deeply with the shadows, with those carried by our lineage, held in our bodies, and woven through unspoken histories. We listen to what has been buried. We mourn what has been lost. And we make space for what is ready to emerge.

Practices for Ancestral Connection during the Dark Moon

1. ACKNOWLEDGE HIDDEN FAMILY HISTORIES

Bring light to what has long been hidden. Speak or write the truths that may have been silenced or forgotten. Let this act of remembrance become an offering.

2. RELEASE INHERITED BURDENS

Let go of shame, guilt, silence, or sorrow that no longer belongs to you. With breath and ritual, liberate yourself from the emotional weight of generations past. This is the clearing of the vessel.

3. INTEGRATE ANCESTRAL WISDOM

Amid the darkness, reflect on the strengths that survived. Gather the medicine of your lineage, the courage, the creativity, the resilience, and allow it to alchemize within you.

4. HONOR THE DARK MOON THROUGH RITUAL

- **Silent Meditation & Ancestral Listening:** Sit in darkness or by candlelight. Invite the presence of those who came before you. Let their quiet wisdom rise.
- **Offerings to Ancestors:** Pour Water into a bowl. Light a single flame. Place objects or food they loved. Let these simple acts become sacred gestures of connection.
- **Writing & Reflection:** Journal about the grief you carry or wish to release. Write a letter to an ancestor. Burn or bury what you are ready to let go.
- **Grief and Release Ceremonies:** Create ritual space for mourning. Sing, weep, shake, or sit still. Allow the body to express what words cannot. This is grief as alchemy, turning pain into presence.

The *Dark Moon* is not empty, it is **full of the unseen**. It is the deep well from which *Ancestral* memory rises and into which old stories dissolve. By honoring this sacred phase, you step into the mystery as a **vessel** of *transformation*, shaped by the past, preparing to hold the next phase of your *lineage's elixir*.

Part Three

THE BODY

BODY MAGIC

Integrating Somatics, Astrology, and Ancestral Mysticism

Body Magic in Ancestral Alchemology

Astrology as a Guide to the Body

strology **bridges** the **celestial** and the **physical**, mapping the influence of the *stars* directly onto the body. Each zodiac sign governs specific anatomical regions, forming a cosmic **blueprint** that links the *cosmos* to the *Earthly* vessel. When this **ancient** wisdom is paired with somatic awareness and *Ancestral* insight, it becomes a **potent** tool for **healing**, **integration**, and **rewriting** inherited narratives.

EXAMPLES OF ASTROLOGICAL BODY CONNECTIONS:

- *Gemini* - **Shoulders and arms** - Echoes of communication, connection, and the emotional burdens carried across generations.
- *Leo* - **Heart and spine** - Radiance, creative courage, and the vulnerability held at the center of *Ancestral* pride or pain.

Astrology invites us to explore these subtle correspondences through **movement**, **ritual**, and *conscious* **embodiment**, transforming physical *imprints* into gateways for *Ancestral* remembrance and personal *transformation*.

SOMATICS:
Unlocking the Body's Wisdom

Derived from the Greek word *soma*, meaning "living body," **somatics** is the **art** of listening to the **body** as a *wise*, expressive, and intuitive guide. Our physical forms store **memory**, **emotion**, and *Ancestral* echoes within **muscle**, **breath**, and **bone**. Through gentle awareness and movement, somatic practices offer a way to unravel tension, process trauma, and reconnect to the body as a *sacred* ally.

WHY SOMATIC PRACTICES MATTER:

- Deepens awareness of bodily sensations and inherited patterns
- Release trauma stored in tissues and the nervous system
- Restore holistic balance through embodied presence

PRACTICES TO EXPLORE:

1. **Feldenkrais Method** - Subtle, mindful movements that enhance ease and alignment
2. **Body-Mind Centering** -Tactile exploration of internal systems and fluid awareness
3. **Alexander Technique** - Releasing habitual tension and reclaiming graceful movement

The **body** is an active **vessel** of power and a *magical* terrain for **reclamation**. Through somatic **ritual**, we transmute what we carry into vitality and inner *sovereignty*.

EMBODIMENT:
Living Fully in the Body

Embodiment is the *sacred* practice of fully inhabiting the **body**, *aligning* **thought**, **emotion**, and **movement** into one *integrated*, authentic *expression*. It invites us to return to ourselves, not as fragmented beings, but as whole, breathing **vessels** of experience, memory, and *Ancestral essence*.

WHY EMBODIMENT MATTERS:

- Cultivates unity between mind, body, and spirit
- Fosters emotional intelligence through presence
- Supports authentic, expressive, spirit-led living

PRACTICES TO EXPLORE:

- **Dance** – Freeform or guided movement to channel emotion and ancestral rhythm
- **Yoga** – Breath-infused practices that align intention, structure, and flow
- **Expressive Arts** – Painting, music, voice, or tactile creation as somatic storytelling

Embodiment *transforms wisdom* into action. It **roots** *Ancestral* insight into the now, allowing us to carry forward the elixir of what has been healed, felt, and known through the body.

Embodiment of Ancestral Mysticism

Ancestral energy is not just inherited, it is lived, moved, and expressed. Through embodied practices, we alchemize the lessons and stories passed down to us, turning them into sacred ingredients for our **Ancestral Alchemical Elixir**. In this work, we become both the wildcrafters and the vessels.

WAYS TO EMBODY ANCESTRAL MYSTICISM

- **Ritual Movement** – Dance or flow with zodiacal energies. Invoke Pisces through undulating, wave-like motion; channel

Aries through sharp, fiery expressions. Let the elements move you.

- **Storytelling as Incantation** – Speak or write your family's stories. Let their joys, losses, and teachings become ritualized memory. This act weaves ancestral timelines into the present moment.
- **Altar Work as Anchor** – Create a sacred space with heirlooms, astrological symbols, and natural elements tied to your family line. Let this be a place of daily devotion, reflection, and energetic grounding.

ASTROLOGY AND THE BODY

A Cosmic Ancestral Bridge

*A*strology connects celestial influences with *Ancestral* narratives, showing us how the **stars** can shape our *physicality* and inherited energies.

EXAMPLES OF ASTROLOGICAL-SOMATIC INTEGRATION:

- **Aries (Head):** Embody leadership or address struggles with self-assertion through head-focused movement or meditation.
- **Taurus (Throat):** Explore inherited values and expression through vocal exercises or singing.

This *Cosmic Ancestral* bridge reminds us that our bodies carry the echoes of our *ancestors'* lives, offering insight and pathways for growth. It gives us a way to uncover the **patterns**, explore and rewrite *Ancestral* **patterns,** and also add to our collective *Ancestral* story. *Decoding* the **elemental patterns** and energies using the *Ancestral Alchemology* method reveals how ancestral energies influence your body. It offers a *blueprint* for aligning practices with *zodiacal* and *elemental* insights. It invites us to work with the elements and signs represented in our *lineage* to deepen our *connection* to our **roots**.

PRACTICAL WAYS TO WORK WITH ASTROLOGY, THE BODY, AND ANCESTRAL ENERGY

1. Move with Intention: Align your physical practices with the *astrological* energies within your body.

For example:

- **Leo:** Heart-opening yoga poses or expressive dance to embody confidence and creativity.

- **Capricorn:** Grounding movements like mindful walking or mountain poses to enhance stability and resilience.

2. Honor Your Ancestors: Design rituals that align with astrological themes and cycles, such as lighting a candle during the New Moon in your zodiac sign to set intentions or offering gratitude during a Full Moon for the strength and resilience passed down through your lineage.

3. Integrate Somatic Awareness: Tune into your body's sensations during celestial events like eclipses or retrogrades. Notice how these cosmic shifts impact your physical and emotional states. Use breathwork, gentle movement, or journaling to maintain balance and foster a deeper connection to yourself and your ancestry, helping you stay centered and in control amidst the cosmic chaos.

CONNECTING YOUR *SOMATIC* AND *ANCESTRAL* PRACTICES with **astrology** taps into a universal flow, the timeless *cosmic* **rhythms** guiding humanity for ages. This isn't just about uncovering inherited *trauma* or family **patterns**; it's about embracing your **true self**, honoring your **roots**, and creating space for deep **healing** and *transformation*. By *weaving* **celestial** *wisdom* into **embodied** action, you **bridge** the **past** and **present**. You honor your ancestors' *resilience* and lessons, release what hinders your growth, and embrace your *unfolding* journey. **Astrology** and *somatic* work remind us we're connected to the *cosmos* and our *lineage*, offering a dynamic map for navigating life with **clarity**, **balance**, and **purpose**, *rooted* in stellar *wisdom* and *Ancestral* strength.

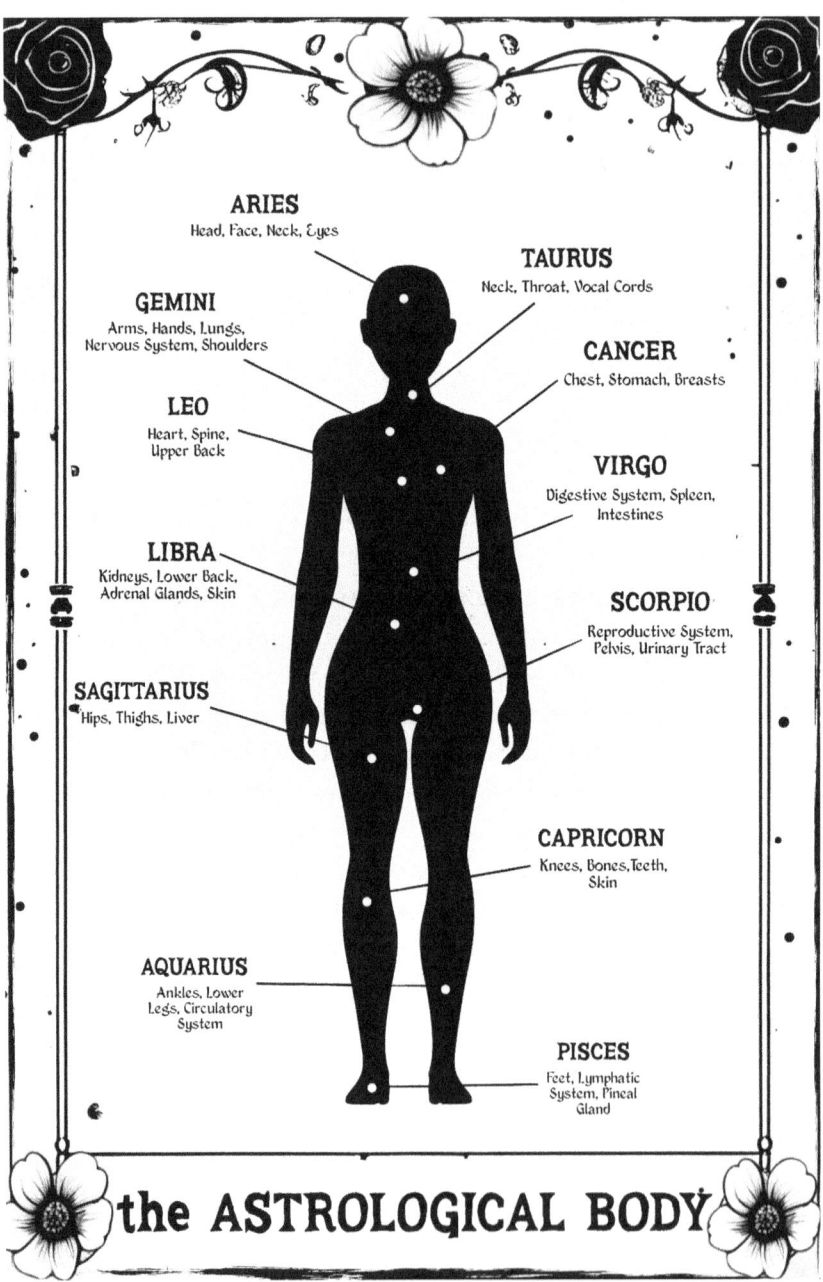

ARIES
Head, Face, Neck, Eyes

TAURUS
Neck, Throat, Vocal Cords

GEMINI
Arms, Hands, Lungs,
Nervous System, Shoulders

CANCER
Chest, Stomach, Breasts

LEO
Heart, Spine,
Upper Back

VIRGO
Digestive System, Spleen,
Intestines

LIBRA
Kidneys, Lower Back,
Adrenal Glands, Skin

SCORPIO
Reproductive System,
Pelvis, Urinary Tract

SAGITTARIUS
Hips, Thighs, Liver

CAPRICORN
Knees, Bones, Teeth,
Skin

AQUARIUS
Ankles, Lower
Legs, Circulatory
System

PISCES
Feet, Lymphatic
System, Pineal
Gland

the ASTROLOGICAL BODY

ARIES
Embodiment of FIRE
& Ancestral Focus

BODY AREAS: HEAD, FACE, NECK, EYES

HARNESSING ARIES' FIERY ENERGY ALLOWS FOR THE RELEASE of stored tension, enhanced clarity, and a deeper alignment with the ancestral imprints held in the head, face, and neck, the regions ruled by Aries. This somatic connection goes beyond awareness; it becomes a form of empowerment. When we embody the essence of Aries ancestors, those who led with instinct, courage, and bold vision, we awaken a reservoir of inherited drive within ourselves. This pioneering force often manifests as intensity or overthinking, particularly in the jaw, temples, and upper shoulders. These areas may carry ancestral determination or unresolved momentum. Mindful engagement with these zones through movement, breath, and presence invites release, steadiness, and inspired action. By tending to Aries' body potion, we transmute tension into vitality and forge a direct link between personal evolution and ancestral fire.

MOVEMENT AND EMBODIMENT PRACTICES

- **Somatic Movement:** Gentle head rolls, jaw stretches, and slow neck rotations to release stored tension and promote alignment.
- **Self-Massage:** Use a calming/cooling essential oil to massage the temples, neck, and shoulders, soothing overactive *Aries* energy and promoting relaxation.

CHAKRA CORRESPONDENCE

1. **Primary Chakra:** *Third Eye* chakra (Ajna) - Tap into *Aries'* *clarity, intuition*, and *visionary thinking*. Practices like forehead massage or visualization exercises can amplify focus and insight.
2. **Secondary Chakra:** *Solar Plexus* chakra (Manipura) - supports *Aries'* determination and **Fiery** drive. Engaging in core-strengthening exercises or meditative practices focused on personal empowerment is a powerful way to harness *Aries'* energy for personal growth.

ARIES Season *Practice*

When the **Sun is in Aries**, marking Aries season, or when the **Moon moves through Aries**, the essence of activation stirs within and around us. This is a sacred window to engage the Aries-governed body areas: the head, face, and upper neck. These energetic zones become ignition points for courage, clarity, and instinctual fire, especially for those with Aries strongly woven into their **MoonTree Chart**, or when working with the lineage of an Aries ancestor. In *Ancestral Alchemology*, *Aries* energy often flows through the elixir of lineage as themes of boldness, innovation, and the ancestral will to initiate change. These Ancestral sparks live within us as sacred Fire, ready to be stirred through movement, ritual, and intention. Somatic practices that awaken the headspace, such as dynamic breathwork, chanting, jaw release, or invigorating neck stretches, help activate this **Aries Body Potion**, channeling Fire into focus. By attuning to this energy with mindful embodiment, we honor the Ancestral trait of fearless becoming. We ignite our creative flame, anchor into selfhood, and walk forward with renewed vitality, held by the firelight of those who came before.

TAURUS
Embodiment of EARTH
& Ancestral Expression

BODY AREAS: NECK, THROAT, VOCAL CORDS

THE INTENTION HERE IS TO SUPPORT YOU IN HARNESSING Taurus' earthy, grounding energy, not only to ease tension and open the Throat Chakra, but to cultivate authentic communication rooted in presence. Through somatic practices focused on the neck, throat, and vocal cords, the regions ruled by Taurus, we connect to the ancestral legacy of stability, nurturance, and resilience. This is a body potion of calm strength, one that supports clarity in expression and confidence in being. Taurus' steady nature, while deeply supportive, can sometimes manifest as tension or constriction in these areas, reflecting the weight of responsibility or the holding of unspoken truths. By gently tending to these zones, we invite spaciousness where there has been holding, and release where words long to be spoken. In this embodied alchemy, Taurus's Ancestral essence becomes a source of rooted power, cultivating patience, emotional clarity, and grounded self-expression, helping you feel steady, capable, and connected.

MOVEMENT & EMBODIMENT PRACTICES

- **Somatic Movement:** Gentle **humming** for vocal release and **slow neck rolls** to dissolve tension and *"sediments"*.
- **Self Massage:** Massage the **neck** with a grounding essential oil to release tension and promote relaxation. This also connects to the body's *imprints* through and *Taurus essence*, listening and exploring the *Ancestral* **connection** and messages.

CHAKRA CORRESPONDENCE

1. **Primary Chakra:** *Throat* Chakra (Vishuddha) - This chakra encourages a focus on authentic *communication* and *self-expression*. Practices like **chanting** or **journaling** can help deepen *clarity* and *expression*.
2. **Secondary Chakra:** *Root* Chakra (Muladhara) - This secondary chakra aligns with *Taurus's* **grounding** and **stabilizing** *essence*, cultivating a deep *connection* to **security**, **resilience**, and the **physical world.** Exploring and *integrating* **grounding** practices into a daily *ritual*/routine, like **walking barefoot** on the **Earth** or **visualizing roots** anchoring you, supports a sense of *stability* and being deeply *cared* for.

TAURUS Season *Practice*

During Taurus season, or when the Moon passes through Taurus, the celestial alignment enhances the potency of somatic rituals. These windows invite us to work intentionally with the Taurus-governed body areas, especially the throat and neck, as sacred entry points into grounded expression and *Ancestral* memory. For those with Taurus prominence in their *Moon Tree Chart*, or when connecting with a Taurus ancestor, these practices become especially potent. In lineages shaped by Taurus energy, the **Ancestral Elixir** often carries notes of patience, nurturance, and emotional steadiness. By tending to the neck and throat with breath, voice, and presence, we stir this **Taurus Body Potion**, honoring inherited strength and making space for expression that is both soft and solid. These embodied rituals offer more than physical ease, they cultivate a legacy of calm resilience and unwavering support, rooted in the slow magic of Earth.

GEMINI
Embodiment of AIR
& Ancestral Curiosity

BODY AREAS: ARMS, HANDS, LUNGS, NERVOUS SYSTEM, SHOULDERS

WILDCRAFT GEMINI'S INTELLECTUAL AND COMMUNICATIVE essence as a body potion for mobility, breath, and mental clarity. This lively Air sign governs the arms, hands, lungs, and nervous system - areas often stirred by overstimulation or the restlessness of a curious mind. In the body, these regions may carry the energetic imprint of scattered focus or ancestral stories left unfinished, unspoken, or unshared. Gemini thrives on movement, conversation, and the exchange of ideas. Through intentional breathwork, mindful hand and arm movements, and practices that calm the nervous system, we begin to distill Gemini's airy elixir into clarity and connection. These somatic explorations create a bridge between intellect and embodiment, aligning us with the ancestral and astrological rhythms of Gemini - and with the wisdom carried through our lineage's voice, hands, and breath.

MOVEMENT & EMBODIMENT PRACTICES

- **Somatic Movement:** Gentle shoulder rolls, wrist and hand stretches, and hand flexion exercises to release tension and improve dexterity.
- **Self Massage:** Massage the hands and forearms to stimulate circulation and focus.

CHAKRA CORRESPONDENCE

1. **Primary Chakra:** *Throat* Chakra (Vishuddha) - Strengthens and taps into *Gemini's* focus on **communication, self-**

expression, and connection through **vocal exercises** or **journaling**.

2. **Secondary Chakra:** *Heart* Chakra (Anahata) - Taps into *Gemini's* quick, **Airy** energy, cultivating **compassion**, **openness**, and **grounded** relationships.

GEMINI Season *Practice*

During **Gemini season**, when the **Sun lights up this Air sign**, or when the **Moon moves through Gemini**, the energy of communication, curiosity, and mental agility is amplified. These are powerful windows to engage in somatic practices that align with Gemini's dynamic essence, especially for those with Gemini influences in their MoonTree Chart or when honoring a Gemini ancestor. In such lineages, the arms, hands, and lungs may carry ancestral imprints of quick-thinking minds, expressive gifts, and the need to move or speak what was once left unsaid. Working with these body areas through breath, movement, and mindful nervous system support helps awaken the **Gemini Body Potion**, an airy elixir of clarity, adaptability, and creative flow. These rituals stir inherited gifts, encouraging vibrant exchange and personal insight. They help us embody the ancestral wisdom of motion and message, honoring a lineage shaped by words, wit, and the breath of connection.

CANCER
Embodiment of WATER
& Ancestral Nurturing Energy

BODY AREAS: CHEST, STOMACH, BREASTS

CANCER, THE ZODIAC'S INTUITIVE NURTURER, GOVERNS THE chest and stomach regions deeply tied to emotional digestion, breath, and the sacred art of care. These body areas often hold the sediments of inherited emotion: grief unspoken, love unexpressed, or the protective instincts of Ancestral caregivers. By tending to this Watery terrain through somatic and Ancestral practices, we stir Cancer's **Body Potion**, a gentle elixir of emotional presence, inner security, and resilience.

Opening the chest, softening the belly, and attuning to breath flow activates a healing current. These embodied rituals invite us to feel held by our bodies, our breath, and the wisdom of those who came before us. When we embody Cancer's essence in this way, we harmonize sensation with spirit, transforming inherited tenderness into a strength that radiates from the inside out.

MOVEMENT & EMBODIMENT PRACTICES

- **Somatic Movement:** Relaxing chest-opening exercises, deep breathing, and abdominal massage to relieve tension and encourage emotional processing.
- **Self-Massage:** Relieve tension and connect with your emotions with a self-touch chest and stomach massage.

CHAKRA CORRESPONDENCE

1. **Primary Chakra:** *Heart Chakra* (Anahata) - This chakra reflects Cancer's nurturing essence and emotional depth.

Heart-opening practices like breathwork or gentle yoga amplify love and empathy.
2. **Secondary Chakra:** *Sacral Chakra* (Svadhisthana) - Aligns with Cancer's Water element, nurturing emotional flow and creativity.

CANCER Season *Practice*

During **Cancer season**, when the **Sun illuminates Cancer's emotional terrain**, or when the **Moon moves through Cancer**, it's a sacred time to return to nurturing practices that soothe the heart and abdomen. These moments are especially resonant for those with Cancer prominence in their **MoonTree Chart**, or when honoring the presence of a Cancer ancestor. In these lineages, the chest and stomach often hold the **emotional waters** of caregiving, intuitive strength, and the quiet labor of love. Somatic practices that open the chest and calm the belly activate the **Cancer Body Potion**, a gentle elixir of protection, nourishment, and ancestral compassion. These rituals honor the legacy of those who held space before us, weaving inner security with a collective capacity to care. As we work with Cancer's energy, we soften into emotional equilibrium and root ourselves in a lineage defined not just by feeling, but by the strength it takes to hold and heal.

LEO
Embodiment of FIRE
& Ancestral Radiance

BODY AREAS: HEART, SPINE, UPPER BACK

LEO, THE RADIANT FLAME OF THE ZODIAC, GOVERNS THE heart, spine, and upper back, centers of emotional vitality, strength, and self-expression. This Fire sign governs from the center, where spirit meets courage, and often reflects ancestral patterns around worth, leadership, and visibility. Tension in the upper back or chest may reveal the weight of inherited expectations or the desire to be seen and valued. Somatic practices that open the heart space and strengthen the spine activate the **Leo Body Potion**, an elixir of confidence, charisma, and authentic presence. These movements help release emotional burdens and reignite the inner flame. By aligning body and spirit with Leo's essence, we cultivate resilience and creative boldness while honoring the ancestral spark that continues to burn within us.

MOVEMENT & EMBODIMENT PRACTICES

- **Somatic Movement:** Relieve tension and restore balance with gentle backbends, shoulder rolls, and heart-opening shapes.
- **Self-Massage:** Chest and upper back massage invigorates the senses and relieves tension.

CHAKRA CORRESPONDENCE

1. **Primary Chakra:** *Heart Chakra* (Anahata) - is the primary chakra that aligns with Leo's essence of love, emotional courage, and self-expression. This alignment amplifies compassion and charisma, enhancing the *Leo* experience.

2. **Secondary Chakra:** *Solar Plexus Chakra* (Manipura) - Reflects Leo's personal power, confidence, and dynamic energy, fostering a strong sense of self, and connects to the Fire element.

LEO Season *Practice*

During **Leo season**, or when the ***Sun*** or ***Moon*** *illuminates Leo*, it's a **potent** time to engage in embodiment practices that awaken the fire of creativity, courage, and self-expression. These movements become especially meaningful when honoring Leo ancestors or exploring Leo influences in your *Moon Tree Chart*. Families with a strong Leo presence often carry the ancestral flame of boldness, charisma, and radiant leadership. Somatic rituals focused on the heart and spine activate the **Leo Body Potion**, an alchemical blend of vitality, visibility, and creative power. These practices help transmute ancestral tensions into personal courage, inviting individuals to step fully into their light. As we work with *Leo's essence*, we cultivate a lineage infused with expressive brilliance and emotional strength, crafting an elixir of confidence and **authenticity** that uplifts the collective spirit.

VIRGO
Embodiment of Earth & Ancestral Hearth

BODY AREAS: DIGESTIVE SYSTEM, SPLEEN, INTESTINES

VIRGO'S GROUNDED, METICULOUS ENERGY GOVERNS THE **digestive system**, the gut, and the vital rhythms that keep us nourished. As the keeper of the **hearth within**, Virgo invites us to tend to the systems that sustain us, body, mind, and environment. This Earth sign carries the ancestral essence of healing, care, and sacred service, often rooted in practices of purification, devotion, and subtle refinement. Tension in the abdomen or digestive tract may reflect the emotional weight of perfectionism or the ancestral pressure to maintain order and balance. Somatic practices that soften and support these areas help activate the **Virgo Body Potion**, an elixir of clarity, compassion, and embodied discernment. Through gentle movement, breath, and presence, we align with Virgo's nurturing essence, restoring harmony and honoring the quiet strength of those who tended both land and lineage before us.

MOVEMENT & EMBODIMENT PRACTICES

Somatic Movement: Gentle abdominal twists, core activation, and intuitive belly massage to support digestion and relaxation.

Self Massage: Massage the abdomen with oils to ease tension and promote digestive balance.

CHAKRA CORRESPONDENCE

Primary Chakra: Solar Plexus Chakra (Manipura) - Virgo's emphasis on purification and vitality aligns with the Solar Plexus, enhancing personal power and digestion.

Secondary Chakra: Root Chakra (Muladhara) - Reflects Virgo's grounding energy, fostering stability, security, resilience, and the Earth element.

VIRGO Season *Practice*

During **Virgo season**, or when the **Moon moves through Virgo**, it's a potent time to return to the hearth, both within the body and across the lineage. Somatic practices that align with Virgo's nurturing, health-conscious nature are especially impactful for those with Virgo prominence in their **MoonTree Chart**, or when honoring Virgo ancestors known for their service, wisdom, or care. Focusing on the abdomen and digestive system activates the **Virgo Body Potion**, an elixir of discernment, restoration, and sacred rhythm. These movements help metabolize emotional residue and physical tension, offering healing from the inside out. As we align with Virgo's essence, we tend the ancestral hearth, nurturing resilience and grounded presence. Through this daily alchemy of care, we craft a legacy woven with integrity, nourishment, and humble devotion.

LIBRA
Embodiment of AIR
& Ancestral Harmony

BODY AREAS: KIDNEYS, LOWER BACK, ADRENAL GLANDS, SKIN

LIBRA CARRIES THE ESSENCE OF HARMONY, RELATIONAL balance, and sacred reciprocity, governing the **kidneys, lower back, and skin**, areas where the body processes both physical filtration and emotional fairness. This Air sign is attuned to beauty and equilibrium, and those with strong Libra placements may carry ancestral imprints tied to justice, diplomacy, and the art of keeping peace. Tension in the lower back or kidneys can reflect the inherited weight of over-accommodation or unresolved relational dynamics. Somatic practices that soothe and support these regions activate the **Libra Body Potion**-an elixir of grace, discernment, and heart-aligned boundaries. These movements invite balance, emotional clarity, and the healing of inherited relational wounds. Through this embodied alchemy, we connect to the ancestral longing for harmony and offer ourselves the support once extended to others.

MOVEMENT & EMBODIMENT PRACTICES

- **Somatic Movement:** Relieve lower back tension and improve mobility with gentle pelvic tilts and hip rolls.
- **Self-Massage:** Massage the lower back, promoting relaxation and rejuvenation.

CHAKRA CORRESPONDENCE

- **Primary Chakra:** *Heart Chakra* (Anahata) - in alignment with Libra's emphasis on relationships and emotional harmony, reflects the heart's capacity for love and connection, associated with Libra's Air element.

- **Secondary Chakra:** *Sacral Chakra* (Svadhisthana) - encourages Libra's creativity and emotions, cultivating balance and adaptability.

LIBRA Season *Practice*

During **Libra season**, when the **Sun or Moon moves through Libra**, it's a sacred time to prioritize embodiment practices that restore balance and relational grace. These rituals are especially meaningful for those with Libra influences in their **MoonTree Chart**, or when honoring the diplomatic legacy of Libra ancestors, those who carried the weight of harmony and offered peace as a way of life. By focusing on the **kidneys, lower back, and skin**, we activate the **Libra Body Potion**, an alchemical blend of beauty, discernment, and quiet strength. These practices help filter ancestral tension, recalibrate inner equilibrium, and soothe the inherited imprints of over-giving or people-pleasing. Through Libra's airy essence, we invite elegance back into our nervous system, crafting a legacy infused with fairness, grace, and heart-aligned connection, one that strengthens belonging across generations.

SCORPIO
Embodiment of WATER
& Ancestral Rebirth

BODY AREAS: REPRODUCTIVE SYSTEM, PELVIS, URINARY TRACT

SCORPIO EMBODIES TRANSFORMATION, EMOTIONAL DEPTH, intensity, and the sacred art of rebirth. It governs the **pelvis, reproductive system, and urinary tract**, gateways of power, intimacy, and release. These regions often carry ancestral imprints tied to survival, sensuality, grief, and resilience. For those with Scorpio prominence, either in their chart or through lineage, this energy may express itself as stored tension in the sacral center, where unspoken emotions, suppressed desires, and generational wounds reside. Engaging with Scorpio's essence awakens the **Scorpio Body Potion**, an elixir of deep emotional integration, shadow healing, and regenerative strength. Through somatic rituals that tend the pelvis and reproductive space, we honor both vulnerability and power, creating room for renewal at the root of our being. This sacred work connects us with the deeper tides of ancestral memory, turning inherited pain into the fertile soil of transformation.

MOVEMENT & EMBODIMENT PRACTICES

- **Somatic Movement:** Relieve sacral tension through gentle hip circles and pelvic tilts. Fluid, instinctive motions that bring forth and release emotional energy.
- **Self Massage:** Massage the lower abdomen and hips, supporting emotional release and promoting relaxation.

CHAKRA CORRESPONDENCE

- **Primary Chakra:** *Sacral Chakra* (Svadhisthana) - Scorpios' focus on intimacy, creativity, and transformation aligns with this energy center, promoting emotional flow and renewal.
- **Secondary Chakra:** *Root Chakra* (Muladhara) - Supports grounding and stability during intense emotional processes, anchoring Scorpio's transformative energy.

SCORPIO Season *Practice*

During **Scorpio season**, or when the **Sun or Moon moves through Scorpio**, devote time to **transformative embodiment practices** that engage the pelvis and sacral region, the sacred cauldron of renewal. These movements become especially powerful when honoring Scorpio ancestors or working with Scorpio placements in your **MoonTree Chart**, inviting you into the deeper layers of ancestral remembrance and emotional integration. Focusing on the **reproductive system and sacral center** activates the **Scorpio Body Potion**, an alchemical elixir of resilience, depth, and regenerative power. These rituals help transmute inherited grief, emotional suppression, or trauma into embodied wisdom. By aligning with Scorpio's essence, we become vessels of healing and evolution, tending to the shadowed places not just for ourselves, but for all who came before and all who will follow.

SAGITTARIUS
Embodiment of FIRE
& Ancestral Adventure

BODY AREAS: HIPS, THIGHS, LIVER

SAGITTARIUS GOVERNS THE **HIPS, THIGHS, AND LIVER**, carries the essence of motion, vitality, and the eternal quest for truth. This sign invites us to stretch beyond boundaries, physically, emotionally, and spiritually, toward greater meaning and embodied wisdom. Tapping into **Sagittarius' fiery energy** awakens a **Body Potion of expansion, optimism, and purposeful movement**. It's a dance between freedom and rootedness, between personal growth and Ancestral momentum. Tension held in the **hips and thighs** may reflect inherited longings for movement, echoes of migrations, exiles, and spiritual searches encoded in the body. The **liver**, a powerful center of detoxification and renewal, resonates with Sagittarius' drive to burn away what no longer serves and make space for new vision. Somatic practices that engage these regions help transmute restlessness into direction, supporting physical and emotional flow while honoring the legacy of Sagittarian ancestors who sought truth across landscapes and lifetimes.

MOVEMENT & EMBODIMENT PRACTICES

- **Somatic Movement:** Gentle hip circles and leg movements improve mobility and release tension. Mindfully explore and move through nature, a Sagittarius-like approach to walking or hiking.
- **Self-Massage:** To boost circulation and ease tension, use warming oils to massage your hips and thighs.

CHAKRA CORRESPONDENCE

- **Primary Chakra:** *Root Chakra* (Muladhara) - Reflects Sagittarius' adventurous spirit, vitality, and grounding energy, thus promoting stability, resilience, and expansive exploration.
- **Secondary Chakra:** *Solar Plexus Chakra* (Manipura) - Aligns with the Fire element and reflects Sagittarius' adventurous nature, supporting confidence, willpower, and purposeful action.

SAGITTARIUS Season *Practice*

During **Sagittarius season**, when the **Sun or Moon moves through Sagittarius**, attune your practices to the hips, thighs, and liver, gateways of movement, expansion, and vitality. These somatic rituals are especially powerful when honoring Sagittarius ancestors or working with Sagittarian energies in your **MoonTree Chart**. They stir the **Sagittarius Body Potion**, an elixir of freedom, fire, and the will to explore beyond the known. By connecting with these areas, you connect with the ancestral spirit of visionaries, travelers, and seekers, those who embraced the unknown with courage and wonder. Movement becomes medicine. Breath becomes a compass. Through these practices, we transmute inherited patterns of restlessness or restriction into resilience, curiosity, and joy. This is how we wildcraft a legacy of growth: one rooted in wisdom, guided by truth, and ever open to the adventure of becoming.

CAPRICORN
Embodiment of EARTH
& Ancestral Discipline

BODY AREAS: KNEES, BONES, TEETH, SKIN

CAPRICORN GOVERNS THE **KNEES, BONES, TEETH, AND skin**, carries the essence of endurance, structure, and grounded wisdom. This earthy archetype offers us a **Body Potion of resilience**, distilled through generations of perseverance and responsibility. By connecting with Capricorn's energy, we honor the steady scaffolding passed down through our lineage, the slow-built strength that supports our becoming. Tension in the knees and skeletal system often reflects the **weight of expectation**, our own and that of those who came before us. The teeth and skin, protectors of our inner world, also echo Capricorn's pragmatic, protective nature. Somatic rituals focused on these areas invite us to release rigidity, restore flexibility, and align with the sacred architecture of Ancestral resilience. In doing so, we awaken the quiet power of grounded ambition and build from a place of reverence.

MOVEMENT & EMBODIMENT PRACTICES

- **Somatic Movement:** Improve joint mobility and strength through gentle knee bends and squats. To improve bone health and grounding, consider weight-bearing exercises such as walking or mindful resistance training.
- **Self Massage:** Massage the knees and legs to relieve tension and nourish these areas.

CHAKRA CORRESPONDENCE

- **Primary Chakra:** Root Chakra (*Muladhara*) - Connects into Capricorn's grounding energy, stability, and resilience.

- **Secondary Chakra:** Crown Chakra (*Sahasrara*) - Aligns with Capricorn's ambition and disciplined nature, connecting to higher wisdom, purpose, and a sense of spiritual alignment with their goals.

CAPRICORN Season *Practice*

During **Capricorn season**, when the **Sun or Moon moves through Capricorn**, turn toward practices that support the **knees, bones, skin, and teeth**, the structural pillars of your being. These rituals harmonize with Capricorn's steady rhythm, cultivating resilience, stability, and inner fortitude. When working with Capricorn placements in your **MoonTree Chart** or honoring Capricorn ancestors, somatic practices that center on these regions become a sacred offering, rooted in reverence for the ancestral blueprint of endurance and responsibility. Through these movements, you stir the **Capricorn Body Potion**, an elixir of perseverance, structure, and quiet power. You align with the wisdom of those who built with patience, carved paths through challenge, and stood as living stones in the architecture of your lineage. Embodying Capricorn's essence invites you to walk your path with grounded clarity, becoming both the mountain and the one who climbs it.

AQUARIUS
Embodiment of AIR
& Ancestral Innovation

BODY AREAS: ANKLES, LOWER LEGS, CIRCULATORY SYSTEM

AQUARIUS GOVERNS THE **ANKLES AND CIRCULATORY system**, serving as a vessel for movement, innovation, and visionary thought. This is the elixir of future-forward energy, fluid yet focused, woven with adaptability and radical care. By tuning into Aquarius' rhythm, we access the pulse of collective wisdom, finding new pathways for connection, insight, and ancestral evolution. Tension in the ankles or disruptions in circulation may signal a buildup of unexpressed ideas or Ancestral energy seeking movement and flow. These body areas, essential for both grounding and motion, echo the Aquarian gift of bridging the Earthly with the visionary. Somatic rituals that focus on enhancing flexibility, vitality, and energetic circulation invite you to wildcraft the **Aquarius Body Potion**, one infused with liberation, clarity, and alignment with the greater good. When we embody the Aquarian current, we dance with the unseen blueprints of those ancestors who dreamed beyond their time. We become conduits of change, flowing with purpose, carrying the pulse of innovation from the past into the future.

MOVEMENT & EMBODIMENT PRACTICES

- **Somatic Movement: Improve mobility and release tension with gentle ankle circles.** Improve circulation and vitality with cardio exercises like jogging, cycling, and swimming.
- **Self-Massage: Relieve tension and boost circulation in your lower legs and ankles with a cooling oil massage.**

CHAKRA CORRESPONDENCE

- **Primary Chakra:** *Crown Chakra* (Sahasrara) - Taps into Aquarius' connection to universal consciousness and visionary inspirations.
- **Secondary Chakra:** *Throat Chakra* (Vishuddha) - Reflects Aquarius' innovative and humanitarian spirit, supporting authentic communication and visionary expression.

AQUARIUS Season *Practice*

During **Aquarius season,** when the ***Moon*** is in Aquarius, turn your attention to somatic practices that promote balance, flow, and visionary clarity. These rituals stir the energetic waters of innovation, encouraging personal transformation and collective connection. They are especially potent for those exploring Aquarius themes within their *Moon Tree Chart,* or when honoring Aquarius ancestors whose spirits were marked by adaptability, originality, and radical hope. Somatic focus on the **ankles and circulatory system** activates the energetic pathways that carried your ancestors' dreams, those who walked ahead with courage, often dancing at the edge of the unknown. These movements become part of your alchemical potion, blending physical release with ancestral remembrance. By embodying Aquarius' essence, you channel currents of forward-thinking wisdom, helping to circulate fresh possibilities through your body and your lineage. Each gesture becomes a prayer for the future, a ripple of freedom, curiosity, and heart-centered evolution.

PISCES
Embodiment of WATER
& Ancestral Intuition

BODY AREAS: FEET, LYMPHATIC SYSTEM, PINEAL GLAND

PISCES, THE FINAL SIGN OF THE ZODIAC, IS ASSOCIATED WITH the **feet, lymphatic system, and pineal gland**, the sacred meeting places of the mystical and the material. It carries the essence of **compassion, intuition, and dreamlike perception**, inviting us to surrender, dissolve boundaries, and commune with the unseen. Engaging with Pisces' watery energy is an invitation to craft the final drops of your ancestral elixir, those that bind spirit to Earth. The **feet** anchor this transcendent sign, reminding us that even the most ethereal visions must be rooted to be lived. The **lymphatic system and pineal gland** reflect Pisces' sensitivity and spiritual depth, guiding the flow of emotional and energetic purification. Tension or overwhelm in these areas can mirror Ancestral imprints of emotional absorption, lacking boundaries, or the burden of carrying others' pain. Through grounding somatic practices that stimulate the feet and encourage energetic movement, we support detoxification, invite spiritual clarity, and deepen our connection to both the body and the vast Ancestral dreaming field. In working with Pisces, we become vessels of tenderness, healing, and divine remembrance.

MOVEMENT & EMBODIMENT PRACTICES

- **Somatic Movement:** Gently roll your feet and stretch your toes to ease tension and improve mobility. Water - mimicking circular motions boosts lymphatic flow and energetic balance.
- **Self-Massage:** Soak your feet in warm Water, visualizing the Water washing away emotional tension and bringing you peace and clarity.

CHAKRA CORRESPONDENCE

- **Primary Chakra:** Third Eye Chakra (Ajna) - This Chakra mirrors Pisces' intuitive depth, visionary dreamscapes, and spiritual perceptiveness, cultivating clarity and inner wisdom.
- **Secondary Chakra:** Sacral Chakra (Svadhisthana) - By tapping into this Chakra, Pisces can enhance their emotional depth, creativity, and connection with Water.

PISCES Season *Practice*

During **Pisces season**, when the **Moon** moves through Pisces, attune to practices that ground the spirit while inviting intuitive flow. These moments are especially potent for those with Pisces energy present in their **MoonTree chart**, or when honoring ancestors who carried the Piscean essence, empaths, dreamers, mystics, or healers. Somatic rituals that focus on the **feet and lymphatic system** offer sacred support to the elixir of your lineage, honoring the compassion, sensitivity, and spiritual depth passed through generations. These practices not only anchor the spirit in embodied presence but also open the channel for ancestral wisdom to move through you like a gentle current. By engaging with Pisces' mystical Waters, you become a bridge between realms, distilling inherited intuition into a living practice. These rituals create space for release, reflection, and spiritual remembrance, ensuring that your path flows forward with grace, rooted in reverence and guided by the unseen.

OUR ENERGY BODIES

The SUBTLE BODY

*O*ur *energy* body is a **vibrant**, pulsing system of **intelligence**, **memory**, and **essence**, not merely a concept. It reflects the full spectrum of our *physical, emotional,* and *spiritual* states, **woven** together by the threads of *Ancestral* influence, *cosmic rhythm,* and vital **life** force, *prana*. At its foundation lies a beautiful synergy, the *celestial* guidance of the ***Sun*** and ***Moon***, the breath of **Air** moving through the **heart**, and the *sacred* inheritance of those who came before us. With each breath, we engage in an *alchemical dance*, drawing in **solar** clarity and **lunar** intuition. These **subtle** *energies* travel through the **nadis**, the energetic rivers of the body, *harmonizing* our intuition and intellect. They merge the logic of the **present** with the intuitive wisdom of the **past**, *cultivating* a vibrant, balanced, and *embodied* **life**.

The AURA

A LIVING ELIXIR OF LIGHT

THE **AURA** IS A *SACRED*, ENERGETIC FIELD, A RADIANT *ELIXIR* of light, that *surrounds* and flows through us. It is both a *shield* and a *mirror*, reflecting our inner landscape while shaping how we experience the world around us. Like the *shimmer* of a **potion** responding to its **ingredients** and environment, our **Aura** carries the *signature* of our *physical* health, *emotional* states, *mental* clarity, and *spiritual* connection. It is alive with **movement, memory,** and **meaning**. This energetic field is an extension of the body, a *fluid* **record** of who we are and who we've been. It holds the **imprint** of our experiences, our dreams, and our *transformations*. When we *tap into* our **Aura**, we engage in a *sacred* act of remembering. We listen to the breath of the **ancient self.** We open a dialogue between *body* and *spirit*, between **self** and **source**. Our **Aura** is also where we can *sense* the whispers of the *ancestors*. It carries threads of *wisdom* that **shimmer** through our presence, revealing not only how we move through life, but how those before us did, too.

Ancestral Aura

A BRIDGE OF MEMORY AND ELEMENTAL INHERITANCE

The *Ancestral* **Aura** is a more subtle field, woven not only of your own *energies* but of those who came before you. It holds the *vibrational* **echo** of your *lineage's* **triumphs**, **griefs**, **strengths**, and **spiritual** *essence*. It is not yours alone. It is **shared, remembered**, and *alive*. This **radiant** field extends beyond *individual* identity. It is a *current* of memory that connects you to *Ancestral archetypes*, **elemental** *lineages*, and the *sacred* **elixir** of becoming. In *Ancestral Alchemology*, the *Ancestral* **Aura** offers a path to access *ancient spirit* memory, **energetic** inheritance, and *transformation* through *Ancestral* presence. The *Ancestral* **Aura** is **alchemical**, its **ingredients** drawn from **Fire**, **Water**, **Earth**, and **Air**. These *elements*, passed down through *generations*, flow in distinct proportions through your family's story. Your *Moon Tree Chart* reveals how these *elemental* forces shape your **Ancestral Elemental Archetypes**, and how they converge to form your *Ancestral Alchemical Elixir*, a metaphorical **potion** composed of inherited *strength*, refined through *shadow*, and infused with *joy, love,* and *remembrance*. This field bends time. Within it, the **past** *breathes* into the **present** and speaks to the **future**. As you *consciously* attune to this **radiant** space, you become the **vessel** through which *transformation* flows. You **reclaim** the *wisdom* that has been waiting. You **wildcraft** the legacy of your *lineage*, tapping into *Ancestral mysticism* and crafting your *unique* **magic**.

The Seven Layers of the Aura

EACH LAYER OF THE **AURA** HOLDS **VIBRATION**, **MEMORY**, AND **purpose**. These **seven** *layers* together form a *sacred* architecture connecting the **body** to the **spirit** and the **self** to **ancestors**. They serve as a **mirror** and a **map**, aiding in understanding where *strength* lies, where *stories* are held, and where *transformation* is needed. The **Aura** is a *dynamic* blend of **memory**, **healing**, and **love**. The *Ancestral* **Aura** contributes to the *sacred essence* of those who came before, enriching the experience. These **luminous** *layers* serve as guides, providing *healing*, *guidance*, and *illumination* along the journey of remembrance.

1. ETHERIC Body

DESCRIPTION: THIS LAYER IS the closest to the skin and is directly linked to physical health, reflecting vitality and life force.

Ancestral Echo: It holds imprints of physical resilience and memories of survival, labor, and ancestral strength stored in the body.

2. EMOTIONAL Body

DESCRIPTION: A FLUID AND responsive field that flows with your moods and feelings.

Ancestral Echo: It carries inherited emotional patterns - grief stored in the blood, joy transmitted through lullabies, and unspoken stories resonating beneath the surface.

3.
MENTAL
Body

DESCRIPTION: THIS IS THE realm of thoughts, beliefs, and perceptions.

Ancestral Echo: encapsulates familial beliefs, cultural conditioning, and ancestral worldviews that have been passed down through generations.

4.
ASTRAL
Body

DESCRIPTION: THE HEART'S bridge is where relational energy, love, and spiritual connection flow.

Ancestral Echo: It holds cords to Ancestral kin, whether they lived or were imagined, linking you to familial love throughout time and space.

5.
ETHERIC
Template

DESCRIPTION: THE ENERGETIC blueprint of the physical form includes its structure, flow, and spiritual DNA.

Ancestral Echo: holds the energetic architecture passed down through the lineage, influencing how energy moves, heals, or becomes stuck.

6.
CELESTIAL
Body

DESCRIPTION: IT IS A RADIANT layer that oversees spiritual intuition, vision, and light.

Ancestral Echo: It opens the pathway to mystical dreaming, divine insight, and guidance from ancestral guardians and star-lineage connections.

7.
CAUSAL
Body

DESCRIPTION: THE OUTERMOST field, luminous and vast, holds your spirit's purpose and spiritual alignment.

Ancestral Echo: weaves your lineage's essence into the greater cosmos, anchoring your ancient self and guiding your future path.

The NADIS

CHANNELS OF COSMIC ENERGY

The **Nadis** are *sacred* energetic channels that carry **Prana**, or *life force*, through the *subtle body*, connecting the **physical, emotional**, and **spiritual** planes like *filaments* of **starlight** and **memory**. These *energy* rivers link us to the *cosmos* and our *Ancestral lineages*. Among the many **Nadis** within us, **Ida** and **Pingala** are the *primary* **polarities** *spiraling* around the central channel, **Sushumna Nadi**, the *sacred* channel of **awakening**. They symbolize the inner **dance** of *Sun* and *Moon*, **masculine** and *feminine, intuition* and *logic*, reflecting the *Ancestral* balance within our **breath**. With each *inhale* and *exhale*, we merge **cosmic** intelligence, harmonizing the nurturing *essence* of the *Moon* (**Ida**) with the activating **Fire** of the *Sun* (**Pingala**). The **Air** *element*, resonating with the *Heart chakra* and influenced by *Venus*, acts as the bridge for these *energies*, carrying them through the **breath** and into the **body** for *transformation* to take place.

IDA

- **Energy:** Feminine, cooling, intuitive
- **Celestial Influence:** Lunar (*Moon*)
- **Essence:** Flows through the **left nostril and left side of the body,** guiding inward movement, emotional depth, and ancestral reflection.
- **Function:** Connects us to dreaming, creativity, inner wisdom, and the receptive mysteries of the feminine lineage.

PINGALA *nadi*

- **Energy:** Masculine, warming, activating
- **Celestial Influence:** Solar (*Sun*)
- **Essence:** Flows through the **right nostril and right side of the body**, illuminating clarity, focus, and outward momentum.
- **Function:** Fuels vitality, action, discipline, and the expressive power of the masculine Ancestral stream.

WHEN **IDA** AND **PINGALA** FLOW IN BALANCE, THEY AWAKEN **Sushumna Nadi,** the central channel of *Kundalini* energy and *alchemical* alignment. This *sacred* opening allows *prana* to flow freely, igniting insight, vitality, and *Ancestral* remembrance. This **activation** allows us to *embody* both **lunar** and **solar** aspects of our *ancestry*, becoming conduits for *healing, transformation*, and the *conscious* **remembrance** of our *lineage*. To walk the *alchemical* path of harmony, we must tend to the *sacred* breath. These practices invite us to balance the *polarities* within, **Sun** and **Moon**, *action* and *rest, doing* and *being*. By harmonizing **Ida** and **Pingala**, we *nourish* the nervous system, increase *subtle* awareness, and connect with the **rhythms** of *Nature* and our *lineage*.

WAYS THAT WE CAN DO THIS:

1. ALTERNATE NOSTRIL BREATHING (NADI SHODHANA)

This ancient *Pranayama* technique purifies and harmonizes the flow of **Ida** and **Pingala**, creating spaciousness in the mind and steadiness in the **heart**. Known for its *calming* and centering effects, it invites us to **breathe** with the *cosmos*, balancing **Solar** and **Lunar** *essences*, grounding the body, and clearing energetic stagnation.

HOW TO PRACTICE:

- Sit comfortably with a tall spine and relaxed shoulders.
- Rest your left hand gently on your knee.
- Bring your right hand to your face: use your thumb to close your **right nostril**, and inhale deeply through the **left**.
- Close your **left nostril** with your ring finger, release the thumb, and exhale through the **right**.
- Inhale through the **right**, switch, and exhale through the **left**.
- Continue this alternating rhythm for 5–10 minutes.
- Allow each inhale to bring presence, and each exhale to bring release.
- Let this breath weave balance through your nervous system, awaken clarity, and align you with the elixir of the moment.

2. MEDITATION ON SOLAR & LUNAR ENERGIES

To *embody* the sacred dance of **Ida** and **Pingala**, we turn to the *celestial* bodies themselves. Meditating on the *Sun* and *Moon* invites balance between outward **action** and inward **reflection**, charging the inner *energy* body with *vitality* and *grace*.

HOW TO PRACTICE:

- Sit in stillness, eyes closed, feet rooted, or hips grounded.
- Visualize **golden sunlight** entering your **right nostril**, flowing down the spine, igniting warmth, courage, and focus.
- As you exhale, imagine **silvery moonlight** entering your **left nostril**, flowing gently through your body, bringing emotional ease, intuitive clarity, and calm.
- Breathe this rhythm of fire and water, allowing the inner elixir to balance and blend within.
- This visualization awakens your inner energies, aligning your body and spirit with Ancestral and cosmic wisdom.

CARING FOR YOUR ENERGY BODY
Daily Rituals of Embodied Alchemy

Tending to your energy body is a sacred act of devotion—an opportunity to cleanse, restore, and reweave your field with the elements, your ancestors, and the breath of the cosmos. These practices are the daily stirrings of your Ancestral Elixir, nurturing vitality, awareness, and harmony.

Aura Cleansing:
Cleanse stagnant or scattered energy with sacred smoke (such as mugwort, cedar, or palo santo), sound tools (singing bowls, bells, or rattles), or a simple energetic sweep using your hands. Let the elements restore balance and radiance to your luminous field.

Daily Breathwork:
Begin each morning with a breath practice—like Nadi Shodhana—to align the nadis and harmonize the inner channels. Breathe consciously to awaken the body, quiet the mind, and center your spirit in rhythm with the day.

Nature as Medicine:
Walk barefoot on the Earth. Stretch under the warmth of the Sun. Meditate beneath the Moon. Let your body remember its elemental origins and return to a natural state of flow and ease.

Ancestral Connection:
Create a sacred space or altar infused with Ancestral presence—candles, heirlooms, natural objects, or symbolic offerings. Invite their guidance as you breathe life into their stories, write your own and walk as the living legacy.

The CHAKRAS

SACRED GATEWAYS OF TRANSFORMATION

THE **CHAKRAS** ARE **SEVEN** LUMINOUS *ENERGY* CENTERS situated along the **spine**. Each one functions as a turning **wheel** of **prana**, overseeing various aspects of the **physical**, **emotional**, and **spiritual** *self*. These centers are more than just *energy* points; they are gateways that allow you to connect with your *energetic* **imprint** and *essence* while **exploring** the *energetic essence* of your *lineage*. Among the many *energy* centers present in the **subtle body**, these **seven** are **fundamental** to your *energetic* structure. When these centers are in *harmony*, they facilitate the exchange between your **inner** and **outer** worlds, aligning your physical body with the *wisdom* of your *spirit*. In *Ancestral Alchemology*, the **Chakras** are viewed as **portals** to *Ancestral* memories. Each energy center holds your *unique* **narrative,** but also the *energetic* **remnants** of inherited **patterns** and **potentials**. Through practices involving *movement, breathwork, vocalization*, and *rituals*, you can **activate** a pathway for integrating *Ancestral* energies. This process helps in clearing *blockages*, enhancing your *essence*, and reestablishing your *connection* to the *sacred lineage* that resides within you.

CHAKRA	LOCATION	ESSENCE
Root Chakra (Muladhara)	Base of the Spine	Grounding, Stability, and Survival
Sacral Chakra (Svadhisthana)	Below the Navel	Creativity, Sensuality, and Emotional Flow
Solar Plexus Chakra (Manipura)	Upper Abdomen	Confidence, Willpower, and Courage
Heart Chakra (Anahata)	Center of the Chest	Love, Compassion, and Connection
Throat Chakra (Vishuddha)	Throat	Communication, Truth, and Self-expression
Third Eye Chakra (Ajna)	Between the Eyebrows	Intuition, Insight, and Imagination
Crown Chakra (Sahasrara)	Top of the Head	Spiritual Connection, Enlightenment, and Universal Consciousness

The Seven Major Chakras

THE CHAKRAS

The Seven Major Chakras

CHAKRAS THROUGH AN ANCESTRAL LENS

Ancestral Frequencies

*T*he **Chakras** are *sacred* energy centers, inner *elixirs* of **movement** and **memory**, spiraling along the spine and acting as *gateways* between the **physical** and the **unseen**. Each **Chakra** holds *Ancestral* resonance, *embodying* the experiences of those who came before us: their **resilience, creativity, grief, wisdom,** and **love.** Viewed through the lens of *Ancestral Alchemology,* these wheels become *Ancestral* portals of *exploration* and *transformation.* By connecting with the **Chakras** as **vessels** of inherited *energy,* we can delve into the *Ancestral* frequencies **embedded** within our *lineage.* This practice leads us towards profound self-awareness, healing, and rediscovering our unique *Ancestral* **magic.**

Root Chakra (Muladhara)

Element:
Earth

Ancestral Keywords:
**Stability
Security
Grounding
Survival
Wisdom**

THE FOUNDATION OF BELONGING

Serving as a **vessel** for *Ancestral* memories, the *Root Chakra* is an *Earthy energy* center located at the **base** of the **spine.** It ties us to the **land,** our **bones,** and the **survival** narratives passed down through *generations.* This core holds the *essence* of our family's origins - their **journeys, struggles,** and the **principles** they upheld. Here, we receive their *fortitude, determination,* and *commitment* to perpetuity.

Connecting with our *Root Chakra* immerses oneself in the energy of our *ancestors*, sensing their *essence* in the **Earth** beneath us. Through this *connection*, we tap into the **grounding** power of inherited *resilience*, the **heartbeat** of *Ancestral wisdom*, and the comfort of belonging.

Sacral Chakra (Svadhisthana)

Element:
Water

Ancestral Keywords:
**Creativity
Emotions
Desire
Flow**

THE WATERS OF MEMORY AND CREATION

The *Sacral Chakra* serves as a *sacred* reservoir of emotional *memories*, where the *essence* of our *lineage* flows. Located **below** the **navel**, it vibrates with unspoken **emotions**, sensual **creativity**, artistic **expression**, and *intergenerational* **stories**. This core holds the **passions, joys, sorrows,** and ability to **craft** *beauty* from the *chaos* within our *Ancestral* lines. Connecting with this *Chakra* awakens the *Ancestral* currents within your being, igniting **intuitive** energy, **sacred** longing, and the **creative** abilities *imprinted* in your *ancestry*. By moving, performing *rituals*, and *expressing* yourself through your **body**, you tap into the deep **well** of your *lineage*, transmuting inherited emotional **patterns** into *art*, *empathy*, and *joy*.

Solar Plexus Chakra (Manipura)

Element:
Fire

Ancestral Keywords:
**Courage
Inner Strength
Willpower
Personal Power**

THE FIRE OF WILL AND INHERITED POWER

The *Solar Plexus Chakra* serves as the core of *Ancestral* **Fire**, housing the **courage, ambition,** and **determination** of your *lineage*. This *Chakra* is located **above** the **navel** point. It retains the *essence* of those who navigated **challenges**, shouldered **duties**, and forged ways through **struggles**. Their *resilience* resides in you, **shining** from your *inner self*. Engaging with this *Chakra* means **lighting** the *transformative* **flame** that has been passed down over the *ages*. You are *encouraged* to convert *doubt* inherited from the **past** into self-assurance, to change **survival** into **empowerment**, and to assert your role as a *beacon* of **dynamic** initiative in your family *lineage*.

Heart Chakra (Anahata)

Element:
Air

Ancestral Keywords:
Love
Harmony
Connection
Forgiveness

THE ELIXIR OF LOVE, FORGIVENESS, AND LINEAGE CONNECTION

At the **center** of the **chest**, we find the *Heart Chakra*, the *sacred* chalice where your *lineage's* **love**, **grief**, and **healing** converge. It carries the **echoes** of your *Ancestors'* **joys** and **losses**, their capacity for **empathy** and **forgiveness**, and their longing for *connection* that **transcended** time and distance. To tend this center is to open yourself to the *emotional* currents passed through *generations*, to **soften** where **hardness** grew from *heartbreak*, to **forgive** where **silence** *lingered*, and to offer **love** where **wounds** once *lived*. Here, we become **Alchemists** of the **heart**, *transmuting* inherited *sorrow* into *compassion* and **love** into *legacy*.

Throat Chakra (Vishuddha)

Element:
Ether / Akasha
(space, vibration, resonance)
From the four *Elements*:
AIR

Ancestral Keywords:
Expression
Truth
Storytelling
Sacred Voice

THE ELIXIR OF EXPRESSION, TRUTH, AND ANCESTRAL VOICE

The *Throat Chakra* resonates with the **echoes** of our *ancestors*, safeguarding their **narratives**, **melodies**, and *spiritual* **insights**. Located in the **throat**, it urges us to **communicate** *genuinely* and *intentionally*, encouraging that the **stories** of our *ancestors* continue to *inspire* the **present** and shape the **future**. This *Chakra* encourages you to *rediscover* silenced **voices**, *respect* the *wisdom* passed down through *generations*, and create a *heritage* of **honesty** through the power of **sound**, *language*, and *music*.

Third Eye Chakra (Ajna)

Element:
Light

From the four *Elements*:
ALL Elements
(integration, perception and energetic synthesis)

Ancestral Keywords:
**Intuition
Insight
Vision**

THE ELIXIR OF INTUITION, VISION, AND ANCESTRAL SIGHT

AT THE **CENTER** OF THE forehead, between the eyebrows, we find the *Third Eye Chakra* serving as a gateway to *Ancestral* **intuition** and **foresight**, holding the **visionary** thread of your *lineage*. This includes the **dreams**, **spiritual** *gifts*, and *inner* **knowing** that have been passed down through *generations*. By tuning into this *energy* **portal**, you can tap into **multidimensional** *awareness*, explore inherited *insights*, and understand the deeper purpose **imprinted** in your family line.

THE ELIXIR OF ANCESTRAL WISDOM, UNITY, AND DIVINE REMEMBRANCE

The *Crown Chakra*, located at the **top** of the **head**, plays a vital role in **bridging** the gap between the *wisdom* of our *ancestors* and the *universal consciousness* that **permeates** all *existence*. This *energy* center serves as a gateway to the *sacred* **teachings** passed down through *generations*, allowing us to tap into the **cosmic** *rhythm* of **life**. By activating the *Crown Chakra*, we can understand and appreciate our **timeless** *Nature*, recognizing the infinite *connection* that binds together our *lineage*, *spirit*, and the **ultimate** *Source* of all creation. Through the *Crown Chakra*, we gain access to profound *insights* and *spiritual* truths that **transcend** individual experiences, enabling us to **align** with the higher *frequencies* of the universe and attain a deeper sense of **purpose** and *fulfillment*.

Crown Chakra (Sahasrara)

Element:
Thought / Akasha (Ether)

From the four *Elements*:
AIR

Ancestral Keywords:
Universal Connection and Spiritual Transcendence

Part Four

THE ELEMENTS

THE FOUR ELEMENTS

Forces of Nature

THE ELEMENTS

The Four Elements

The **four** fundamental *elements*, **Earth**, **Water**, **Air**, and **Fire**, are *natural* forces that represent the *essence* of our existence. They *intertwine* with us, blending us into the design that is *nature*, reminding us we are not apart from it, but an integral **part** of it. The **Earth** that anchors us is the same **Earth** that sustained our *ancestors*. The **Water** coursing through us reflects the *rivers* and *oceans* that carried their *histories*. The **Air** that fills our *lungs* is the life-giving *breath* passed down through *generations*, and the **Fire** that ignites our *passions* is the *eternal* spark handed down through time. We **embody** these *elements* just as they **embody** those who came before us. Each *element* possesses distinct **qualities, offerings,** and **enchantment**. The interplay of these *elements* bridges our inner *world* with the cosmos, **grounding** us in the natural *rhythms* of **life** and tapping us into our *Ancestral roots*. Acknowledging our *shared* origins, delving into our bond with the *natural* world, and paying homage to the *elemental* forces that are **imprinted** in our *lineage, Ancestral* **path,** and ourselves. We uncover our **magic** in nature and *discover* that nature's **magic** *dwells* within us.

EARTH IS OUR *FOUNDATION*, AN **ANCHOR** OF **STABILITY** AND **grounding** that holds body and spirit within the embrace of the natural world. It carries *Ancestral memory* in the soil beneath our feet, holding stories, traumas, and legacies like **seeds** awaiting to bloom. **Earth** offers resilience and nourishment, the quiet strength that allows us to *grow*, *transform*, and plant the intentions of *renewal*.

Earth Energies

The **Earth** carries the enduring *wisdom* of our *ancestors*, echoing their **strength**, **perseverance**, and **practical** ingenuity. Within its layers lie traditions, values, and lessons passed down through *generations*. It is both a physical and spiritual *tether*, keeping us *rooted* in their energy while empowering us to carry their legacy forward. **Earth** *cultivates* presence and *connection* to the here and now. It offers the steadiness needed to move toward our goals with grounded *intention*, and it supports the gentle release of outdated **patterns**, creating space for new growth to emerge.

PRACTICES TO CONNECT WITH THE EARTH ELEMENT

- **Grounding Rituals** – Reconnect with the **Earth** by walking barefoot on soil, lying beneath the open sky, or tending to a garden. Let these simple acts restore your connection to *nature* and your *ancestors*.
- **Reflection & Writing** – Journal about areas of your life that

feel *untethered*. Explore inherited values or traditions and how they influence your current **path**.

- **Rooting Meditation** – Visualize *roots* extending from your body deep into the **Earth**. Draw strength, resilience, and *Ancestral wisdom* up through those *roots*.
- **Creative Expression** – Engage in hands-on activities like pottery, building, or *cultivating* a *sacred* space that honors the *essence* of **Earth** – stability, nourishment, and growth.

AFFIRMATION

"I am grounded, resilient, and deeply *nourished* by the **Earth's** and my *ancestors'* strength and *wisdom*."

Like ancient roots intertwined beneath the surface, Earth reminds us of the unseen connections to our past, sustains us in the present, and nurtures the seeds of the future we are creating.

WATER▽

IN THE DEPTHS OF **WATER** LIES THE POWER TO **CLEANSE**, **renew**, and **transform**, linking us to our *ancient selves* and the ongoing *rhythms* of **life**. **Water** carries the *essence* of emotional *wisdom* and adaptability. It washes away stagnation, soothes **unseen** wounds, and makes space for change to unfold. Like the shifting currents of a river, **Water** moves with clarity and grace, accompanying us through **life's** transitions and teaching us how to *soften*, *shed*, and *flow*.

Water Energies

Water invites fluidity, guiding us to adapt with grace as **life** shifts and reshapes. It **purifies** and **rejuvenates** emotional energy, drawing us inward to connect with our *intuition*, inner depths, and the quiet *wisdom* that lives beneath the surface. **Water** also carries the emotional currents of our *lineage*, resilient, tender, and enduring. It reflects *Ancestral memory*, the adaptability of those who came before, and their strength in navigating life's tides. With its flowing nature, **Water** offers a connection to their stories and opens a path for healing the emotional **patterns** we inherit.

PRACTICES TO CONNECT WITH THE WATER ELEMENT

- **Ritual Cleansing** – Immerse yourself in a warm bath with herbs or salts. Let the **Water** hold your emotions, release burdens, and restore balance.
- **Moon Water Ritual** – Collect **Water** under the *Full Moon*.

Use it in reflection, healing, or *ritual* practice as a way to hold *lunar light* in liquid form.

- **Creative Exploration** – Express your emotional landscape through journaling, painting, or music. Let **Water** guide your *intuitive* flow.
- **Ancestral Connection** – Sit beside a river, lake, or ocean. Reflect on your *lineage's* emotional resilience and invite their presence into your **heart**.

AFFIRMATION

"I flow with the *cleansing* power of **Water**, releasing what no longer serves and embracing *renewal* and *healing*."

In the depths of Water lies the power to cleanse, connect and transform, linking us to the emotional essence of our ancestors and the continuity of life's cycles

AIR

AIR IS THE *BREATH* OF **LIFE, SUBTLE, VITAL,** AND **EVER-moving.** It brings *clarity* to the mind, sweeping away *stagnation* and inviting fresh perspective. As the element of *communication* and thought, **Air** carries our words, ideas, and insights, bridging understanding between ourselves and others. It moves through us with a **lightness** that *disperses* what no longer serves, making space for *inspiration* and *renewal* to emerge.

Air Energies

Air sparks **inspiration**, awakening **curiosity**, **creativity**, and the flow of new ideas. It supports meaningful connection through open and honest communication, while also nurturing mindfulness, bringing clarity, focus, and spaciousness to our inner world. **Air** carries the collective knowledge and stories of our ancestors, their *wisdom*, adaptability, and vision. It holds their ability to innovate, speak truth, and communicate across time. Through **Air**, we honor the *insights* they've passed on while stepping into our own *intellectual* and *spiritual* evolution. The movement of **Air** reminds us that their thoughts and teachings still travel, carried gently on the *unseen* winds.

PRACTICES TO CONNECT WITH THE AIR ELEMENT

- **Breathwork** – Practice deep, **conscious** breathing or *pranayama* to center your *energy* and invite spacious clarity into the mind. Let each *breath* be a *clearing* **wind**.

- **Creative Expression** – Write, speak, or create art that channels **Air's** essence—*communication*, *inspiration*, and *movement*. Let your voice move with freedom and truth.
- **Meditation** – Sit with your *breath* as your guide. With each **inhale**, welcome *insight* and presence; with each **exhale**, release mental *clutter* and stagnant thought.
- **Storytelling** – Share *Ancestral* stories aloud, journal reflections, or give voice to the *wisdom* you carry. Let your words be carried on the **winds** of *memory*.

AFFIRMATION

"I take deep **breaths**, welcoming clarity, inspiration, and the *wisdom* of my *ancestors* into my life."

The whispers of Air carry the wisdom of our ancestors and the spark of inspiration, guiding us towards transformation and the freedom to explore new horizons.

FIRE

FIRE IS THE SPARK OF LIFE, A TRANSFORMATIVE FORCE THAT fuels **passion**, **ambition**, and creative **expression**. It burns through stagnation, clearing space for *renewal* and bold action. **Fire** awakens confidence and courage, inviting us to step into our power and bring vision into form. It reminds us that within challenge lies *opportunity*, and within us burns the light to *illuminate*, *create*, and *transform*.

Fire Energies

Fire brings *illumination*, guiding us with *insight* and clarity. It sparks **energy**, **courage**, and **vitality**, fueling *transformation* through *resilience* and growth. **Fire** *embodies* the spirit and **determination** of our *ancestors*, their *creative* spark, *boldness*, and ability to *rise* through challenge. **Fire** calls us to honor that *lineage* by pursuing our *passions* with confidence and **daring** to *cultivate* new paths. Through its *flame*, we connect to our *ancestors'* strength and *awaken* our **own**, *inspiring* the motivation to love, create, and live with purpose.

PRACTICES TO CONNECT WITH FIRE

- **Candle Rituals** – Light a candle as a *sacred* symbol of *transformation*. Gaze into the flame as you set intentions for growth, *renewal*, or courage. Let it reflect the **Fire** within.
- **Creative Expression** – Channel **Fire's** energy through *art*, *writing*, or *movement*. Allow your *creative* spark to move freely, *illuminating* what longs to be seen.

- **Invigorating Movement** – Engage in *energizing* practices like yoga, dance, or *embodied* breathwork. Let your body become the **flame** – *alive*, *vital*, and *awake*.
- **Ancestral Reflection** – Reflect on your *ancestors'* strength and *determination*. Call in their *resilience* as fuel for your journey, honoring the **Fire** they carried and passed on to you.

AFFIRMATION

"I *cultivate* the *transformative* power of **Fire**, fueling my *passion*, *courage*, and *creativity* to pursue my dreams."

The Fire within us shines brightly, transforming challenges into chances and dreams into reality, illuminating the path for growth and change.

Reflection and Journaling Questions

1. **WHICH ELEMENT FEELS MOST ALIVE WITHIN YOU RIGHT** now, and how does it mirror your current path or challenges?

- Explore how this *element* shows up in your thoughts, *emotions*, or actions. How might it reflect the strengths or struggles of your *ancestors*?

2. **How can you work with the elements to restore balance in areas that feel stuck, disconnected, or in need of renewal?**

- Reflect on which *elemental* energies could support healing, movement, or growth. Consider how these forces relate to *Ancestral* patterns or *wisdom* passed down through your lineage.

3. **What Ancestral connections arise when you reflect on each element?**

- Contemplate how **Earth**, **Water**, **Fire**, and **Air** may have influenced your *ancestors' essences*. In what ways can honoring these *connections* deepen your *rituals* and daily practices?

4. **How might you create seasonal or everyday rituals that honor both the elements and your lineage?**

- Consider ways to *infuse* your routines with *elemental* presence, through grounding practices, storytelling, flower essences, movement, or *offerings* to the *land* and your *ancestors*.

5. WHAT DOES ELEMENTAL BALANCE LOOK AND FEEL LIKE for you?

- Envision a harmony between **Earth**, **Water**, **Fire**, and **Air** within your body and life. What practices help you *cultivate* that *balance*?

THESE QUESTIONS ARE HERE TO GUIDE YOUR REFLECTION, TO deepen your connection with nature, awaken *Ancestral* remembrance, and explore how *elemental wisdom* can support your *healing*, *embodiment*, and *creative* path forward.

In the Nature of Art, Within the Art of Nature

ELEMENTAL ESSENCES

The Alchemy of Dual Elemental Combinations

Decoding Ancestral Blueprints

*E*lemental Essences* are born from the union of two primary *elements*, forming energetic blends that hold **transformative potential**. Each *essence* carries a distinct frequency, an **alchemical** *signature* shaped by the interplay of its *elemental* components. For example, the fusion of **Water** and **Fire** creates **Steam**, a dynamic *essence* embodying emotional *intensity* and adaptability in motion. These **dual-element** combinations appear within our *astrological* charts and act as **keys** to *Ancestral memory*. They help us *decode* **patterns**, uncover *gifts*, and tend to *generational* healing. Each essence becomes a thread within your **Ancestral Elemental Blueprint**, a path of remembrance and energetic exploration.

Elemental Essences also offer subtle *insight* into the ways we relate to others and our *lineage*. By blending the *elemental* energies of the ***Sun*** and ***Moon*** signs, we begin to see how these forces *dance* together in relationship.

FOR EXAMPLE

- A friend who is an **Aries Sun (Fire)** with a **Cancer Moon (Water),** when *energetically* blended with someone who is a **Pisces Sun (Water)** with a **Cancer Moon (Water)**.

- Their **Sun sign elements** form **Steam** (Fire + Water), while their **Moon sign elements** create **Ocean** (Water + Water).

This *method* reveals the *energetic* **undercurrents** within relationships, offering a deeper understanding of how *elements* merge, interact, and awaken growth, reflection, and **shared** *transformation*. It opens a gateway for *magic, connection*, and *Ancestral* resonance.

Elemental Essences in Ancestral Alchemology

In *Ancestral Alchemology,* **Elemental Essences** are tools for *uncovering* and working with the *energetic* signatures of your *lineage*. They help decode your **Ancestral Elemental Blueprint**, revealing the vibrational patterns that are shared in your family across *generations*.

For example, if your *Moon Tree Chart* reveals an **Ancestral Elemental Archetype** composed of **Water–Fire–Earth**, the corresponding *Elemental Essences* might be:

- *Steam* (**Water** & **Fire**): *Transformation*, adaptability, and emotional power.
- *Lava* (**Fire** & **Earth**): *Creation*, resilience, and grounded passion.
- *Mud* (**Earth** & **Water**): *Nurturing*, grounding, and the balance of stability with flow.

These *essences* offer a tangible way to connect with inherited *energies*, serving as a bridge to **healing**, **integration**, and *Ancestral* **remembrance**. Through this work, you awaken the *gifts* carried through your *lineage*, gently repattern inherited wounds or stagnant *energies*, and transform your **Ancestral Alchemical Elixir** into a source of **love**, **wisdom**, and **renewal**. This practice moves in both directions, *flowing* **backward** to tend the *roots* of your **ancestry**, and **forward** to infuse your **life** with vitality and *magic*.

Creating the Ancestral Alchemical Elixir

ELEMENTAL ESSENCES FORM A VITAL PART OF THE **Ancestral Alchemical Elixir**—a vibrational blend that aligns you with your *roots*, *lineage*, and the deeper layers of your *Ancestral Aura*. This *elixir* holds the energy and potential passed down through your bloodlines, becoming a living tool for awakening ancestral gifts and transmuting inherited cycles into sources of strength and renewal.

TO CRAFT THIS *ELIXIR*, WE ENGAGE WITH MAGICAL correspondences unique to each *Elemental Essence*. Flowers and herbs carry the essence's frequency, such as *lotus* for **Water**, *marigold* for **Fire**, or *cedar* for **Earth**, while movements and embodied practices help activate the energies in the body. For example, grounding your hands in **Mud** (**Earth** & **Water**) or practicing breathwork in a steamy space (**Water** & **Fire**) can amplify the essence's vibration. *Ritual* tools like candles, incense, and oils attuned to each element enhance the sensory and energetic field, anchoring the *essence* into *Ancestral* practices. Through these acts, the *elixir* becomes tangible, an energetic *offering* that flows **healing** and beauty into your *roots*.

WITHIN THE *MOONTREE CHART*, DOMINANT *ELEMENTAL Essences* reveal *Ancestral* **patterns** that extend beyond the personal. A *lineage* rich in **Steam** (**Water** & **Fire**) may reflect themes of emotional resilience and transformation, while a family deeply *rooted* in **Mud** (**Earth** & **Water**) might carry nurturing strength along with inherited challenges of stagnation or attachment. **Distilling** these *essences* allows us to name what's been passed down and begin the work of conscious *transformation*. By working with these *elemental* blends, we create practices that heal *Ancestral* wounds, awaken dormant **gifts**, and reconnect us with the *wisdom, resilience*, and **creative** force of those who came before. *Elemental Essences* offer a framework, both structured and deeply personal, to explore the **unseen** threads of *lineage* and spirit. Through this lens, we don't merely witness the **past**; we reshape it, taking the raw *elemental* material of our history and *transforming* it into a legacy of **love** and **purpose**.

THIS **ALCHEMICAL** PROCESS IS ALIVE. IT'S AN *INVITATION* TO honor your family's unique *energy*, to engage with *nature* and the *cosmic* cycles, and to **embody** *healing* in motion. When we embrace *Elemental Essences*, we stand at the meeting point of *ancestry* and presence, breaking *cycles*, tending *roots*, and becoming **vessels** of *transformation* for the *generations* to come.

As the alchemist seeks gold not in metal,
but in meaning,
We combine elemental forces to
transmute the raw substance
of our ancestry into radiant insight
and remembrance

The Essences

Wind Essence
(Air + Air)

Keywords
Clarity, Movement, Communication, Curiosity, Perception

THE **WIND** IS THE *ESSENCE* OF MOTION AND transformation, born from the merging of two **Air** elements. It carries clarity, breathes movement, and amplifies the power of communication. **Wind** flows with intention—connecting, inspiring, and stirring transformation. It moves through the unseen, carrying ideas across time and space, weaving the **past** into the **present**, and delivering ancestral wisdom into the **future**. Like a current of thought, **Wind** sharpens perception, awakens curiosity, and invites exploration. It travels freely, unhindered by form, reminding us of the value of perspective and the necessity of fluid thinking. **Wind** is both whisper and force, a *sacred* messenger that clears stagnant energy and opens the mind to new possibilities. **Wind** carries the voices of those who came before, mystery, stories, and insight lifted and carried across generations. It flows through time like breath itself, reconnecting us to the ancestors. Seen as a holy current, Wind brings messages from the *unseen* **realms** and guides those who are ready to listen. When we work with the **Wind**, we honor the brilliance and resilience of our *lineage*. Through breath, song, and spoken word, we remember that knowledge is meant to be moved, shared, carried forward, and kept alive.

ENERGIES AND INFLUENCES

- **Clarity & Focus** – Clears mental fog, refining perception, and deepening insight.
- **Movement & Flow** – Encourages momentum, fluidity, and the unfolding of ideas.
- **Connection & Communication** – Bridges past and future through the exchange of wisdom

THE SHADOW SIDE OF THE WIND ESSENCE

When out of *balance*, its energy may *manifest* as:

- **Scattered Focus** – Difficulty grounding *thoughts* or taking decisive action.
- **Instability** – *Restlessness* or excessive mental activity with no clear direction.
- **Detachment** – A tendency to skim the surface or *avoid* emotional depth due to constant motion.

Magical Workings and Ritual

HARNESS THE ENERGY OF THE *WIND* THROUGH PRACTICES that enhance *clarity*, *movement*, and *connection*:

1. **Breathwork Practices** – Practice breathing techniques to *clear* mental fog, *recalibrate* your energy, and invite *spaciousness* into the mind.
2. **Journaling for Insight** – Record fleeting thoughts, *distill* clarity, and explore new perspectives through *stream-of-consciousness* writing.

3. **Sound & Space Cleansing** – Use incense, singing bowls, bells, or wind chimes to clear stagnant *energy* and *magically* attune your space to *inspiration*.
4. **Meditation on Movement** – Visualize ***Wind*** flowing through your body and mind, *dissolving* blocks and opening *energetic* pathways for *renewal* and *magic*.

Scientific and Symbolic Perspective

- **Motion & Transformation** – **Wind** arises from *shifts* in pressure, much like ideas *stirred* by inner or outer change.
- **Dispersal & Influence** – Just as **Wind** carries *seeds* across vast distances, thoughts and *intentions* shape the landscape of *consciousness*.
- **Unseen Power** – Though *invisible*, **Wind** holds immense force, bridging timelines and connecting the **past**, **present**, and **future**.

WIND REMINDS US THAT CHANGE IS A CONSTANT, THAT knowledge must move, and that *communication* is a *sacred* bridge between **realms**. It moves with both force and grace, inviting us to trust *momentum* while staying attuned to the *Ancestral wisdom* carried in the currents.

Mountain Essence
(Earth + Earth)

Keywords
Stability, Endurance, Groundedness, Ancestral Wisdom, Resilience

WHEN TWO **EARTH** *ELEMENTS* CONVERGE, THEY FORM THE **Mountain**, an *essence* of unwavering **strength**, deep **patience**, and **ancient** *wisdom*. Steadfast and enduring, **Mountain** holds the stillness of time, offering a grounded space for reflection, resilience, and inner fortitude. It stands as a symbol of presence, unmoving through shifting seasons and uncertain terrain. **Mountain** energy teaches us that true growth is steady and rooted, not rushed. It is the guardian of *Ancestral wisdom*, holding the perseverance and quiet determination of those who came before. By aligning with its grounded nature, we cultivate long-term strength, align with the rhythm of the **Earth**, and build a foundation capable of carrying us through the long journey. **Mountains** have long been regarded as sacred, silent witnesses to generations of transformation. Their stone and soil carry stories, prayers, and echoes of endurance. Engaging with this *essence* connects us to our *Ancestral* strength, reminding us that our **roots** run as deep as the **Earth** itself. Whether through ritual, meditation, or simply honoring the land beneath our feet, we ground into the *wisdom* of those who walked before us and integrate their **resilience** into our path.

ENERGIES AND INFLUENCES

- **Steadiness & Strength** – Offers stability, patience, and the quiet endurance needed to move through life's challenges.
- **Wisdom & Reflection** – Encourages deep introspection and presence during seasons of transformation.

- **Rooted Ambition** – Inspires the pursuit of high goals while remaining firmly grounded in the present moment

THE SHADOW SIDE OF THE MOUNTAIN ESSENCE

When out of *balance*, it may *express* as:

- **Rigidity** – Resistance to change, clinging to outdated beliefs or inherited patterns
- **Isolation** – Emotional withdrawal or detachment from others, rooted in a need for over-self-reliance
- **Overwhelm** – Viewing life's challenges as immovable, leading to inertia or heaviness.

Magical Workings and Ritual

HARNESS *MOUNTAIN* ENERGY FOR GROUNDING AND endurance-building practices:

1. **Grounding Meditation** – Envision yourself as a *Mountain – roots* descending deep into the **Earth**, crown reaching toward the sky. Let your breath anchor you in both *realms*.
2. **Earth Rituals** – Use stones, crystals, or soil to connect with the mountain's grounding energy. To *venerate* your *ancestors*, construct a small altar or make an **Earth** offering.
3. **Endurance Practices** – Walk mindfully through *Nature*, hold stillness in *meditation*, or commit to long-term goals that require *patience*, *presence*, and *persistence*.
4. **Intentional growth:** Match your *ambitions* to steady, sustainable progress; build your path with *purpose* and *stability*.

Scientific and
Symbolic Perspective

- **Tectonic Formation** – *Mountains* rise slowly from immense pressure, *symbolizing* the gradual *strengthening* that comes through time and inner *resilience*.
- **Volcanic birth:** The eruption-formed *Mountains* serve as a reminder that *transformation* can be both **fiery** and **foundational**.
- **Erosion & Resilience** – Though shaped by Wind, Water, and time, the Mountain endures, just as we evolve through life while remaining rooted in our essence.

MOUNTAINS TEACH US THAT ENDURANCE IS *CULTIVATED* layer by layer. Their strength lies not in resisting change, but in remaining **rooted** through it – **rising** with *patience*, and standing as quiet witnesses to what was, what is, and what may come.

Ocean Essence
(Water + Water)

Keywords
Emotional Depth, Intuition, Flow, Renewal, Collective Memory.

THE *OCEAN* IS A VAST RESERVOIR OF EMOTION, INTUITION, and *Ancestral wisdom*. Formed by merging two **Water** elements, it embodies **fluidity, depth,** and **renewal** *cycles*. The *Ocean* reflects the vastness of the **subconscious**, holding *stories, memories,* and emotions that **ebb** and **flow** through time. It invites us to surrender to movement, trust in the tides of *transformation*, and embrace the deep currents of our inner world. Like the waves that **rise** and **recede**, the *Ocean* teaches us the rhythm of **life**, moments of stillness and surges of intensity, all part of a greater unfolding. It **creates** space for healing and self-discovery, reminding us that beneath the surface lies a wellspring of **resilience**, insight, and boundless *connection*. The *Ocean* is an *Ancestral* bridge, carrying the **echoes** of those who came before us. As rivers flow into the *sea*, our *lineage* weaves through time, creating an **unbroken** *thread* of **memory** and experience. Many traditions view the *Ocean* as a **vessel** of *wisdom*—a force that holds the *essence* of past *generations* and their emotional **imprints**. By working with *Ocean Energy*, we engage with this collective current, acknowledging inherited **patterns**, honoring resilience, and tapping into the transformative power of ancestral healing. Through **ritual, meditation,** or still **reflection**, we allow the *Ocean* to guide us in letting go of what no longer serves us while carrying forward the *wisdom* that sustains us.

ENERGIES AND INFLUENCES

- **Emotional Insight & Depth** - The *Ocean* embodies many

emotions, encouraging deep reflection and intuitive connection.

- **Flow & Surrender** - It teaches us to trust in movement, embracing life's natural cycles of change and renewal.
- **Ancestral Memory** - The *Ocean* carries past stories, connecting us to collective wisdom and transformation.

THE SHADOW SIDE OF THE OCEAN

When out of *balance*, it may *express* as:

- **Emotional Overwhelm:** The vastness of the *Ocean* can feel all-consuming, making it challenging to find stability.
- **Evasion of Truth:** Its ever-shifting nature may lead to avoidance or an inability to confront deep emotions.
- **Instability:** Without grounding, the *Ocean's* currents can pull us into uncertainty and emotional *turbulence*.

Magical Workings and Ritual

CONNECT WITH THE *OCEAN'S* ENERGY THROUGH PRACTICES that encourage emotional flow, renewal, and connection:

1. **Movement Practices:** Engage in fluid dance or yoga sequences that reflect the *Ocean's* ebb and flow.

2. **Cleansing Rituals:** Take a saltwater bath or incorporate sea elements into your rituals to release emotional burdens.

3. **Meditative Visualization:** Imagine waves washing over you, carrying away stagnation and inviting clarity.

4. **Ancestral Reflection:** Journal about recurring emotional patterns or meditate on the resilience of your lineage.

Scientific and Symbolic Perspective

- **Cradle of Life:** Covering 70% of the Earth's surface, the Ocean is a source of creation, transformation, and renewal.
- **Cyclical Motion:** Waves, tides, and currents reflect the movement of emotions, reminding us that nothing remains the same forever.
- **Connection & Flow:** The *Ocean* links continents, ecosystems, and generations as our lineage flows through time.

THE *OCEAN* TEACHES US TO MOVE WITH LIFE RATHER THAN resist it, to find strength in surrender, and to trust in the currents that guide us forward. Beneath its surface lies an infinite well of wisdom, waiting for those willing to dive deep.

Blaze Essence (Fire + Fire)

Keywords
Transformation, Passion, Courage, Renewal, Creativity.

THE *BLAZE ESSENCE* **EMBODIES** PURE, UNTAMED **FIRE**, A *transformative* force inspiring bold **creation**. Born from the fusion of two **fiery** *elements*, it consumes stagnation, fuels passion, and ignites decisive **action**. This *essence*, both **destructive** and **regenerative**, teaches that to grow, one must let go of the **past**, embrace self-expression without fear, and **create** something new. *Blaze* clears the path for *reinvention*, igniting **purpose** with fierce, unwavering energy; it urges passionate, confident action, empowering us fully. Moreover, *Blaze* represents *Ancestral* **Fire**, their **resilience**, **struggles**, and **creativity**, connecting us to the *flames* guiding them through darkness, the *sacred* **Fires** of their *rites*, and their **indomitable** *spirit*. This reminds us we're not alone in *transformation*; we inherit the **courage** and **drive** of our *Ancestors*. Honoring their struggles and triumphs, we harness their **Fire**, trusting our inherent capacity for **creation** and **renewal**. Working with this *element*, we **reclaim** our **Fire**, our **voice**, **purpose**, and **power** to forge new paths.

ENERGIES AND INFLUENCES

- **Passion & Drive:** Blaze ignites creativity, ambition, and the courage to take action.
- **Transformation & Renewal:** It consumes the old, creating new beginnings.
- **Resilient Power:** Blaze embodies destruction and creation, a force that cannot be contained.

THE SHADOW SIDE OF BLAZE

When out of balance, it can manifest as:

- **Impulsivity:** Acting without thinking, which can lead to reckless decisions.
- **Overwhelm:** Being overwhelmed by intense emotions or unchanneled energy.
- **Destruction:** Recklessly depleting resources, damaging relationships, or squandering opportunities.

Magical Workings and Ritual

HARNESS BLAZE'S ENERGY THROUGH PRACTICES THAT channel passion, transformation, and creative expression:

1. **Fire Rituals:** Light a candle or small Fire as part of a ceremony to release old patterns and set bold new intentions.

2. **Movement Practices:** To embody Blaze's intensity, engage in fiery dance or dynamic yoga sequences, such as Sun Salutations.

3. **Creative Expression:** Translate Blaze's inspiration into tangible forms through art, writing, or music.

4. **Visualization Meditation:** Imagine a flame burning within you, clearing away blockages and illuminating your path.

Scientific and
Symbolic Perspective

- **Combustion and Energy Release:** Flame grows through heat and light, symbolizing the exponential power of transformation.
- **Amplification and Expansion:** Fire spreads through conduction and radiation, mirroring the momentum of passion and inspiration.
- **Destruction and Renewal:** Wildfires clear the land, allowing new growth, just as flames dismantle the old to create space for evolution.

———

FIRE TEACHES US THAT IT IS NOT ONLY A FORCE OF destruction but also a symbol of rebirth. It drives us forward, illuminates our path, and fuels transformation. When embraced with intention, Fire becomes the force that shapes our destiny.

Lava Essence (Fire + Earth)

Keywords
Transformation, Resilience, Creation, Renewal, Fertility.

LAVA, BORN FROM EARTH'S FIERY DEPTHS, EMBODIES creation and transformation. A symbol of resilience, it forges new landscapes from destruction, paving the way for growth. Upheaval, it teaches, isn't an ending, but a vibrant new beginning. Fire breaks through, reshaping the old to make room for the new, infusing the process with fierce determination, adaptability, and creative regeneration. To create fertile ground for renewal, we must sometimes release the old, embracing challenges and the fire within. Lava's essence is evolution, destruction's alchemy, birthing something stronger, richer, and enduring. It embodies Ancestral resilience: enduring hardship, transforming challenges into wisdom, and creating lasting legacies. It reflects their determined spirit, strength of survival, and the fertile ground they cultivated for future generations. Harnessing lava's energy honors their perseverance, empowers us to create, rebuild, and thrive. As lava reshapes the land, so too can we reshape our lives, building on the lessons of our ancestors, forging our own paths.

ENERGIES AND INFLUENCES

- **Transformation & Renewal:** Lava paves the way for new beginnings, reminding us that change catalyzes growth.
- **Resilience & Strength:** It embodies endurance, demonstrating that the power to rebuild comes from destruction.
- **Creation & Fertility:** Lava enriches the Earth as it cools, forming a foundation for future abundance.

THE SHADOW SIDE OF LAVA

When out of balance, it can manifest in the following ways:

- **Overwhelming Emotions:** The intense, fiery nature of Lava can lead to impulsive actions and emotional instability if it's not grounded.
- **Resistance to Change:** A fear of upheaval may lead to stagnation or attachment to outdated patterns.
- **Destructive Tendencies:** Unchecked Lava energy can damage relationships, deplete resources, and negatively impact personal well-being.

Magical Workings and Ritual

HARNESS THE ENERGY OF LAVA THROUGH PRACTICES THAT promote transformation, grounding, and creation:

1. **Transformation Rituals:** Safely burn a piece of paper on which you have written your fears or limiting beliefs, symbolizing release and renewal.
2. **Grounding Practices:** Work with volcanic stones such as basalt or obsidian to stabilize fiery energy.
3. **Manifestation Work:** Visualize obstacles melting away and reshaping into stepping stones for personal growth.
4. **Cleansing & Renewal:** Use volcanic ash or clay in a ritual to represent rebirth and new beginnings.

Scientific and
Symbolic Perspective

- **Molten Creation:** Lava rises from deep within the Earth, symbolizing the courage to face challenges and embrace transformation.
- **Cooling & Solidification:** As Lava cools, it forms new land, illustrating the balance between intensity and stability.
- **Volcanic Fertility:** Weathered Lava enriches the soil over time, demonstrating how upheaval can lead to renewal and abundance.

LAVA TEACHES US THAT TRANSFORMATION REQUIRES BOTH passion and a solid foundation. It reminds us that even in moments of destruction, we have the power to rebuild, stronger, wiser, and more deeply connected to the energies that shape us.

Mist Essence
(Water + Air)

Keywords
Introspection, Emotional Clarity, Connection, Perception, Flow.

MIST EMBODIES THE GENTLE DANCE BETWEEN WATER'S emotional depth and air's expansive awareness. It softens perceptions, creating space for reflection, insight, and connection. Neither fully formed nor dissipated, mist inhabits the liminal, a threshold revealing glimpses of the unseen, carrying whispers from the past, dissolving boundaries between knowing and feeling. It moves effortlessly between worlds, reminding us that clarity arises not from rigidity, but openness and presence. Mist teaches us to embrace mystery, listen to whispers over shouts, and trust the wisdom of stillness. It invites us to honor the spaces between moments of quiet reflection, subtle emotions, and ancestral stories waiting to be unearthed. Long viewed as a veil between realms, mist carries voices and visions from the past, lingering where memory and presence intertwine, holding ancestral echoes and wisdom. Mist-shrouded landscapes are often considered sacred places where spirits communicate, dreams deliver messages, and the physical and spiritual worlds feel intertwined. Working with mist's energy, we learn to trust intuition, sense the unidentifiable, and honor the intangible guidance of our lineage. Mist reminds us that some truths unfold gently, like dawn breaking through fog, not forced into harsh light.

ENERGIES AND INFLUENCES

- **Emotional Clarity & Perception:** Mist reveals what is hidden, offering understanding through reflection.
- **Flow & Connection:** It moves effortlessly between realms, linking the past and present.

- **Softened Awareness:** Mist dissolves rigid thinking, allowing intuition and insight to emerge.

THE SHADOW SIDE OF MIST

When out of balance, it can manifest as:

- **Confusion:** The absence of clear boundaries can make it challenging to find a direct path forward.
- **Emotional Obscurity:** Feelings may remain elusive, leading to uncertainty and avoidance.
- **Lack of Grounding:** The ethereal quality of Mist can result in a sense of drifting or feeling unanchored.

Magical Workings and Ritual

ENGAGE WITH THE ENERGY OF MIST THROUGH PRACTICES that foster reflection, insight, and connection.

1. **Flowing Movement Practices:** To harmonize your emotions and thoughts, incorporate gentle dance, slow-flow yoga, or Tai Chi.

2. **Mist & Aromatherapy:** Utilize diffusers with essential oils such as lavender or eucalyptus to create a calming and clarifying atmosphere.

3. **Dream Work & Intuition Practices:** Maintain a dream journal to explore the subconscious messages that Mist's energy may carry.

4. **Breathwork & Meditation:** Visualize the Mist surrounding you, dissolving confusion and revealing hidden truths.

Scientific and
Symbolic Perspective

- **Condensation & Suspension:** Mist forms when warm, moist Air cools, creating suspended droplets. This phenomenon mirrors the balance between thought and feeling.
- **Light Diffusion:** Mist softens and scatters light, representing the gentle revelation of hidden insights.
- **Movement & Adaptability:** Mist shifts with Air currents, embodying fluidity and the dynamic nature of perception.

MIST TEACHES US THAT NOT EVERYTHING NEEDS TO BE FULLY visible to be understood. It exists in the in-between, offering wisdom in whispers. It represents the soft unveiling of truths that emerge when we create space for them to be felt rather than forced.

Dust Essence
(Earth + Air)

Keywords
Memory, Impermanence, Wisdom, Dispersal, Connection.

DUST, A SILENT HISTORIAN, TRAVELS ON THE WINDS OF change, yet always finds its way back to Earth. Born from Earth's stillness and Air's movement, it holds echoes of time, fragments of the past suspended between then and now. Dust reminds us that nothing is permanent, that even the smallest particle has a story, and nothing is truly lost, only transformed. It drifts through landscapes, settling in forgotten places, imprinted with the lives of those who came before. Dust encourages us to honor the past while embracing the flow of time, showing how history lives in the present. It invites reflection, urging us to uncover the wisdom hidden in the overlooked and unspoken. Dust whispers of our ancestors' paths walked, homes built, and wisdom passed down. It rests in sacred spaces, in old books, in Ancestral homes, holding traces of the past. Engaging with dust is an act of remembrance, acknowledging the stories woven into the particles around us. Working with its energy connects us to the unseen threads of history, drawing strength from the past while letting it flow into the present. Ancestry isn't just in records and names, but in the land, the air, and the smallest grains that endure.

ENERGIES AND INFLUENCES

- **Memory & Preservation:** Dust holds remnants of the past, providing insights into what once was.
- **Impermanence & Movement:** It reminds us that nothing is permanent and encourages us to remain open to change.

- **Connection Across Time:** Dust creates a bridge between generations, linking us to ancestral wisdom and forgotten knowledge.

THE SHADOW SIDE OF DUST

When out of balance, it can manifest in the following ways:

- **Scattered Focus:** A tendency to shift between thoughts without clarity or direction.
- **Emotional Detachment** is a feeling of disconnection from the present or an avoidance of deeper emotional engagement.
- **Unfinished Cycles:** The re-emergence of unresolved ancestral patterns that lack integration.

Magical Workings and Ritual

ENGAGE WITH THE ENERGY OF DUST THROUGH PRACTICES that honor memory, clarity, and connection:

- **Journaling for Reflection:** Write about themes of impermanence, change, and the ancestral wisdom found in forgotten places.
- **Breath Practices:** Utilize intentional breathwork to clear mental clutter and regain focus.
- **Cleansing Rituals:** Burn incense or work with wind energy to disperse stagnant thoughts or emotions.
- **Ancestral Meditation:** Visualize Dust carrying echoes of the past, revealing messages and insights through its movement.

Scientific and
Symbolic Perspective

- **Erosion & Fragmentation:** Dust forms from the breakdown of larger structures, symbolizing the gradual dissolution of rigid patterns over time.
- **Atmospheric Suspension:** Wind carries Dust across vast distances, illustrating how knowledge and history travel through generations.
- **Deposition & Regeneration:** Eventually, Dust settles, nourishing the Earth and fostering new growth, which symbolizes how past experiences shape the future.

DUST TEACHES US THAT EVEN THE MOST MINOR REMNANTS hold significance. It represents the traces of what once was, the movement of memory, and the quiet keeper of stories waiting to be rediscovered.

Aetherflame Essence (Fire + Air)

Keywords
Visionary Energy, Inspiration, Creativity, Psychic, Illumination.

AETHERFLAME, CELESTIAL FIRE OF INSIGHT, IGNITES discovery, fuels inspiration, and propels ideas into action. Born from the fusion of fire's radiance and air's boundless reach, it embodies the unseen forces driving thought, artistry, and transformation. Burning with visionary brilliance, it reveals paths and illuminates potential. Delicate yet powerful, like an ember carried on the wind, it kindles profound awareness and awakens latent talents. It invites purposeful channeling of inspiration, ensuring passion fuels lasting creation, not merely flickers. It teaches us to burn away doubt, embrace possibility, and trust our inner Fire's brilliance. Aetherflame represents the torch of Ancestral wisdom, a powerful force carrying knowledge, vision, and resilience through generations. It symbolizes the flame passed down through storytellers, philosophers, artists, and seers, inspiring new insights and awakening creativity. Inspiration, it reminds us, is woven into our lineage, shaped by ancestral voices. Engaging with Aetherflame honors ancestral fiery intelligence, bold ideas, visionary dreaming, and the lighting of paths for future generations. In this energy, we bridge ancient knowledge and future vision, carrying forward past brilliance while igniting new understanding.

ENERGIES AND INFLUENCES

- **Inspiration & Illumination:** Aetherflame provides clarity to ideas and uncovers hidden potential.
- **Creative & Intellectual Fire:** It fuels artistic expression, enhances psychic awareness, and deepens insight.

- **The Spark of Vision:** Aetherflame is the guiding light that ignites passion and purpose.

THE SHADOW SIDE OF AETHERFLAME

When out of balance, it can manifest in the following ways:

- **Overstimulation:** An overwhelming influx of ideas or intuitive insights without a clear direction.
- **Burnout:** Exhaustion from exerting creative or spiritual energy too intensely without grounding oneself.
- **Restlessness:** A struggle to focus or commit as energy dissipates too rapidly.

Magical Workings and Ritual

ENGAGE WITH AETHERFLAME BY FOCUSING ON ITS brilliance and maintaining balance through the following practices:

- **Candle Rituals:** Light a gold or crimson candle to channel inspiration and enhance psychic clarity.
- **Fire and Air Invocation:** Use incense, breathwork, or flame gazing to deepen your connection with Aetherflame's energy.
- **Manifestation Through Action:** Direct Aetherflame's power into creative work, such as writing, speaking, or leadership.
- **Psychic Expansion:** Practice divination, dream interpretation, or intuitive development to refine your perception.

Scientific and Symbolic Perspective

- **Combustion & Oxygen Flow:** Fire relies on Air to burn, just as ideas need movement and breath to take shape.
- **Heat Expansion & Energy Transfer:** Flames radiate outward, symbolizing the spread of inspiration and knowledge.
- **Plasma & Ionization:** High-energy flames can produce plasma, mirroring the activation of heightened awareness and expanded perception.

AETHERFLAME REPRESENTS THE RADIANT SPARK OF INSIGHT, a Fire that does not consume but reveals. It reminds us that vision is not merely about seeing; it is about igniting the mind, illuminating the unseen, and carrying forward the brilliance that has always burned within us.

Mud Essence
(Earth + Water)

Keywords
Nurturing, Rebirth, Fertility, Emotional Depth, Foundation.

MUD, BORN FROM EARTH'S STEADFASTNESS AND WATER'S flow, embodies nourishment, change, and life's cycles. It's fertile ground where creation starts, offering stability and the power to adapt. Mud teaches balance, showing that true growth blends structure and flexibility. Resilience is its essence; even in life's chaos, something new constantly emerges. Like seeds in damp soil, Mud fuels transformation, supporting our growth while grounding us. It's a cradle of renewal, where past and future intertwine, shaping our narratives. Mud holds ancestral memory, whispering stories of those before us. Used in rituals, from burials to ancient homes, it links us to ancestral lands and traditions. Through Mud, we honor hardship and resilience, shaping it as a symbol of transformation. Working with it, planting, molding, or simply touching, connects us to Earth's wisdom. We find grounding in the past and strength for the future within its embrace.

ENERGIES AND INFLUENCES

- **Emotional Depth & Renewal:** Mud nurtures the heart and spirit, creating a space for healing and transformation.
- **Balance & Adaptability:** It teaches us to stay grounded while allowing emotions to flow.
- **Bridge Between Past & Future:** Mud carries ancestral stories and encourages growth from past lessons.

THE SHADOW SIDE OF MUD

When out of balance, it can manifest in the following ways:

- **Stagnation:** An excess of Earth energy can cause feelings of being stuck or resistant to change.
- **Emotional Overwhelm:** Too much Water can cloud clarity, making it difficult to find direction.
- **Uncertainty:** Its shifting nature can create instability, leaving one feeling ungrounded.

Magical Workings and Ritual

HARNESS THE ENERGY OF MUD THROUGH PRACTICES THAT honor both stability and fluidity:

- **Grounding Practices:** Walk barefoot, press your hands into the Earth, or engage in slow, intentional dance to connect with both stability and flow.
- **Rituals of Transformation:** Plant seeds in the soil as a symbolic act of new beginnings and renewal.
- **Tactile Expression:** Work with clay or natural Earth materials to process emotions through creative touch.
- **Ancestral Reflection:** Meditate on Mud as a connection to your lineage, drawing strength from the stories and resilience in the land.

Scientific and Symbolic Perspective

- **Formation and Fertility:** When soil absorbs Water, it transforms into a malleable, life-giving substance, similar to how emotions can soften rigid patterns, enabling transformation.
- **Cycles of Decay and Growth:** Mud supports plant life, reflecting the continuous process of renewal and rebirth.
- **Layers of Memory:** Over time, sediment accumulates and preserves history, just as ancestral wisdom is passed down through generations.

MUD SERVES AS A CONVERGENCE OF STRUCTURE AND movement, history, and renewal. It reminds us that transformation is often chaotic; it is raw and deeply connected to our past and future.

Steam Essence (Fire + Water)

Keywords
Transformation, Purification, Adaptability, Renewal, Revelation.

STEAM, BORN FROM THE VITALITY OF FIRE AND THE FLUIDITY of Water, symbolizes transformation, purification, and revelation. It rises from deep emotions to bring clarity, guiding us gracefully through life's transitions. This gentle and powerful force teaches us the art of release and renewal, reminding us that change requires a balance between surrender and empowerment. Steam illustrates the sacred interplay of opposites, the heat of Fire and the fluidity of Water, creating something entirely new. It embodies the Mist rising from sacred springs, the transformative breath in purification rites, and the vapor that carries prayers and wisdom across realms. It invites us to embrace life's changes, allowing our emotions to rise and be illuminated by Fire's energy. Steam has long been a conduit for ancestral healing, deeply woven into traditions such as sweat lodges, ritual baths, and purification ceremonies. The enveloping warmth acts as a bridge between realms, carrying intentions to the spirit world while fostering deep introspection. Within this embrace, we release stagnant energy, honor the wisdom of those who came before us, and renew ourselves with clarity and strength. By engaging with Steam, we acknowledge the struggles and triumphs of our lineage, integrating their teachings into our path. This process of ancestral connection empowers us, cultivating resilience and a deeper understanding of our roots.

ENERGIES AND INFLUENCES

- **Emotional Release & Clarity:** Steam supports letting go, renewal, and deep transformation.

- **Balance & Adaptability:** It teaches how to move through change while staying grounded.
- **Bridge Between Realms:** Steam unveils the hidden, carries ancestral messages, and reveals the unseen.

THE SHADOW SIDE OF STEAM

When out of balance, it can manifest as:

- **Overwhelm:** Too much rising energy can create emotional turbulence and mental fog.
- **Burnout:** Constant transformation without grounding can leave you drained.
- **Illusion:** Steam can blur what's real, making it easy to get lost in uncertainty or avoidance.

Magical Workings and Ritual

MAGICAL WORKINGS & RITUALS:

- **Purification:** Release stagnant energy by taking a Steam bath, sitting in a sauna, or soaking in natural hot springs. Let the heat cleanse both body and mind.
- **Clarity Meditation:** As Steam rises, imagine carrying away what no longer serves you, making space for deeper insight and wisdom.
- **Breath & Heat Activation:** Engage in breathwork, sauna rituals, or dynamic movement to stoke inner transformation and vitality.
- **Ancestral Connection:** Steam holds the voices of the past. Use it in rituals to call upon ancestral wisdom and receive its guidance.

Scientific and Symbolic Perspective

- **Fire & Water in Motion:** Heat turns Water into Steam, mirroring emotional release and revelation.
- **Hidden Energy:** Steam holds stored power, releasing it in moments of change.
- **Cycles of Renewal:** Steam moves through Air and Water, showing the ever-shifting balance of nature.

ELEMENTAL ESSENCE CORRESPONDENCES

Category	Correspondence	Description
Keywords		Freedom, Movement, Adaptability, Inspiration, Clarity, Breath, Communication, Expansion.
Plant Allies & Gemstones	Fennel, Orris Root, Moonstone, Yew, Marigold	Communication
	Lemon Balm, Frankincense, Citrine, Quartz	Clarity
	Sage, Tiger's Eye	Insight (Perception)
	Vanilla, Opal, Dragon's Blood, Lily of the Valley	Inspiration
	Quartz, Dandelion	Air Element
Colors	White, Pale Blue, Silver, Lavender, Grey	
Chakras	Throat Chakra (Vishuddha)	Fluidity in communication, clarity of expression, and the power of spoken and unspoken words
	Third Eye Chakra (Ajna)	Mystical, intuition, insight
	Heart Chakra (Anahata)	Emotional balance, deep connection with others, and the ability to flow with change. Air element.
Yoga Poses	Fish Pose (Matsyasana)	Clarity, Expression, Fluidity, Airy Lightness.
	Camel Pose (Ustrasana)	Expansion, Release, Lightness, Breath, Openness
Pranayama (Breathing Practices)	Alternate Nostril Breathing (Nadi Shodhana)	Harmony, Airflow, Mental Clarity, Balance
	Bhastrika (Bellows Breath)	Power, Activation, Life force, Energy, Clarity
Mudras (Hand Gestures)	Vayu Mudra (Air Gesture)	Balances the Air element in the body and promotes clarity and adaptability.
	Jnana Mudra (Wisdom Gesture)	Inspires intellectual clarity, knowledge expansion

Wind Essence Correspondence Chart

Category	Correspondence	Description
Keywords		Stability, Endurance, Resilience, Strength, Grounding, Patience, Stillness, Earth element
Plant Allies & Gemstones	Hyacinth, Sycamore, Amethyst, Lavender	Stability / Grounding
	Pine, Oak, Sunflower, Thistle, Quartz	Strength
	Chamomile, Onyx	Patience
	Cedar, Smoky Quartz	Stillness / Calm / Peace
	Malachite, Ivy, Moss	Earth element
Colors	Browns, Greens, Slate Grey, Ochre	
Chakras	Root Chakra (Muladhara)	Foundation, Stability, Ancestral Connection, Earth element
	Crown Chakra (Sahasrara)	Spiritual Presence and Cosmic Connection
Yoga Poses	Mountain Pose (Tadasana)	Stillness, Presence, Stability, Rootedness, Strength
	Child's Pose (Balasana)	Wisdom, Reflection, Rest, Protection, Surrender
Pranayama (Breathing Practices)	Long Deep Breathing	Grounding, Presence, Stillness.
	Equal Breathing (Samavritti)	Equilibrium, Inner Stillness, Balance, Deep Presence
Mudras (Hand Gestures)	Earth Gesture (Prithvi Mudra)	Earth element connection, Grounding, Stability
	Prayer Gesture (Anjali Mudra)	Connection, Balance, Alignment, Grounding.

Mountain Essence Correspondence Chart

Category	Correspondence	Description
Keywords		Emotional Depth, Intuition, Connection, Flow, Renewal, Healing, Water element connection
Plant Allies & Gemstones	Honeysuckle, Ash Tree, Lapis Lazuli, Rosemary	Intuition
	Sandalwood, Rose, Bloodstone, Dandelion	Emotional Connection
	Apple, Poppy, Patchouli, Quartz, Topaz	Renewal / Rebirth
	Birch, Morning Glory, Moonstone	Water element
Colors	Blue, Turquoise, Silver, Grey, Black	
Chakras	Sacral Chakra (Svadhisthana)	Emotions, Flow, Creativity, Water element, Intuition
	Heart Chakra (Anahata)	Expansion, Connection
	Throat Chakra (Vishuddha)	Expression, Connection.
	Third Eye Chakra (Ajna)	Intuition, Deep knowing
Yoga Poses	Low Lunge (Anjaneyasana)	Fluidity, Openness, Emotional Expression
	Cat-Cow Flow (Bitilasana Marjaryasana)	Embody the Ocean's wave-like rhythm. Fluidity, Flow and Intuitive movement
	Pigeon Pose (Eka Pada Rajakapotasana)	Deep Waters, Emotional Release
Pranayama (Breathing Practices)	Ocean Breath (Ujjayi)	Mimics ocean sound with breath, fluidity, flow
	Cooling Breath (Sheetali)	Cooling and calming, Water element
Mudras (Hand Gestures)	Jala Mudra (Water Gesture)	Connects to Water element, Enhances Intuition

Ocean Essence Correspondence Chart

Category	Correspondence	Description
Keywords		Passion, Transformation, Vitality, Courage, Illumination, Creative Power, Intensity, Radiance
Plant Allies & Gemstones	Mustard, Fire Opal, Red Rose	Passion
	Ginger, Thyme, Tiger's Eye, Bergamot	Courage
	Tourmaline, Nutmeg	Intensity (to increase)
	Cherry, Maple, Rosemary, Aquamarine, Lily	Creativity
	Ash Tree, Cumin, Carnelian	Fire Element
Colors	Red, Bright Orange, Yellow, Gold	
Chakras	Solar Plexus Chakra (Manipura)	Inner Fire, Transformation, Boldness, Willpower, Self-mastery, Strength, Fire Element, Confidence
	Sacral Chakra (Svadhisthana)	Creation, Desire, Movement, Emotional Intensity, Raw Energy, Passion, Sensuality
Yoga Poses	Boat Pose (Navasana)	Core Fire, Willpower, Focus, Solar Plexus
	Pigeon Pose (Eka Pada Rajakapotasana)	Release, Flowing Fire, Creative Energy, Sacral & Solar Plexus Chakras
	Goddess Pose (Utkata Konasana)	Primal Power, Sensual Fire, Embodied, Solar Plexus, Sacral and Root Chakras
Pranayama (Breathing Practices)	Kapalabhati (Skull Shining Breath)	Fire Element, Purification, Inner Fire, Heat, Transformation
	Bhastrika (Bellows Breath)	Activation, Raw Energy, Power, Fire Element
Mudras (Hand Gestures)	Agni Mudra (Fire Gesture)	Digestion, Confidence, Solar Plexus, Fire Element
	Surya Mudra (Sun Gesture)	Vitality, Boosts Energy, Passion, Sun connection

Blaze Essence Correspondence Chart

Category	Correspondence	Description
Keywords		Balance, Intuition, Clarity, Emotional Flow, Adaptability, Mystery, Subtle Transformation
Plant Allies & Gemstones	Chamomile, Blue Lace Agate	Harmony and Calm
	Lemongrass, Moonstone	Adaptability and Balance
	Lavender, Clear Quartz	Purity and Clarity
	Eucalyptus, Aquamarine	Cleansing and Renewal
	Lilac, Selenite	Hope and Transience
Colors	Soft Silver, Soft Blue, Gray, White	
Chakras	Heart Chakra (Anahata)	Emotional Flow and Balance
	Throat Chakra (Vishuddha)	Gentle, Clear Communication
	Third Eye Chakra (Ajna)	Intuitive Clarity and Subtle Awareness
Yoga Poses	Cat-Cow Pose (Marjaryasana)	Reflects Mist's gentle flow
	Seated Twist (Ardha Matsyendrasana)	Purification and Balance
	Thread the Needle (Urdhv Mukha Pasasana)	Promotes Introspection and Release
	Supported Fish Pose (Matsyasana)	Enhances Emotional Flow and Clarity
Pranayama (Breathing Practices)	Ujjayi Breath (Ocean Breath)	Mimics Mist's rhythm and Calmness
	Sheetkari (Hissing Breath)	Promotes Clarity
	Nadi Shodhana (Alternate Nostril Breathing)	Balances energy flow
Mudras (Hand Gestures)	Jala Mudra (Water Gesture)	Water Element and Emotions
	Gyan Mudra (Wisdom Gesture)	Enhances Awareness and Harmony
	Hridaya Mudra (Heart Gesture)	Promoted Emotional Connection

Mist Essence Correspondence Chart

Category	Correspondence	Description
Keywords		Rebirth & Renewal, Fertility, Fire Element, Earth Element
Plant Allies & Gemstones	Cedar, Poppy, Lilac, Citrine	Rebirth / Renewal.
	Violet, Geranium, Onyx	Fertility
	Jasmine, Aloe, Cinquefoil, Peridot, Amethyst	Destruction (To heal)
	Vervain, Tiger's Eye	Fire Element.
	Mugwort, Malachite, Patchouli	Earth Element.
Colors	Molten Orange, Deep Red, Black	
Chakras	Solar Plexus Chakra (Manipura)	Confidence and Transformative energy
	Root Chakra (Muladhara)	Grounded Intensity and Stability
	Sacral Chakra (Svadhisthana)	Creative Passion and Flow
Yoga Poses	Chair Pose (Utkatasana)	Builds Heat and Strength
	Crescent Lunge (Anjaneyasana)	Reflects Balance and flow
	Plank Pose (Phalakasana)	Embodies Lava's intensity
	Reverse Warrior (Viparita Virabhadrasana)	Combines Boldness and Grace
Pranayama (Breathing Practices)	Bhastrika (Bellows Breath)	Builds Inner Heat and Vigor
	Kapalabhati (Skull Shining Breath)	Invigorates and Transforms
	Ujjayi Breath (Ocean Breath)	Balances fiery energy with Steadiness
Mudras (Hand Gestures)	Agni Mudra (Fire Gesture)	Activates Transformation
	Rudra Mudra (Power Gesture)	Aligns Vitality and Boldness
	Surya Mudra (Sun Gesture)	Amplifies fiery energy

Lava Essence Correspondence Chart

Category	Correspondence	Description
Keywords		Clarity, Adaptability, Reflection, Grounded Thought, Purification, Subtle Energy
Plant Allies & Gemstones	Lavender, Sage, Tourmaline, Pine	Grounding
	Jasmine, Garlic, Rosemary, Clear Quartz	Purification
	Dandelion, Peppermint, Tiger's Eye	Clarity / Thought
	Bergamot, Thyme, Opal, Meadowsweet	Air Element
	Mugwort, Fern, Malachite	Earth Element
Colors	Beige, Yellow, Brown, Gold	
Chakras	Throat Chakra (Vishuddha)	Clear and grounded Communication
	Root Chakra (Muladhara)	Stability and connection to Earth
	Third Eye Chakra (Ajna)	Insight and reflective clarity
Yoga Poses	Extended Side Angle Pose (Utthita Parsvakonasana)	Balances stability with expansive thought
	Triangle Pose (Trikonasana)	Reflects Dust's grounded Flow and Movement
	Child's Pose (Balasana)	Encourages reflection and connection to Earth
Pranayama (Breathing Practices)	Dirga Pranayama (Three-Part Breath)	Steady, grounded breathing for Clarity
	Samavritti (Equal Breathing)	Balances energy and Focus
	Bhramari Pranayama (Bee Breath)	Soothes the mind and cultivates reflection
Mudras (Hand Gestures)	Vayu Mudra (Air Gesture)	Encourages mental flow and Clarity
	Prithvi Mudra (Earth Gesture)	Enhances grounding and Balance
	Jnana Mudra (Wisdom Gesture)	Promotes Introspection and Insight

Dust Essence Correspondence Chart

Category	Correspondence	Description
Keywords		Creativity, illumination, transformation, dynamic, energy, Fire element, Air Element
Plant Allies & Gemstones	Honeysuckle, Cherry, Rose, Moonstone	Creativity
	Marigold, Iris, Hawthorne, Bloodstone	Energy
	Violets, Lotus, Amethyst	Transformation
	Lily of the Valley, Yarrow, Aventurine	Air Element
	Hibiscus, Mustard, Peony, Red Jasper	Fire Element
Colors	Gold, Red, Orange	
Chakras	Third Eye Chakra (Ajna)	Intuition and higher perception
	Crown Chakra (Sahasrara)	Divine inspiration and cosmic awareness
	Solar Plexus Chakra (Manipura)	Personal power and the spark of Transformation
Yoga Poses	Wild Thing Pose (Camatkarasana)	Creativity and Freedom
	Camel Pose (Ustrasana)	Openness and illumination
	Reverse Tabletop (Ardha Purvottanasana)	Upward expansion and energetic alignment
	Twisted High Lunge (Parivrtta Anjaneyasana)	Grounded strength with visionary energy
Pranayama (Breathing Practices)	Bhastrika (Bellows Breath)	Dynamic energy and focus
	Nadi Shodhanam (Alternate Nostril Breathing)	Balances intuitive and logical energies
	Hakini Mudra (Intuition Gesture)	Enhances focus and higher awareness
Mudras (Hand Gestures)	Surya Mudra (Sun Gesture)	Amplifies solar and personal power
	Jnana Mudra (Wisdom Gesture)	Encourages deep wisdom and visionary insight

Aetherflame Essence Correspondence Chart

Category	Correspondence	Description
Keywords		Grounding, Nurturing, Fertility, Emotional Depth,Foundation, Rebirth / Renewal.
Plant Allies & Gemstones	Oak, Ash Tree, Thyme, Honeysuckle, Wheat, Bloodstone, Topaz	Rebirth / Renewal
	Hawthorn, Pomegranate, Lady's Mantle, Rose Quartz, Carnelian, Mushroom (Male),	Fertility
	Elder Tree, Lavender, Tourmaline, Onyx, Patchouli, Sandalwood	Grounding, Foundation
	Mullein	Nurturing
Colors	Brown, Green, Deep Blue, Gray	
Chakras	Root Chakra (Muladhara)	Foundation, Grounding, Stability, Earth element
	Sacral Chakra (Svadhisthana)	Creativity, Fertility, Water element, Potential, Emotional depth
	Heart Chakra (Anahata)	Nurturing, Calming, Renewal
Yoga Poses	Legs Up the Wall Pose (Viparita Karani)	Renewal, Nurturing, Restoration, Root and Heart Chakras
	Garland Pose (Malasana)	Root and Sacral Chakras, Grounding, Rebirth, Connection to Earth
	Tree Pose (Vrksasana)	Grounding, Foundation, Stability
Pranayama (Breathing Practices)	Dirgha Pranayama (Three-Part Breath)	Grounding, Calming, Nurturing
	Ujjayi Pranayama (Victorious Breath)	Rebirth, Release, Calming
Mudras (Hand Gestures)	Prithvi Mudra (Earth Gesture)	Calm, Grounding, Stability, Earth element
	Yoni Mudra (Womb Gesture)	Sacral Chakra, Fertility, Connection to Earth, Balance

Mud Essence Correspondence Chart

Category	Correspondence	Description
Keywords		Transformation, Purification, Renewal, Balance, Adaptability, Revelation.
Plant Allies & Gemstones	Marigold	Transformation
	Rose (white), Peppermint, Mustard	Purification
	Honeysuckle, Willow	Adaptability
	Poppy, Apple, Cedar	Renewal (also Rebirth)
	Pomegranate (flowers)	Balance
Colors	Opalescent, Teal, Light Gray, Pale Blue	
Chakras	Sacral Chakra (Svadhisthana)	Emotional Flow, Creativity, Adaptability, Water Element, Transformation,
	Solar Plexus Chakra (Manipura)	Fire Element, Clarity, Digestion, Willpower, Renewal, Transformation
	Heart Chakra (Anahata)	Warmth, Transformation, Release, Expansion, Purification
Yoga Poses	Cat-Cow Pose (Marjaryasana-Bitilasana)	Sacral Chakra, Fluidity, Release, Creativity (Renewal)
	Cobra Pose (Bhujangasana)	Solar Plexus, Heart Chakra, Transformation, Strength, Renewal, Fluidity
	Twisting Low Lunge (Parivrtta Anjaneyasana)	Transformation, Activation, Solar Plexus, Sacral Chakra
Pranayama (Breathing Practices)	Nadi Shodhana (Alternate Nostril Breathing)	Balances flow and Clarity. Connects to Water and Fire Elements
	Sheetali / Sitali (Cooling Breath)	Calms and purifies the mind, mirroring Steam's cleansing qualities
Mudras (Hand Gestures)	Jala Mudra (Water Gesture)	Connects to Water & Fire elements (thumb & little fingers)
	Agni Mudra (Fire Gesture)	Digestion, Energy, Warmth, Regulates Body Temperature

Steam Essence Correspondence Chart

These *correspondences* offer just a few options; **explore** them and your *intuitive* methods for **incorporating** these **Elemental Essences.** Use what you have available to you.

ANCESTRAL ELEMENTAL ARCHETYPES

Echoes of the Past

*T*he *Ancestral Elemental Archetypes* are living forces that imbue your journey, your essence, **distilled** from the *elemental* **imprints** of your lineage. *Rooted* in the *Moon Tree Chart*, these *archetypes* emerge from the predominant *elemental* energies of the **Sun**, **Moon**, and **Venus** within your family tree. They reveal the *inherited* currents flowing through your *Ancestral* line, offering *insight* into **strengths, challenges,** and **pathways** of *transformation*. Each *archetype* expresses a distinct fusion of **Earth**, **Water**, **Fire**, and **Air**, an *Ancestral* **body potion** blended over *generations* and still influencing your path. For instance, someone with the **Water-Water-Earth** *archetype*, known as **The Sacred Wellkeeper,** carries the deep emotional intelligence of **Water**, anchored by **Earth's** grounded resilience. This blend reflects a *lineage* of **nurturers**, **healers**, and **guardians** of *sacred* knowledge, gifts, and challenges that echo through time, **infused** into your living *elixir*.

WE OFTEN THINK OF THE *ELEMENTS* ONLY AS EXTERNAL forces, **Earth** beneath our steps, **Water** in flowing rivers, **Fire** in the sun's warmth, and **Air** stirring the skies. But these forces *live* within us. They shape our **emotions**, **instincts**, and *Ancestral* inheritance. This isn't about *fixed* beliefs or doctrine, it's about **remembering** the *elemental* **ingredients** that have always moved through our *bodies*, our *lineages*, and our *stories*. These *elemental* energies **infuse** your inner *elixir*, reminding you that you are a living **vessel**, a **body potion** crafted by *Ancestry* and *Nature*. When you honor these *messengers*, you deepen your connection to both your *lineage* and the **cyclical** *wisdom* that flows through all of **life**. Discovering your **Ancestral Elemental Archetype** reveals how these energies have moved through your *lineage*, how they shaped those who came before and how they continue to *pulse* through your own energetic field. This perspective invites a deeply **embodied** relationship with the *Ancestral* essences still with you on your path, allowing you to engage with them in a way that is both tangible and *alchemical*. Each **Ancestral Elemental Archetype** acts as a **body potion recipe,** an *alchemical* formula **encoded** in your *lineage* that holds tools for *healing, gifts, talents, lessons, memories, mysticism,* and your **unique magic.** These *archetypes* come alive through intentional practices, *rituals,* **embodied** *movement,* and *astrological* alignments, that awaken your inner **potion** and connect you with the same *cycles* once honored by your *ancestors,* now living within and around you.

Part of you, part of them, We are Nature.

These practices carry *Ancestral wisdom* and *intention,* helping you **embody** a more *grounded* and connected way of being through the guidance of these **Ancestral Elemental Archetypes**. Your *Moon Tree Chart* reveals the three dominant *elements* of your *Ancestral* energetic **blueprint**. These *elements,* along with their *Elemental Essences,* like *Steam* (**Fire** & **Water**), *Mud* (**Earth** & **Water**), *Mist* (**Air** + **Water**), and *Blaze* (**Fire** + **Fire**), bring deeper nuance to your *archetype.* Each *essence* holds a distinct energetic *imprint,* influencing how your *lineage's* *essence* expresses itself through you. Take *The Sacred Wellkeeper* (**Water–Water–Earth**), for example. This *archetype* carries a legacy of *intuitive* **healers** and **nurturers**. In this *lineage, Elemental Essences* like *Mud* (rooted emotional depth) and *Steam* (passionate flow) enrich our understanding of *transformation* and exploration.

ENGAGING WITH THESE *ELEMENTAL ESSENCES* ALLOWS A **direct**, **embodied experience** of *Ancestral* **memory** and *energetic* inheritance. Exploring your *archetype* enables you to reconnect with *Nature* by sensing how *elemental* forces move within and around you. It also involves honoring *Ancestral wisdom* by crafting *rituals* and practices that align with the **patterns** held in your *lineage*. Additionally, you can facilitate *transformation* by working with **lunations, flower essences**, and **embodied** movement to activate these *archetypal* **gifts**. This work and path is about **remembrance, reclamation**, and the conscious reshaping of your *Ancestral* story. The *Ancestral Elemental Archetypes* remind us that we are part of a living *lineage*. We carry their whispers, their strengths, struggles, and unspoken truths. These archetypes offer a sacred structure through which to meet those echoes, honoring what came before while *alchemizing* the path ahead. To **unveil** and work with your *archetype* is to stir the *essence* of your lineage into conscious form, turning inherited energies into something alive, purposeful, and intentional. This is the **heart** of *Ancestral Alchemology*: a call to honor what has been, transmute what is, and fully embody the **elixir** of *Ancestral* wisdom flowing through your being.

Ritual Guide for Archetypes

THE **RITUAL** FRAMEWORK OF *ANCESTRAL ALCHEMOLOGY* TO connect with *Ancestral Elemental Archetypes* and *Essences*. All rituals in this collection follow a shared structure, one **rooted** in *Ancestral* reverence, *elemental* resonance, and *embodied* remembrance. While each *Ancestral Elemental Archetype* carries its own unique frequency, they all build upon this universal ritual framework.

ANCESTRAL VENERATION

Begin every **Body Potion** ritual by **honoring the ancestors** connected to the archetype's *elemental lineage*. This may be as simple as closing your eyes and sensing their presence, or as *ceremonial* as lighting a candle, placing offerings, or speaking their names aloud.

For Example: *"I honor the ancestors of [line or archetype focus], those who came before me, who whisper through my bones and breath. I welcome* *their wisdom, strength, and presence as I walk this path of remembrance and transformation."*

This invocation creates an energetic container, anchoring your ritual in reverence and rootedness.

ASTROLOGICAL ENERGIES & SOMATIC ACTIVATION

Each archetype draws from your *Moon Tree Chart*, specifically from the **Sun, Moon, and Venus** placements across *generations*. These placements correspond with distinct areas of the **body**, creating a **somatic bridge** to *Ancestral* memory. Through conscious breath, embodied movement, and meditative stillness, you awaken these energetic portals. This practice invites you to feel the lineage not only in your mind or **heart**, but in your *living, breathing Soma*, connected, in spiral, in all of time. **Magically.**

ZODIAC Sign	Body Area	Suggested Movements
ARIES	Head	Gentle head and neck movements
TAURUS	Neck / Throat	Throat-opening stretches
GEMINI	Arms / Hands	Fluid hand motions and gestures
CANCER	Chest	Heart-centered breath and movement
LEO	Upper Back	Expansive chest openers
VIRGO	Abdomen	Core awareness and digestive focus
LIBRA	Lower Back	Soft spinal stretches
SCORPIO	Pelvis	Rooted pelvic grounding
SAGITTARIUS	Hips / Thighs	Hips/Thighs - Open, dynamic hip movements
CAPRICORN	Knees	Stable, supported posture
AQUARIUS	Ankles	Circulating ankle stretches
PISCES	Feet	Mindful, grounding footwork

Body Areas and Zodiac Signs

LUNAR PHASES & ANCESTRAL TIMING

These rituals can be practiced at any time, but their **potency** increases when aligned with:

- The predominant *Moon* phase in your *Moon Tree lineage*
- A significant *Ancestral* date (*birth, death*, or meaningful *milestone*)
- A **lunation** that aligns with the *archetype's essence* (e.g., Full *Moon* for *illumination*, **Dark Moon** for release)

Let the *Moon* guide your timing, her cycles are the heartbeat of *Ancestral* alchemy.

ANCESTRAL CONNECTION & REFLECTION

This part of the ritual deepens your link to the *archetype* and invites integration:

- **Meditative Focus**: Enter stillness. Visualize the *archetype's* energy as a glowing current flowing through you from behind, ahead, and all around. You may see yourself as a torchbearer or **vessel**, carrying *Ancestral medicine* forward with grace. Let yourself *feel* their presence, **witnessing, guiding, loving**.

Reflective Inquiry: Journaling is a *powerful* part of this process.

To begin, freely and *intuitively* write answers to the following prompts, allowing insights to emerge in any form they choose:

1. What *Ancestral* **gift** or wisdom is moving through this *archetype*?
2. How does this *energy* want to express itself through me?
3. What **insight, vision**, or **transformation** is calling?
4. What action can I take to **ground** it in my current life?

CLOSING & INTEGRATION

Complete your **ritual** with *gratitude* and *grounding*. Sense how the *elements*, **movement**, and **insight** have **stirred** your *inner elixir*. Place your hands over your **heart**, and take a few slow breaths, feeling what is now **present**. If your **ritual** includes creating or using a **flower essence**, this is the moment to place it on your altar, offer it to your *ancestors*. End by showing *respect* for the energies you called upon.

RECITE WORDS SIMILAR TO:

"I thank the ancestors, the elements, and this archetypal energy. May what has been remembered root deeply within me. May I carry it with clarity, compassion, and purpose."

THESE STEPS FORM THE **RITUAL COMPASS** OF *ANCESTRAL Alchemology*, a guide that evolves with you. Adapt its shape as needed, but stay rooted in its essence: **connection, embodiment, and remembrance**.

the CELESTIAL SEEKER

Elemental Trio: **Air, Air, Air**

Keywords:
Curious. Adaptable. Eloquent. Clairvoyant. Communicative.

LIMITLESS CURIOSITY AND PROFOUND INSIGHT characterize the *Celestial Seeker,* guided by the element of **Air**. This *archetype* is naturally connected to higher wisdom, *flourishing* in pursuing concealed **truths**, deciphering **symbols**, and articulating intricate **ideas** clearly. Transitioning between *realms* of **thought** and **intuition**, they act as translators of the *invisible* and the unspoken. Whether in the roles of **communicators**, **visionaries**, or **guides**, *Celestial Seekers* shed light on understanding through articulate *communication*. When they *harmonize* their intellectual vigor with *grounding* and emotional presence, they become influential sources of **inspiration** and change for both themselves and their communities.

ANCESTRAL ESSENCE

The *Celestial Seeker* **embodies** the *essence* of their **Ancestral** *lineage*, which includes **mystics**, **scholars**, **visionaries**, and **orators**. These *ancestors* provided wisdom to their communities by interpreting *dreams*, *symbols*, and abstract *concepts*. Acting as messengers, they connected the rational with the intuitive and the spoken with the *unseen*. **Embodying** this archetype involves respecting their legacy by trusting insights, *communicating* truth clearly, and continuing their pursuit of knowledge and *connection*.

The Celestial Seeker - Ancestral Elemental Archetype

SHADOW THREAD

HOWEVER, A STRONG *CONNECTION* BETWEEN THOUGHT AND perception presents some challenges. Identifying these challenges *facilitates* **integration**:

- **Emotional Detachment:** Overemphasis on intellect may lead to disconnecting from emotions, making it difficult to navigate emotions or show empathy.

- **Restlessness:** Constant pursuit of new ideas can lead to dissatisfaction or instability.
- **Scattered Focus:** Lack of grounding may cause their energy to scatter, resulting in burnout or unfinished projects.

Awareness of these **patterns** helps the *Celestial Seeker* balance intellect with *emotions* and body. A *grounding* **ritual**, such as deep breathing while visualizing *clarity* in the **Wind** and letting thoughts settle into *stillness*, can help realign.

- Affirmations like *"I honor both what I know and what I feel"* can be mentally or verbally repeated to come back into alignment.

JUST LIKE THE **WIND** CARRIES MESSAGES OVER VAST distances, the *Celestial Seeker* embodies **Air's** *clarity* and *movement*, converting curiosity into wisdom and channeling restlessness into *inspired* exploration.

ELEMENTAL ALCHEMY

- **AIR** + **AIR** = *Wind Essence* (Clarity of Thought, Perception, and Expansive Intellectual Energy)

This ritual harmonizes intellectual curiosity, intuitive perception, and Ancestral wisdom. It supports **clarity**, **adaptability**, and the graceful **expression** of deep insights through the expansive qualities of **Air**.

Celestial Seeker
Alchemical Elixir Recipe & Ritual

Instructions

Step 1: Prepare the Space
- Add **Air**-corresponding items: feathers, incense (Lavender or Peppermint), or a tuning fork.
- Include one **Earth** item (stone, soil, or small plant) for *grounding*.
- *Always practice Fire safety when working with candles / incense.*

Ingredients

- **3 x Wind Essence** – For clarity, adaptability, intuition, and intellectual flow.
- **1 x Curiosity** - Visualize Air opening new mental pathways and deeper perception.
- **1 x Communication** – Envision a breeze carrying your voice, expressing truth and wisdom.
- **1 x Clairvoyance** - Picture a soft current revealing unseen insights and inner knowing.

Step 2: Set Intention
- Begin with **Vayu Mudra** (index finger to base of thumb – for clarity & calm).
- Transition to **Jnana Mudra** (index finger to thumb, palms up – for *wisdom*).
- **Honor *ancestors*:** Speak names aloud or hold their presence in your *heart*.

Recite:
"I honor the wisdom and vision of my ancestors.
I call upon their insights to guide me as I seek clarity, connection, and balance in my journey."

Step 3: Embodiment Practice
1. Awaken the Body:
- Gentle stretches or movements, intuitively guided.

2. Elemental Breath & Movement:
- Choose Air-aligned breathwork (see Wind Essence section).
- Move with intention to promote clarity and flow.

3. Chakra Focus:
- Heart (Anahata) & Third Eye (Ajna): for expansion, perception, intuition.

THE CELESTIAL SEEKER'S ELIXIR

→ Refer to **pg 200** for Wind Essence practices, poses, and correspondences.

4. Suggested Embodiment Shapes / Poses:
- Standing Side Stretch (Parsva Tadasana): opens chest, invites clarity.
- Cat-Cow (Marjaryasana-Bitilasana): activates spine, bridges thought + voice.
- Reverse Warrior (Viparita Virabhadrasana) – enhances heart flow + focus.

5. Dance & Intuitive Movement:
- Explore airy, flowing gestures.
- Include stillness and fluid movement to embody thought, voice, and insight.

Step 4: Astrology & Body Awareness
- Use your *MoonTree Chart* to identify ancestral body correspondences.
- Pair movements, breathwork, or visualization with these areas for deeper connection.
  Lunar Phase:
- Align ritual with the current lunar phase for deeper ancestral resonance.

Step 5: Reflection & Writing
- Meditation / journaling.
- Reflect on **Ancestral** communication *patterns*.
- Practice automatic writing / receive intuitive messages.

Step 6: Ancestral Offering
- Offer flowers or flower *essences* aligned with the *Celestial Seeker:*
  - *Dandelion* – clarity & renewal
  - *Clover* – adaptability & flow
  - *Lavender* – calm & insight
  - *Lilac* – intuitive clarity
  - *Daisy* – clear expression
  - *Rose* – clairvoyance & higher perception
- Light a candle to welcome and invite Ancestral connection and clarity.

Step 7: Closing
- End with gratitude.
- Acknowledge any insights or energy shifts.
- Let the ritual integrate into your daily thoughts, words, and creations.

Closing Reflection

The *Celestial Seeker* ritual connects you to the intellectual **curiosity**, **clairvoyant** perception, and **eloquence** passed down through your *lineage*. While the details of your *ancestors*' lives may remain a **mystery**, their commitment to wisdom, effective communication, and *intuitive* understanding *echoes* within you. Embracing these energies honors their legacy and unlocks your potential for clear thinking, articulate *expression*, and visionary perception.

** **Fire Safety:** When working with candles and incense, practice caution.*

The ROOTED GUARDIAN

Elemental Trio: **Earth, Earth, Earth**

Keywords:
Grounded. Resilient. Nurturing. The Home. Business.

THE *ROOTED GUARDIAN* REPRESENTS STABILITY, NURTURING, and protection **rooted** in the enduring power of **Earth**. This *archetype* embodies the triple force of tradition, resilience, and belonging. They are stewards of *Ancestral* wisdom and material foundations, **creating** and maintaining spaces that support future *generations* - **physically**, **emotionally**, and **spiritually**. Guided by *Mountain Essence*, the *Rooted Guardian* excels in creating, sustaining, and safeguarding what truly matters: homes, families, communities, and legacies. Whether caring for land, **nurturing** relationships, or developing thriving enterprises, they teach that resilience involves both standing firm and evolving with **purpose**.

ANCESTRAL ESSENCE

The *Rooted Guardian* carries the legacy of **caretakers**, **builders**, and **providers**, *ancestors* who created structures, upheld traditions, and cultivated the resources needed for their *communities* to **flourish**. From tending land and crafting tools to managing *households* and leading with **strength**, their contributions ensured continuity and **care** across *generations*. To **embody** this archetype is to honor that *lineage, rooted* in **prosperity**, **responsibility**, and **stewardship**. The *Rooted Guardian* sustains the wisdom and values passed down through the ages, *weaving* them into the fabric of modern life to support a thriving, *interconnected* **future**.

The Rooted Guardian - Ancestral Elemental Archetype

SHADOW THREAD

WHILE GROUNDED IN STRENGTH, THIS *ARCHETYPE* CAN encounter challenges that arise from its core qualities. Awareness of these **patterns** opens the door to deeper integration:

- **Resistance to Change**: A deep attachment to tradition may create difficulty adapting to new ideas or shifts.

- **Over-Focus on Practicality:** Prioritizing the material world may cause emotional or spiritual needs to be overlooked.
- **Stagnation:** The steady nature of **Earth** can become overly fixed, resisting necessary evolution or growth.

To restore balance, the *Rooted Guardian* must learn to trust both the foundation and the possibility of transformation. A centering practice, inhale deeply, connecting with the strength of the **Earth**; exhale, opening space for new possibilities that can create harmony.

- Affirmations like "*I build with care and grow with intention*" help bridge tradition with renewal.

JUST LIKE THE MOUNTAINS, ENDURING YET EVER-CHANGING, the *Rooted Guardian* embodies **Earth's** resilience. They cultivate grounded strength, build lasting legacies, and adapt to growth. Their presence reminds us: we carry the **past's** roots and **future's** seeds within.

ELEMENTAL ALCHEMY

- **EARTH + EARTH** = *Mountain Essence* (The steadfast strength of grounded resilience, providing support, patience, and enduring stability)

This ritual connects you with the grounding, sustaining, and protective energy of the Rooted Guardian. It supports **stability**, **care**, and **resourcefulness**, while aligning you with Ancestral wisdom and the enduring power of **Earth**.

Rooted Guardian

Alchemical Elixir Recipe & Ritual

Instructions

Step 1: Prepare the Space

- Gather **Earth** elements: *crystals, gemstones, soil, small plants.*
- Add *grounding* scents: **cedar**, **patchouli**, **vetiver**.
- *Create a calm, rooted environment to anchor your energy.*

Ingredients

- **3 x Mountain Essence** – Embodying Earth's strength, steadiness, and resilience.
- **1 x Resilience** – Visualize a mountain's unshakable presence through all seasons.
- **1 x Care** – Feel the nurturing essence of fertile soil, sustaining life and healing.
- **1 x Prosperity** - Imagine a flourishing home, business, and community built on strong, loving foundations.

Step 2: Set Intention

- Begin with Prithvi Mudra (ring finger + thumb) – enhances grounding, resilience.
- Transition to Anjali Mudra (palms at heart) – honors the Earth and ancestors.
- **Honor your *ancestors***: Speak their names aloud or hold their presence in your *heart*.
- Set your **intention** and invite their strength into your ritual.

Recite:

" *I honor my ancestors' stability, prosperity, and resilience. I call upon their wisdom to guide me in creating a strong foundation for my home, work, and lineage.* "

THE ROOTED
GUARDIAN'S
ELIXIR

Step 3: Embodiment Practice

1. Ground the Body
- Begin with slow, earthy movements that connect you to the ground beneath you.

2. Elemental Breath & Movement:
- Choose a steady, grounding breathwork technique (see **Mountain Essence** section).
- Move with *presence, rooting* into the **Earth's** stability

3. Chakra Focus:
- Activate **Root** (*Muladhara*), **Solar Plexus** (*Manipura*), and **Heart** (*Anahata*) for stability, power, and connection.

→ REFER TO **PG 203** FOR MOUNTAIN ESSENCE PRACTICES, poses, and correspondences.

4. Suggested Embodiment Shapes / Poses:
- **Mountain Pose** (*Tadasana*) – strength & rooted presence
- **Tree Pose** (*Vrikshasana*) – grounded growth & balance
- **Goddess Pose** (*Utkata Konasana*) – power, rootedness, and receptivity.

5. Dance & Intuitive Movement:
- Move slowly and deliberately. Reflect the process of building, sustaining, and standing firm.
- Let your body *embody* **Earth's** resilience and care.

Step 4: Astrology & Body Awareness
- Use your *MoonTree Chart* to identify ancestral body correspondences.
- Pair movements, breathwork, or visualization with these areas for deeper connection.
  - *Lunar Phase:*
- Align ritual with the current lunar phase for deeper Ancestral resonance.

Step 5: Reflection & Writing
- Meditation / journaling.
- Reflect on **Ancestral** strength and how they sustained their homes and communities.
- Practice automatic writing / receive intuitive messages and guidance on themes of **stability**, **prosperity**, and **nurturing** care.

Step 6: Ancestral Offering
- Offer flowers or flower *essences* aligned with the ***Rooted Guardian:***
  - **Comfrey** – grounding, resilience
  - **Honeysuckle** – nurturing energy
  - **Mugwort** – Ancestral intuition
  - **Blackberry Blossoms** – grounded support
  - **Mullein** – protective, nurturing presence
  - **Basil Flowers** – prosperity, business growth
- Light a candle as a symbol of gratitude and grounding ancestral presence.

Step 7: Closing
- Offer gratitude for the insights and support received.
- Acknowledge any insights or energy shifts.
- Let the ritual integrate into your daily thoughts, words, and creations.

Closing Reflection

The Rooted Guardian ritual links you to the enduring strength, prosperity, and nurturing energy of your ancestors. While the specifics of their lives may be unclear, their resilience, wisdom, and knack for building solid foundations reside within you. Through grounding practices, symbolic offerings, and reflective writing, you pay tribute to their legacy. The elemental pattern shown in your MoonTree Chart showcases their energetic impact. By harmonizing with these elements, you can establish deep roots, foster growth, and create a strong and prosperous foundation for generations to come. ▽▽▽

*** Fire Safety:** When working with candles and incense, practice caution.*

The EMBERFLOW SEER

Elemental Trio: **Water, Water, Fire (in any order)**

Keywords:
Empathetic. Creative. Transformative. Psychic Ability. Ambition.

THE *EMBERFLOW SEER* EMBODIES A POWERFUL BLEND OF *intuitive* wisdom and transformative **Fire**, guided by the fluidity of **Water** and the bold spark of **Fire**. This *archetype* excels at the *crossroads* of **emotional intelligence** and **visionary** purpose, effortlessly navigating *visible* and *invisible* realms. Channeling from *Ancestral* wisdom and **psychic clarity,** the *Emberflow Seer* ignites impactful and lasting change. Inclined towards **leadership** and **innovation**, they combine deep *compassion* with unwavering *ambition*, encouraging others to follow their instincts, embrace their inner vision, and boldly pursue their **life's** purpose. Their talent lies in converting emotional depth into **magnetic inspiration** and drive, both on a *personal* and *collective* level.

ANCESTRAL ESSENCE

The *Emberflow Seer* follows in the footsteps of **spiritual leaders, intuitive creators**, and **visionary healers** – *ancestors* who influenced their communities with emotional wisdom, *clairvoyant gifts*, and *creative power*. These individuals felt deeply, led boldly, and brought about *transformation* through insight and action. Their legacy is one of *resilience* and intuitive *leadership*, intertwined with a strong sense of purpose. *Embodying* this *archetype* is a way to **venerate** those who paved the way, *transmuting* **emotion** into action, **compassion** into transformation, and **vision** into reality. By assuming this role, the *Emberflow Seer* awakens a *wellspring* of insight and ambition that ripples outward, **cultivating** growth and potential for **future** *generations*.

The Emberflow Seer - Ancestral Elemental Archetype

SHADOW THREAD

PROFOUND DEPTH AND *INTENSITY* PRESENT SOME *ELEMENTAL* shadows as well. Recognizing these **patterns** helps in maintaining balance and achieving grounded and tangible *transformation*:

- **Empathy Overload:** Absorbing others' emotions too deeply can blur *energetic* boundaries and lead to exhaustion.

- **Impulsivity:** A powerful drive may cause *hasty* decisions without aligning with *long-term vision.*
- The Intense fusion of **Water** and **Fire** can cause emotional turbulence, resulting in internal storms that *intentional* nervous system regulation can help in *cultivating* calm within.

Acknowledging these shadows enables the *Emberflow Seer* to transmute *sensitivity* into *resilience* and *impulsiveness* into *focused* power. A helpful practice involves taking *deep breaths*, allowing emotions to surface like **waves** on the inhale, and directing inner **Fire** towards purposeful action on the exhale.

- Affirmations such as *"I transform intensity into strength and insight"* can help ground and empower your energetic flow.

JUST AS *STEAM* EMERGES FROM THE FUSION OF **WATER** AND **Fire**, the **Emberflow Seer** *distills* their *essence* into a **ritual** of *transformation*, harnessing **emotion**, **intuition**, and **creative** energy to drive *bold, compassionate* action. Through this *alchemical* **fusion**, they carry the *mysticism* of their *lineage* into a **future** shaped by vision, purpose, and empowered change.

ELEMENTAL ALCHEMY

- **Water + Water** = *Ocean Essence* – a flowing depth of connection, intuition, and adaptability.
- **Water + Fire** = *Steam Essence* – the dynamic interplay of feeling and action, sparking renewal, transformation, and resilience.

This *ritual* blends emotional **insight**, **psychic** ability, and **ambition**. It helps you align intuition with drive, facilitating transformation through **embodiment**, **visualization**, and **reflection**. Balance spiritual vision with purposeful action through the alchemy of **Steam** and **Ocean**.

Ingredients

- **1 x Ocean Essence** – Deepens emotional insight and enhances psychic awareness.
- **1 x Steam Essence** – Sparks resilience and transformation through inner drive.
- **1 x Clairvoyance** – Visualize your third eye opening to perceive beyond the visible.
- **1 x Creativity** - Picture a fiery spark igniting bold imagination and inspired ideas.
- **1 x Ambition** - Envision rising steam lifting you toward purpose and success.

Emberflow Seer

Alchemical Elixir Recipe & Ritual

Instructions

Step 1: Prepare the Space
- Light a red candle for *creativity* & **Fire** energy.
- Place a bowl of **Water** to anchor emotional depth & *intuition*.
- Use scents such as **Bergamot** (focus), **Cinnamon** (creativity), and **Clove** (psychic activation).

Step 2: Set Intention
- Begin with **Hridaya Mudra** (hands on heart) – compassion and opens **Heart Chakra**.
- Transition to **Shakti Mudra** (ring + little fingers touch, others curled over thumb) – awakens **Sacral** energy, **creativity**, and *flow*.
- Honor your *ancestors*: Speak their names aloud or hold their memory in your *heart*.
- Set your **intention** and invite their strength & vision into your ritual.

Recite:

" *I honor the vision and ambition of my ancestors. I call upon their strength to guide me in manifesting my purpose, blending intuition with decisive action.*"

Step 3: Embodiment Practice
1. **Warm the Body**
- Start with slow fluid movements to awaken energy flow.

2. **Elemental Breath & Movement:**
- Choose breathwork that channels both **Water's** flow and Fire's upward motion (see *Ocean & Steam Essence* section).

3. **Chakra Focus:**
- Activate **Sacral** (*Svadhisthana*), **Solar Plexus** (*Manipura*), and **Heart** (*Anahata*) to support creativity, drive, and emotional depth

→ REFER TO **PGS 206** & **227** FOR ADDITIONAL PRACTICES, poses, breathwork, and correspondences related to Ocean & Steam Essences.

4. Suggested Embodiment Shapes / Poses:
- **Cat-Cow Pose** *(Marjaryasana-Bitilasana)* – release and inner rhythm.
- **Warrior I** *(Virabhadrasana I)* – strength, purpose, and focus.
- **Seated Twist** *(Ardha Matsyendrasana)* – clarity and adaptability.

5. Dance & Intuitive Movement:
- Flow between **Water's** fluid rhythm and **Fire's** dynamic sparks.
- Let movement reflect inner *transformation, ambition and inspiration*

Step 4: Astrology & Body Awareness
- Use your *MoonTree Chart* to determine **astrological** body areas governed and *Ancestral* connections.
- Pair *movements*, *breathwork*, or *visualization* with these areas for deeper connection.
  ***Lunar Phase**:*
- Choose a lunar phase that aligns with either your *MoonTree Chart* results or any Lunar phase you are called to work with..

Step 5: Reflection & Writing
- Meditation / journaling.
- Reflect on **Ancestral visions, ambitions, and spiritual insight.**
- Practice automatic writing / receive intuitive messages and guidance on themes of **leadership**, **creativity**, and **inner transformation.**

Step 6: Ancestral Offering
- Offer flowers or flower *essences* from plant allies aligned with the ***Emberflow Seer:***
  - **Daffodil** (Water) – renewal and intuition
  - **Water Lily** (Water) – clarity and purity
  - **Holy Basil** (Fire) – ambition and sacred focus
  - **Rose** – psychic activation and divine wisdom
  - **Lilac** – adaptability and creativity
  - **Peony** – boldness and visionary ambition
- Light a candle as a symbol of gratitude for your *Ancestral* **strength** and **insight**.

Step 7: Closing
- Offer gratitude for the insights and support received.
- Acknowledge any insights or energy shifts.
- Let the ritual integrate into your visions, decisions and creative pursuits.

Closing Reflection

The *Emberflow Seer* **ritual** invites you to blend the *dynamic* energy of **Water** with the fiery *passion* of **Fire**. This union *empowers* you to access the **psychic talents, foresight,** and **determination** passed down by your ancestors. While the details of their existence may remain a *mystery*, their **strength, wisdom,** and **aspirations** resonate within you. Embracing these *elements* awakens your *intuition, innovation*, and ability to effect real change, unlocking your potential as a **seer, guide,** and **architect** of your own fate.

▽ ▽ △

__Fire Safety:__ When working with candles and incense, practice caution.

The INVENTIVE ORACLE

Elemental Trio: **Water, Water, Air (in any order)**

Keywords:
Creative. Inventive. Oracle. Willpower. Empathetic.

THE *INVENTIVE ORACLE* SEAMLESSLY CONNECTS **REALMS** OF **thought** and **emotion**, blending deep *emotional* intelligence with visionary intellect to craft meaningful and *transformative* expressions. The interplay of **Water** and **Air** guides this *archetype*, moving effortlessly through *subtle* energies and drawing inspiration from the unseen to **unveil** profound truths. With heightened sensitivity and original thinking, the *Inventive Oracle* taps into *Ancestral wisdom* and inner perception to provide insights that ignite clarity and **unlock** new possibilities. Naturally visionary, they delve beyond the surface to discover unique solutions that *merge* **intuition**, **creativity**, and purposeful **innovation**. Encouraging us to balance sensitivity with **strength**, **perception** with **action**, and *inspiration* with **grounded** creation.

ANCESTRAL ESSENCE

The *Inventive Oracle* carries the legacy of *Ancestral essence*, **embodying** the *wisdom* of **seers**, **creative thinkers**, and **intuitive guides** who blended emotional awareness with intellect to aid their *communities* in **flourishing**. These visionaries translated **unseen** *mysteries* into *tangible* support and action, providing *clarity* and *transformation* through their words, **art**, or mere presence. **Expressing** this *archetype* means honoring their **gifts** of **foresight**, **creativity**, and **resilience**. The *Inventive Oracle* perpetuates this tradition by translating inner *wisdom* into purposeful offerings that **light** the way for others.

The Inventive Oracle - Ancestral Elemental Archetype

SHADOW THREAD

THE *INVENTIVE ORACLE* POSSESSES A PROFOUND DEPTH OF perception and *imaginative* thinking that can bring both brilliance and challenge. Being aware of these **patterns** can help in achieving **balance** and **integration**. Here are some common tendencies and how to address them:

- **Emotional Overwhelm:** Intense *sensitivity* may cause exhaustion if you don't maintain energetic boundaries.
- **Scattered Focus:** Dealing with simultaneous emotional flow and mental stimulation can cause indecision or *creative* stagnation.
- **Over-analysis:** Constantly exploring *possibilities* may delay taking tangible action, causing ideas to remain unrealized.

Recognizing and understanding these tendencies can assist the *Inventive Oracle* in honing their **gifts**, **channeling** their *energy* into impactful and sustainable *creations*. A useful practice involves deeply *inhaling* while *visualizing Mist* rising with *brightness*, followed by exhaling with the *intention* to direct insights into focused action.

- Affirmations such as *"I transform inspiration into creation"* can reinforce the balance between **intuition** and **innovation**.

Just as *Mist* arises from the meeting of **Water** and **Air**, the *Inventive Oracle* **distills** emotional and intellectual clarity into *creative* **solutions**. Their *alchemical* practice transforms **vision** into **action** and insight into form, while honoring the *Ancestral wisdom* that flows through their *sensitive* and *imaginative* being.

ELEMENTAL ALCHEMY

- **Water + Water** = *Ocean Essence* – emotional flow, spiritual connection, and adaptability.
- **Water + Air** = *Mist Essence* – intuitive perception meets intellectual clarity, fostering innovation and fluid insight.

This **ritual** harmonizes **emotional flow**, **creative** energy, and intellectual **clarity**. It awakens *perception*, *articulation*, and *innovation*– balancing **sensitivity** with **willpower** to channel *insight* into inspired, *transformative* **action**.

Inventive Oracle

Alchemical Elixir Recipe & Ritual

Instructions

Step 1: Prepare the Space
- Arrange **Water** and **Air** symbols: a bowl of **Water**, *feathers*, *wind chimes*.
- Include *creative* items: **paper & pencil to draw**, **paints** etc representing *invention*.
- Use scents such as **Jasmine** (intuition), **Sandalwood** (clarity & focus), and **Patchouli** (creative grounding).

Ingredients

- **1 x Ocean Essence** – Deepens emotional adaptability and clarity
- **1 x Mist Essence** – Supports mental clarity, perception, and fluid thought.
- **1 x Empathy** – Visualize waves of compassion radiating from the heart, connecting to others.
- **1 x Creativity** - Picture vibrant inspiration flowing around you, sparking invention.
- **1 x Willpower** - Envision a steady river flowing through obstacles, directing insight into action.

Step 2: Set Intention
- Begin with **Yoni Mudra** – activates creative and emotional energy.
- Transition to **Akash Mudra** (middle finger to thumb) – openness to divine insight.
- **Honor your *ancestors***: Speak their names aloud or hold their memory in your *heart*.
- Set your **intention** and invite their creativity & clarity into your ritual.

Recite:

"*I honor the wisdom, creativity, and vision of my ancestors. With clarity and strength, I channel my insights into inspired action and transformative creation.*"

The Inventive Oracle's Elixir

Step 3: Embodiment Practice
1. Connect into your Body
- Begin with movements reflecting **Water's** flow and **Air's** fluid & flowing expansion.
2. Elemental Breath & Movement:
- Choose breathwork that blends *emotional adaptability* and mental **clarity**.
- (see *Ocean & Mist Essence* section).
3. Chakra Focus:
- Activate **Sacral** (*Svadhisthana*), **Heart** (*Anahata*), and **Throat** (*Vishuddha*) for expression, connection, and creativity.

→ REFER TO **PGS 206** & **215** FOR PRACTICES, POSES, breathwork, and correspondences related to Ocean & Mist Essences.

4. Suggested Embodiment Shapes / Poses:
- **Butterfly Pose** *(Baddha Konasana)* – supports emotional *adaptability* and flow.
- **Camel Pose** *(Ustrasana)* – opens **heart** to insight and resilience.
- **Supported Fish Pose** *(Matsyasana)* – encourages *expression* and mental clarity.

5. Dance & Intuitive Movement:
- Alternate between *Airy*, expansive gestures & fluid, flowing **Water**-like motions.
- Follow your movement with **creative expression** (painting, journaling, drawing) to *embody* your inspiration.

Step 4: Astrology & Body Awareness
- Use your *MoonTree Chart* to identify ancestral body correspondences.
- Pair movements, breathwork, or visualization with these areas for deeper connection.
   Lunar Phase:
- Align ritual with the lunar phase that aligns with your **creative** or *healing* intention and your *Ancestral* work. Follow your *intuition*.

Step 5: Reflection & Writing
- Meditation / journaling.
- Reflect on *Ancestral* patterns of **creativity**.
- Practice automatic writing / receive intuitive messages and guidance on themes of **expression**, **innovation**, and **clarity**.

Step 6: Ancestral Offering
- Offer flowers or flower *essences* aligned with the **Inventive Oracle:**
    - **Iris** *(Water)* – adaptability and *intuitive* flow
    - **Daisy** *(Water)* – clarity and gentle perception
    - **Primrose** *(Air)* – self-*expression* and *creative* spark
    - **Lily** – deep emotion and willpower
    - **Lavender** – *clarity*, *creativity*, and *calm*
    - **Vervain** – visionary insight and higher purpose
- Light a *silver or pale blue* candle as a gesture of gratitude for *inherited* **creativity** & **inspiration**.

Step 7: Closing
- Offer **gratitude** for the insights and support received.
- Acknowledge any insights or *energy* shifts.
- Let the ritual integrate into your *projects*, *relationships*, & *creative* endeavours.

Closing Reflection

The *Inventive Oracle* **ritual** prompts you to blend your **emotional** flow with **intellectual** clarity and align your **psychic** abilities with *creative* actions. Even though the details of your *ancestors'* lives may be a *mystery*, their **vision**, **resilience**, and **ingenuity** are present within you. By *embracing* these qualities, you can *unlock* your *potential* to serve as a **mentor**, a **creator**, and **innovator**, *infusing* your **intuition** and **inspiration** into paths of *transformation* for both yourself and those around you.

▽▽△

*** Fire Safety:** When working with candles and incense, practice caution.*

The EMBERHEART PATHFINDER

Elemental Trio. **Fire, Fire, Earth** (in any order)
Keywords:
Courageous. Visionary. Grounded. Creative. Leadership.

THE *EMBERHEART PATHFINDER* IS A VISIONARY trailblazer, combining the fierce spark of **Fire** with the solid strength of **Earth** to create new paths and motivate others to follow. This archetype excels at the intersection of ambition and resilience, turning raw passion into purposeful drive. Led by the intensity of **Blaze Essence** and the transformative power of **Lava Essence**, the *Emberheart Pathfinder* sparks bold action while establishing enduring foundations. They serve as both the catalyst for change and the constant *flame* that sustains it. Through a blend of **dynamic** *creativity* and practical strategy, the *Emberheart Pathfinder* imparts lessons on leading with purpose, acting with **bravery**, and constructing with **diligence**.

ANCESTRAL ESSENCE

The *Emberheart Pathfinder* **embodies** the *Ancestral* **essence** of brave leaders, innovative pioneers, and resilient builders who fearlessly pursued their dreams. They ignited movements, guided with *integrity*, and established a solid foundation for **future** eras. Embracing this *archetype* pays homage to their skill at combining **ambitious** goals with **practical** steps. By carrying on this legacy, the *Emberheart Pathfinder* motivates others to achieve greatness through **bravery**, **ingenuity**, and steadfast **leadership**.

The Emberheart Pathfinder - Ancestral Elemental Archetype

SHADOW THREAD

THE **SHADOW** *ENERGY* OF THIS *ARCHETYPE* POSSESSES GREAT power and **intensity**, but it also brings its own set of challenges. Understanding these **patterns** can help in *achieving* a deeper alignment:

- **Burnout:** If you don't prioritize sufficient *rest* and *restoration*, the combination of **Fire** energies can deplete your *energy*.

- **Impatience:** The urgent nature of **Fire** may clash with the steadiness of **Earth**, leading to *frustration* or *impulsive* decisions.
- **Overextension:** Juggling too many roles or *projects* can disperse *energy*, jeopardizing long-term success.

Recognizing these inclinations allows the *Emberheart Pathfinder* to enhance their leadership skills. A centering *practice* involves taking a *deep inhale*, connecting with the **Earth's** unwavering presence below, and exhaling with intent to focus the **Fire** energy into a clear and *purposeful* flame.

- Affirmations like "*I lead with courage and build with care*" help maintain a balance between **boldness** and **endurance**.

JUST LIKE HOW *LAVA* FLOWS WITH POWER AND PURPOSE, THE *Emberheart Pathfinder* embodies the *essence* of **Fire** and **Earth**, combining them into an alchemical representation of **creative** leadership, **transformation**, and **sustainability**. Their *essence* encourages us to spark lasting change, *rooted* in legacy and fueled by vision.

ELEMENTAL ALCHEMY

- **Fire + Fire** = *Blaze Essence* – bold *inspiration*, decisive *action*, and dynamic *creativity*.
- **Fire + Earth** = *Lava Essence* – grounded *transformation*, blending *passion* with practical strength.

This **ritual** combines the **radiant** energy of **Fire** with the **grounding** power of **Earth**. It *activates* ambition, **creativity**, and **leadership**—anchoring your *inner flame* with stability and *Ancestral* strength.

Ingredients

- **1 x Blaze Essence** – Sparks *creativity* and *passionate* purpose.
- **1 x Lava Essence** – Grounds **Fire** energy, activating practical, steady action.
- **1 x Courage** – Visualize a radiant inner **Fire** fueling *boldness* and confidence.
- **1 x Resilience** - Imagine deep *roots* anchoring your strength & endurance.
- **1 x Vision** - See your *aspirations* lit by **Fire** and held by **Earth**.
- **1 x Creative Flow** - Feel **inspired** ideas becoming tangible outcomes.
- **1 x Leadership** - Sense *Ancestral* wisdom *empowering* you to lead with clarity and strength.

Emberheart Pathfinder
Alchemical Elixir Recipe & Ritual

Instructions

Step 1: Prepare the Space
- Symbols of **Fire** & **Earth**: For **Fire**, a lit candle and for **Earth**, crystals, stones, or some soil.
- Use scents such as **Cinnamon** (**Fire** element & Motivation), **Vetiver** (**Earth** element & grounding)
- Add *warm* colors to your space: **red**, **orange**, **golds** - to *connect* with passion and purpose.

Step 2: Set Intention
- Begin with **Surya Mudra** (ring finger to base of thumb) – activates **Fire** and *vitality*
- Transition to **Prithvi Mudra** (ring finger to thumb tip) – strengthens grounding and resilience.
- **Honor your** *ancestors*: Speak their names aloud or hold their memory in your *heart*.
- Set your **intention** and invite their courage, vision & strength into your ritual.

Recite:
"*I ignite my inner Fire with courage, creativity, and clarity. Rooted in resilience, I honor the strength and wisdom of my ancestors to lead with vision and transform my dreams into reality.*"

Step 3: Embodiment Practice
1. Ground & Energize
- Begin with movements that reflect **Fire's** energy and **Earth's** strength.
2. Elemental Breath & Movement:
- Choose breathwork that blends *grounding* and **creativity** (see *Blaze & Lava Essence* section).
3. Chakra Focus:
- Activate **Solar Plexus** (*Manipura*) and **Root** (*Muladhara*) for **ambition**, **stability**, and **drive**.

→ REFER TO **PGS 209** & **212** FOR PRACTICES, POSES, *breathwork, and correspondences related to Blaze & Lava Essences.*

4. **Suggested Embodiment Shapes / Poses:**
- **Low Lunge** (*Anjaneyasana*) – *grounds* while initiating forward *momentum*.
- **Warrior I** (*Virabhadrasana* I) – builds *strength*, *clarity*, and *direction*.
- **Tree Pose** (*Vrikshasana*) – balances **Fire** with deep *rootedness*.

5. **Dance & Intuitive Movement:**
- Alternate between **dynamic** movements (**Fire**) and **grounded**, deliberate stomping steps (**Earth**) expressing *courage* and *creativity*.

Step 4: Astrology & Body Awareness
- Use your *MoonTree Chart* to identify ancestral body correspondences.
- Pair movements, breathwork, or visualization with these areas for deeper connection.
  Lunar Phase:
- Align ritual with the lunar phase that aligns with your *grounding*, *creative* and *healing* intention and your *Ancestral* work. Follow your **intuition**.

Step 5: Reflection & Writing
- Meditation / journaling.
- Reflect on *Ancestral* patterns of **strength, courage** and **purpose**.
- Practice automatic writing / receive intuitive messages and guidance on themes of *ambition, creativity* and *stability*.

Step 6: Ancestral Offering
- Offer flowers or flower *essences* aligned with the ***Emberheart Pathfinder:***
  - **Hibiscus** (*Fire*) – creative boldness
  - **St. John's Wort** (*Fire*) – courage and clarity
  - **Comfrey** (*Earth*) – practical resilience
  - **Lady's Mantle** – inner strength
  - **Red Clover** – grounding balance
  - **Jasmine** – visionary spark
- Light a **red** or **gold** candle in honor of the *courage*, *creativity*, and *grounded* vision passed to you through your *lineage*.

Step 7: Closing
- Offer **gratitude** for the *insights* and support received.
- Acknowledge any insights or *energy* shifts.
- Let the **ritual** integrate fueling your path forward with *clarity* and grounded **Fire**.

Closing Reflection

The *Emberheart Pathfinder* **ritual** links you to the *powerful* energies of **ambition**, **creativity**, and **leadership** that run in your *lineage*. Despite the *mystery* surrounding your *ancestors*' exact paths, their *bravery*, *strength*, and *courage* are part of your *heritage*. Embracing these qualities helps you *unlock* your capacity to lead with **clarity**, establish meaningful **goals**, and respond with **resilience**. This newfound strength enables you to carve a way *forward* that respects the **past** and shapes the **future**.

△△▽

* Fire Safety: *When working with candles and incense, practice caution.*

the PSYCHIC WEAVER

Elemental Trio: **Water, Water, Water**
Keywords:
Compassionate. Adaptive. Psychic Ability. Rebirth. Creativity.

THE *PSYCHIC WEAVER* EMBODIES EMOTIONAL DEPTH, FLUID *transformation*, and *intuitive* **creation**. Guided by the boundless element of **Water**, this *archetype* channels feeling into *wisdom* and shapes **unseen** *energies* into **healing, vision,** and **artistry**. Moving seamlessly between the **visible** and **invisible**, the *Psychic Weaver* **weaves** together emotion, *Ancestral* memory, and *intuitive* insight into *transformational* experiences. **Rooted** in the vastness of *Ocean Essence*, they serve as a living **bridge** between worlds, offering **renewal, inspiration**, and deep **presence** to all they *inspire*. Their *presence* invites us to release emotional blockages, awaken our **creative** *current*, and **embrace** the *cyclical* power of **rebirth** and *magical* shifts.

ANCESTRAL ESSENCE

The *Psychic Weaver* embodies the legacy of ancient **healers, dreamers**, and intuitive **creators** who were in harmony with the emotional and *mystical* **realms**. They trusted the *wisdom* of **dreams**, expressed stories through **art**, and provided **healing** through *compassion*. Understanding the **unseen** language and the transformational *potential* of emotions, they navigated life's emotional currents. By embracing this *archetype*, one acknowledges the **gift** of emotional navigation passed down by *ancestors*. The *Psychic Weaver* upholds this tradition by blending **intuition, creativity,** and emotional **authenticity** in modern practices of **renewal** and *healing*.

The Psychic Weaver - Ancestral Elemental Archetype

THE SHADOW THREAD

EMBRACING GREAT *SENSITIVITY* AND DEPTH BRINGS profound challenges. Acknowledging these shadow aspects aids in **integration** and clarity. Some *challenges* include:

- **Emotional Overwhelm:** Increased *psychic* awareness can cause *energetic* exhaustion or blurred boundaries.

- **Creative Blockages:** Inner turmoil or *emotional* stagnation can impede **creative** flow, leading to frustration or *self-doubt.*
- **Fear of Change:** The transformative *cycles* of **Water** may trigger *resistance*, hindering the ability to embrace **renewal** and **rebirth** fully.

Awareness of these tendencies helps the *Psychic Weaver* to balance **sensitivity** while maintaining a clear energetic flow. A helpful practice involves taking deep breaths, envisioning the vast **Ocean** within, releasing stagnant energy on exhale, and allowing the tides of renewal to flow.

- **Affirmations** such as *"I honor the flow of change and trust my creative power"* strengthen the *connection* between **intuition**, **creativity**, and emotional wisdom.

JUST LIKE THE **OCEAN** TRANSFORMS AND RENEWS ITSELF, THE *Psychic Weaver* refines the element of **Water** into a dynamic *alchemy* that *cultivates* healing, unleashes **creativity**, and channels profound insights into *mystical* **expression**. Their *essence* guides us to navigate the currents, to **craft** with emotion, and to have trust in the *sacred* process of *transformation*.

ELEMENTAL ALCHEMY

- **Water + Water** = *Ocean Essence* – vast psychic awareness, emotional transformation, and fluid adaptability.

This **ritual** awakens your *lineage's* **emotional** depth, **psychic** wisdom, and *creative* flow. It harmonizes *compassion*, **rebirth**, and *intuitive* perception–activating the transformational essence of the *Psychic Weaver*.

Ingredients

- **2 x Ocean Essence** – Enhances psychic perception, emotional clarity, and adaptability.
- **1 x Creativity** – Visualize a flowing river of inspiration fueling your artistic expression.
- **1 x Rebirth** – Envision a wave clearing stagnant emotions and awakening renewed self-awareness.
- **1 x Compassion** - visualize waves from your heart forming bonds of trust and healing all around you.
- **1 x Vision** - Imagine emotional currents guiding you with clarity and grace.

The Psychic Weaver's Elixir

Psychic Weaver
Alchemical Elixir Recipe & Ritual

Instructions

Step 1: Prepare the Space
- Gather items of **Water**: a bowl of **Water**, *seashells, aquamarine / moonstone.*
- Use scents such as **Thyme** (*Psychic vision*), **Rose** (*dreamwork*) and, **Sandalwood** (*emotional healing & grounding*)
- *Create a calm, rooted environment to anchor your energy.*

Step 2: Set Intention
- Begin with **Padma Mudra** (*Lotus gesture*) – heart-centered, symbolizing rebirth and emotional wisdom
- Transition to **Shakti Mudra** (*Gesture of flow*) – encourages creative release, adaptability and ease.
- **Honor your *ancestors***: Speak their names aloud or hold their presence in your *heart*.
- Set your **intention** and invite their energy to support your intuitive and creative flow.

Recite:
"*I honor the psychic wisdom and creative flow of my ancestors. Through the Waters of rebirth, I release, create, and embrace the unseen guidance that flows through me.*"

Step 3: Embodiment Practice
1. Warm Up
- Gently awaken the body before beginning. Let your own rhythm guide the practice

2. Elemental Breath & Movement:
- Let your breath flow with intention & intuitive rhythm. (choose a breathwork practice from the *Ocean Essence* section).
- Move with *presence, rooting* into the **Earth's** stability.

3. Chakra Focus:
- Activate **Sacral** (*Svadhisthana*), **Heart** (*Anahata*), and **Third Eye** (*Ajna*) for creativity, compassion, and intuitive clarity.

→ REFER TO **PG 206** FOR ADDITIONAL PRACTICES, POSES, *breathwork, and correspondences related to Ocean Essence.*

4. **Suggested Embodiment Shapes / Poses:**
- **Goddess Pose** (*Utkata Konasana*) – ignites emotional strength and creative flow
- **Fish Pose** (*Matsyasana*) – activates psychic vision
- **Child's Pose** (*Balasana*) – connects you to inner waters and ancestral guidance

5. **Dance & Intuitive Movement:**
- Move fluidly, exploring Water's waves and transformational depth.
- Alternate between flowing gestures with bold, expressive waves.
- Sence ancestral mysticism moving through you as you dance emotion into form.

Step 4: Astrology & Body Awareness
- Use your *MoonTree Chart* to identify *Ancestral* body correspondences.
- Pair movements, breathwork, or visualization with these areas for deeper connection.
  Lunar Phase:
- Align ritual with the lunar phase that aligns with your **ritual** intention, *and the phase that helps you connect with your own* **psychic** *energies and Ancestral* work. Follow your **intuition**.

Step 5: Reflection & Writing
- Meditation / journaling.
- Reflect on *Ancestral* patterns of **psychic gifts/energies** and **emotional sytength.**.
- Practice automatic writing / receive *intuitive* messages and guidance from your *ancestors*.

Step 6: Ancestral Offering
- Offer flowers or flower *essences* aligned with the **Psychic Weaver:**
  - **Poppy** (*Water*) – dreamwork and clarity
  - **Rose** (*Water*) – emotional healing and creative passion
  - **Violet** (*Water*) – intuitive adaptability
  - **Gardenia** – compassion and emotional depth
  - **Heather** – psychic connection
  - **Lemon Balm** – renewal and rebirth
- Light a candle in gratitude for inherited wisdom and emotional insight.

Step 7: Closing
- Offer **gratitude** for the *insights* and support received, Acknowledge any *energy* shifts.
- Let the **ritual** integrate into your daily life, stengthening your intuition and building your **psychic** *essence*.

Closing Reflection

The *Psychic Weaver* **ritual** connects you to the fluid **wisdom**, **rebirth**, and creative **expression** carried through your *lineage*. While the specifics of your *ancestors*' journeys may be unknown, their **compassion**, **artistry**, and **psychic** vision flow through you.
By *aligning* with these *elements*, you awaken your capacity to **heal**, **create**, and see **beyond the veil**–becoming a vessel for transformation, *Ancestral* wisdom, and boundless *magical* energy.

▽▽▽

Fire Safety: *When working with candles and incense, practice caution.*

the
EARTHSPRING
STEWARD

Elemental Trio: **Earth, Earth, Water (in any order)**
Keywords:
Resilient. Nurturing. Adaptable. Insightful. Renewal.

THE *EARTHSPRING STEWARD* SERVES AS A PROTECTOR OF growth, healing, and restoration, embodying a harmonious mix of **Earth's** stability and **Water's** adaptability. In tune with nature's rhythms and life cycles, this archetype combines resilience with emotional understanding to create sacred spaces where renewal, wisdom, and well-being thrive. Acting as both a caregiver and a visionary, the Earthspring Steward provides grounded guidance during times of change. Rooted in endurance yet open to evolution, they blend tradition with intuition and structure with fluidity. Whether caring for the land, relationships, or community, they emphasize that true restoration demands patience, presence, and a readiness to navigate life's currents.

ANCESTRAL ESSENCE

The *Earthspring Steward* honors the lineage of caretakers, healers, and wisdom keepers - those who listened deeply to the land, attuned to the emotional and spiritual needs of their communities. These ancestors worked in harmony with both the tangible and unseen, recognizing that healing flows through balance, patience, and intentional presence. To embody this archetype is to carry forward their sacred knowing, transforming ancestral insight into grounded, compassionate action. The *Earthspring Steward* becomes a vessel of clarity, tending to the spaces where harmony and wholeness can **root** and **bloom**.

The Earthspring Steward - Ancestral Elemental Archetype

SHADOW THREAD

WITH DEEP CARE AND INTUITIVE STRENGTH COMES potential challenges. Recognizing these patterns supports growth and energetic balance:

- **Resistance to Change:** A strong bond with tradition may hinder the ability to adapt or welcome transformation.

- **Emotional Overload:** Their compassionate nature may lead to overextension, resulting in depletion or imbalance.
- **Over-nurturing:** Excessive care can blur boundaries, fostering dependency or a lack of self-prioritization.

Awareness of these tendencies helps the Earthspring Steward cultivate clarity within their nurturing, ensuring their care remains empowering and sustainable. A supportive practice to do is to inhale deeply, anchoring into the **Earth's** steady embrace; exhale, allowing the **Waters** of renewal to flow through you with ease and grace.

- Affirmations like *"I nurture with clarity and trust the cycles of renewal"* restore alignment between care, boundaries, and the mysticism and magic of natural rhythms.

JUST LIKE HOW *MUD* IS FORMED FROM **EARTH** AND **WATER**, the *Earthspring Steward* distills their *essence* into an *alchemical* practice that supports healing, growth, and harmony. **Rooted** in tradition and flowing with transformation, they hold space for what is ready to grow, and what is ready to be restored.

ELEMENTAL ALCHEMY

- **Earth + Earth** = *Mountain Essence* – resilience, longevity, and unwavering wisdom.
- **Earth + Water** = *Mud Essence* – emotional stability, flexibility, and nurturing renewal.

This **ritual** connects you with **Earth's** *grounding* strength and **Water's** *emotional* adaptability. It awakens **resilience**, **clarity**, **nurturing** care, and **renewal** through *movement*, *reflection*, and *Ancestral* connection.

Ingredients

- **1 x Mountain Essence** – Embodies enduring wisdom and strength.
- **1 x Mud Essence** – Supports emotional grounding and flexible flow.
- **1 x Insight** – Visualize yourself as a still body of Water, where clarity naturally arises.
- **1 x Renewal** – Picture a gentle rain restoring the Earth, replenishing your spirit.
- **1 x Nurturing Energy** - Envision being both giver and receiver of love and care, radiating balanced support.

The Earthspring Steward's Elixir

Earthspring Steward
Alchemical Elixir Recipe & Ritual

Instructions

Step 1: Prepare the Space
- Arrange symbolic items of **Earth** & **Water**: A small bowl of soil, stones / crystals, a bowl of **Water**
- Use scents such as **Frankincense** (grounding & renewal), **Vanilla** (*strength & nostalgic comfort*) and, **Sandalwood** (*emotional healing & grounding*)

Step 2: Set Intention
- Begin with **Dhyana Mudra** (*Hands in lap, Thumbs touching*) - reflection and insight.
- Transition to **Prithvi Mudra** (ring finger to thumb tip) - enhances grounding and resilience.
- **Honor your** *ancestors*: Speak their names aloud or hold their presence in your *heart*.
- Set your **intention** and invite their nurturing wisdom, grounding energies and Ancestral mysticism into the ritual and your practice.

Recite:
" *I honor the nurturing insight and renewal of my ancestors. I embrace the cycles of growth and reflection, grounding myself in their wisdom and clarity.*"

Step 3: Embodiment Practice
1. **Warm Up**
- Gently awaken the body before beginning. Let your own rhythm guide the practice
2. **Elemental Breath & Movement:**
- Slow, steady breathwork to embody grounding and flow. Blend **Earth's** stability with **Water's** fluid adaptability.
- Choose a breathwork practice from the *Mountain & Mud Essence* section).
3. **Chakra Focus:**
- Activate **Root** (*Muladhara*), **Sacral** (*Svadhisthana*) for *stability*, **renewal**, and *emotional* **magic** & mastery

→ REFER TO **PGS 200** & **203** FOR MORE PRACTICES, POSES, *breathwork*, & *correspondences related to Mountain & Mud Essences.*

4. Suggested Embodiment Shapes / Poses:
- **Child's Pose** (*Balasana*) – inner connection and grounded rest
- **Triangle Pose** (*Trikonasana*) – balances strength and flexibility
- **Low Lunge with Twist** (*Parivrtta Anjaneyasana*) – fuses grounding with emotional flow

5. Dance & Intuitive Movement:
- Flow between **grounded**, steady movements and slow, **fluid** gestures.
- Explore slow **meditative** walking, **rooted** postures and arm waves that mirror the rhythm of soil and stream.

Step 4: Astrology & Body Awareness
- Use your *MoonTree Chart* to identify ancestral body correspondences.
- Pair **movements**, **breathwork**, or **visualization** with these areas for deeper *connection*.
  Lunar Phase:
- Align the **ritual** with a significant *Lunar* phase or *Ancestral* date (e.g., birthday or passing) to amplify connection and renewal, or any other *Lunar* phase that feels aligned to you for this **ritual**. Follow your **intuition**.

Step 5: Reflection & Writing
- Meditation / journaling.
- Reflect on *Ancestral* patterns and themes of **resilience** and **compassion**.
- Practice automatic writing / receive intuitive messages and guidance on themes of *nurturing*, *restoration*, and *emotional wisdom*.

Step 6: Ancestral Offering
- Offer flowers or flower *essences* aligned with the **Earthspring Steward:**
  - **Pomegranate flower** (*Earth*) – **grounding** and enduring strength
  - **Sage** (*Earth*) – *Ancestral* **wisdom** and clarity
  - **Feverfew** (*Water*) – emotional **adaptability**
  - **Chamomile** – gentle **insight** and inner calm
  - **Carnation** – renewal and **rebirth**
  - **Sunflower** – radiant strength and **stability**
- Light a **candle** in *Earthy* tones (brown, green, or deep blue) connecting to the **restorative** energy of your *lineage*.

Step 7: Closing
- Offer **gratitude** for the *insights* and support received.
- Acknowledge any insights or *energy* shifts.
- Let the **ritual** integrate as you carry the *Earthspring Steward's* harmony into your relationships, creative work, and care for self and others.

Closing Reflection

The *Earthspring Steward* **ritual** links you to the grounding energy of the **Earth** and the clarifying flow of **Water**, fostering *wisdom*, *rejuvenation*, and *nurturing* care. While the specifics of your *ancestors'* lives may be unknown, their **resilience**, **compassion**, and **clarity** are present in you. The *elemental* **pattern** uncovered in your *MoonTree Chart* displays their *enduring* legacy. By harmonizing with these *elements*, you *unlock* your capacity for emotional **revitalization**, **understanding**, and **sustainable** beliefs & *magic*. This cultivates spaces where **life** *flourishes* and *Ancestral* wisdom **illuminates** your journey.

▽ ▽ ▽

*** Fire Safety:** When working with candles and incense, practice caution.*

the
CREATIVE
ANCHOR

Elemental Trio: **Air, Air, Earth (in any order)**
Keywords:
Innovative. Grounded. Communicative. Creative. Stable.

THE *CREATIVE ANCHOR* FLOURISHES AT THE INTERSECTION of inspiration and action, blending the expansive intellect of **Air** with the steadfast resilience of **Earth**. This *archetype* embodies **communication**, **creativity**, and **grounded** action, turning ideas into tangible realities that endure. Guided by broad thinking and practical wisdom, the *Creative Anchor* connects **imagination** with **manifestation**, ensuring that **creative** *insights* result in meaningful and sustainable endeavors. **Rooted** in *Ancestral* knowledge and the power of clear expression, they maintain a harmonious balance between mental agility, creative exploration, and unwavering perseverance. The *Creative Anchor* serves as a reminder that authentic raw creativity is not just dynamic but also **practical**, **structured**, and **capable** of shaping resilient, *magical* futures.

ANCESTRAL ESSENCE

The *Creative Anchor* embodies the legacy of artisans, storytellers, builders, and inventors. These ancestors combined broad thinking with focused action to make long-lasting contributions. They used their intellect, skills, and voices to create ideas, share truths, and influence realities that persisted through *generations*. Embodying this *archetype* means recognizing and honoring their valuable traits: exceptional intelligence, imaginative creativity, and effective application. The *Creative Anchor* carries on this heritage by translating inspiration into tangible creations, connecting visionary ideas with practical actions, and shaping a future grounded in wisdom, creativity, and community.

The Creative Anchor - Ancestral Elemental Archetype

SHADOW THREAD

THE INTERSECTION OF AIR'S EXPANSIVENESS AND EARTH'S grounding can pose specific challenges. Being aware of these patterns helps in achieving focused and integrated expression. Some challenges include:

- **Scattered Focus:** where an abundance of ideas makes it hard to prioritize;

- **Impractical Ideation:** where visionary concepts remain unexecuted without grounding.
- **Over-analysis:** where exploring too many possibilities hinders taking action and realizing creative potential.

Recognizing these tendencies allows the *Creative Anchor* to bring clarity and structure to their vision and creativity. A grounding practice you can do involves deeply inhaling while visualizing clear ideas, and exhaling slowly to anchor those ideas into practical steps forward.

- Affirmations like "*I transform vision into reality with clarity and purpose*" help maintain the balance between imagination and execution.

JUST LIKE THE *WIND* STIRS UP *DUST*, THE *CREATIVE ANCHOR* combines **Air** and **Earth** to create an *alchemical* **synergy**. This is where inspiration meets a solid foundation, and dreams begin to take form. Its *essence* pays tribute to the **past**, anchors the **present**, and constructs a **future** infused with **purpose, creativity, love,** and lasting **wisdom**.

ELEMENTAL ALCHEMY

- **Air + Air** = *Wind Essence* – adaptability, intellectual clarity, and expansive thought.
- **Air + Earth** = *Dust Essence* – practical innovation, grounding imagination in reality.

This **ritual** harmonizes creative **thought**, expressive **communication**, and practical **stability**. It balances **inspiration** with grounded **action**, awakening the *synergy* of *imagination* and *structure* for impactful, *Ancestral-aligned* creation.

Ingredients

- **1 x Wind Essence** – Sparks intellectual clarity, innovation, and adaptability
- **1 x Dust Essence** – Grounds creative energy and strengthens practical resilience.
- **1 x Creativity** – Visualize a gentle breeze clearing pathways for new ideas.
- **1 x Communication** – Imagine magical winds carrying your words with magnetic ease & meaning.
- **1 x Stability** - Picture Earth anchoring your expansive thoughts into tangible form

THE CREATIVE ANCHOR'S ELIXIR

Creative Anchor

Alchemical Elixir Recipe & Ritual

Instructions

Step 1: Prepare the Space
- Arrange symbolic items of **Air** & **Earth**: A *feathers, flowing fabrics, incense, crystals, soil, stones.*
- Use scents that blend *grounding* with mental focus such as **Ginger**, **Sandalwoods** and, **Vanilla.**

Step 2: Set Intention
- Begin with **Jnana Mudra** (index finger + thumb, palms up on knees) – invites clarity and *insight*
- Transition to **Prithvi Mudra** (ring finger to thumb tip) – *roots* your vision in stability.
- **Honor your *ancestors***: Speak their names aloud or hold their presence in your *heart*.
- Set your **intention** and invite their *wisdom Ancestral* **mysticism** into the **ritual** and your practice.

Recite:
"*I honor the wisdom of my ancestors and the balance of creativity, communication, and stability within me. I ground my visions with practical actions to manifest meaningful change.*"

Step 3: Embodiment Practice
   1. Warm Up
- Begin with breath and gentle movement to open both body and mind.
   2. Elemental Breath & Movement:
- Combine focused breathwork with movements that *merge* **Air's** *expansiveness* and **Earth's** *grounded* rhythm.
- For additional *movement* and *breathwork* practices, refer to the **Wind & Dust Essence** section).
3. Chakra Focus:
- Activate **Third Eye** (*Ajna*), **Heart** (*Anahata*), and **Root** (*Muladhara*) for *vision*, *insight*, *expressive connection*, structure, steadiness.

→ REFER TO **PGS 200** & **218** FOR ADDITIONAL PRACTICES, *poses, breathwork, and correspondences related to Wind & Dust Essences.*

4. **Suggested Embodiment Shapes / Poses:**
- **Eagle Pose** (*Garudasana*) – *enhances* focus and **creative** vision
- **Warrior II** (*Virabhadrasana II*) – builds **rooted** strength and balance
- **Seated Twist** (*Ardha Matsyendrasana*) – opens *heart* and supports *self-expression*
- **Tree Pose** (*Vrksasana*) – blends **Earth's** steadiness with **Air's** adaptability

5. **Dance & Intuitive Movement:**
- Alternate between Airy, *flowing* gestures and *strong*, **rooted** steps.
- Move with the intention **weaving** *creativity* and structure together through the body.

Step 4: Astrology & Body Awareness
- Use your *MoonTree Chart* to identify ancestral body correspondences.
- Enhance connection through focused **breath**, **movement**, or **visual** attention to these areas.

  Lunar Phase:
- Align the **ritual** with a significant *Lunar* phase or *Ancestral* date (e.g., birthday or passing) to amplify connection and renewal, or any other *Lunar* phase that feels aligned to you for this **ritual**. Follow your ***intuition***.

Step 5: Reflection & Writing
- Meditation / journaling.
- Reflect on *Ancestral* patterns and themes of **expression** and **communication**.
- Practice automatic writing / receive intuitive messages and guidance on themes of *communication*, **manifestation**, and *grounding*.

Step 6: Ancestral Offering
- Offer flowers or flower *essences* aligned with the ***Creative Anchor:***
  - **Lavender** (*Air*) – for **calm** & clarity
  - **Marjoram Flowers** (*Air*) – **communication** and focus
  - **Sage** (*Earth*) – **grounding** Ancestral wisdom
  - **Vervain** – **innovation** and adaptability
  - **Valerian** – for stable **creativity**
  - **Dandelion** – expressive **clarity**
- Light a blue or golden **candle** inviting *Ancestral* support into your **ritual** and practice..

Step 7: Closing
- Offer **gratitude** for the *insights* and support received.
- Acknowledge any insights or *energy* shifts.
- Let the **ritual** integrate as you carry the *Creative Anchor's* clear *thought*, grounded *action*, and inspired *creation*.

Closing Reflection

The *Creative Anchor* **ritual** serves as a bridge to the harmony of **communication**, **creativity**, and **stability** inherited from your *lineage*. Even if the specifics of your *ancestors'* experiences remain a **mystery**, their **inventive** *essence* and **grounded** insight continue to shape your being. By **cultivating** these attributes, you *unlock* your **potential** to bring ideas to **life**, express yourself effectively, and make a lasting impact.

---

* FIRE SAFETY: *WHEN WORKING WITH CANDLES AND incense, practice caution.*

the LUMINOUS TRAILBLAZER

Elemental Trio: **Fire, Fire, Fire**
Keywords:
**Passionate. Visionary. Transformative. Trailblazing.
Inspirational.**

THE *LUMINOUS TRAILBLAZER* EMBODIES THE UNSTOPPABLE force of Fire, symbolizing courageous leadership, visionary momentum, and transformative energy. This archetype sparks bold beginnings and fosters creative innovation, inspiring others to follow. Guided by the dynamic Blaze Essence, the Luminous Trailblazer encourages us to act with passion, lead with purpose, and turn challenges into break-throughs. Embracing this archetype means awakening the purposeful flame within and honoring the courageous lineage that has inspired us with fearless determination.

ANCESTRAL ESSENCE

The *Luminous Trailblazer* follows the path of pioneers, visionaries, and courageous bringers of change - ancestors who defied norms, ignited movements, and paved the way for future generations. Their drive, perseverance, and strength serve as a reminder that change starts with a small spark - a spark that lives within us. Embodying this archetype means continuing the fearless legacy of these trailblazers. The Luminous Trailblazer transforms passion into a mission and motivation into empowerment, leading others to enlightenment and determination.

The Luminous Trailblazer - Ancestral Elemental Archetype

SHADOW THREAD

THE POWERFUL ENERGY OF **FIRE** CAN SOMETIMES LEAD TO imbalances. By recognizing these shadow **patterns**, we can align this *archetype* with *grounded* clarity:

- **Impulsiveness:** Making quick decisions without reflection can cause setbacks or unintended consequences.

- **Burnout:** Working intensely without taking breaks can lead to exhaustion or a decrease in creative energy.
- **Intensity Overload:** Uncontrolled energy may cause emotional volatility or overwhelm others with forceful expression.

Being aware of these tendencies helps the *Luminous Trailblazer* to focus and maintain a sustainable **flame**. To center yourself, try this practice: Inhale deeply, feeling the steady warmth of your inner **Fire**, then exhale slowly, directing its light with intention and purpose.

- Affirmations like *"I ignite change with wisdom and sustain my Fire with care"* reinforce the **balance** between **bold** action and **mindful** presence.

JUST LIKE ***BLAZE ESSENCE*** TRANSFORMS RAW FIRE INTO A radiant purpose, the *Luminous Trailblazer* distills passion into legacy. Their *essence* turns into an *alchemical* force - **fearless**, **authentic**, and **enduring** - guiding the path for future *generations* while honoring the *sacred* **flame** of their *Ancestral* **Fire**.

ELEMENTAL ALCHEMY

- **Fire + Fire** = *Blaze Essence* – the embodiment of passion, transformation, and radiant creative power.

This **ritual** channels the vibrant force of **Fire**, awakening **courage**, creative **power**, and purposeful **momentum**. Through **movement**, **breath**, and *Ancestral* **connection**, you ignite *inner* strength and visionary *leadership*.

Ingredients

- **2 x Blaze Essence** – Amplifies passion, transformation, and bold creativity.
- **1 x Trailblazing Energy** – Visualize your path lighting up with each courageous step forward.
- **1 x Inspiration** – Feel your Fire sparking motivation and awakening others to their purpose.
- **1 x Courage** – Sense your Solar Plexus radiating strength and fearless energy.
- **1 x Resilience** – Picture Fire's warmth renewing your spirit through challenge and growth.

Luminous Trailblazer
Alchemical Elixir Recipe & Ritual

Instructions

Step 1: Prepare the Space
- Arrange symbolic items of **Fire**: *candles, carnelian, garnet* and any other crystals corresponding to the **Fire** *element*.
- Use scents that inspire *energy* and *focus* such as **Bay Leaves**, **Cinnamon** and, **Ginger**.
- Add fiery colors: **red**, **orange**, **gold** – to *evoke* **heat**, **vitality**, and *creative* **drive**

Step 2: Set Intention
- Begin with **Surya Mudra** *(ring finger to thumb, palms up)* – activates **vitality** and **radiance.**
- Transition to **Agni Mudra** *(fists with thumbs extended)* – *empowers* **courage** and inner **strength**.
- **Honor your** *ancestors*: Speak their names aloud or hold their presence in your *heart*.
- Set your **intention** and invite their **trailblazing** ideas, authentic essence and *Ancestral* **mysticism** into the ritual and your practice.

Recite:
"I honor the courageous spirit of my ancestors. I embrace bold action, creative vision, and transformational power."

Step 3: Embodiment Practice
1. **Warm Up**
- Begin with *energizing* stretches and breath to awaken the **Fire** within.

2. **Elemental Breath & Movement:**
- Combine deep breaths with **dynamic** *movement* to engage and *activate* the Fire element within.
- Choose a practice from the ***Blaze Essence*** section to **amplify** intention.

3. **Chakra Focus:**
- Activate **Solar Plexus** (*Manipura*) for confidence, leadership and the **Sacral** (*Svadhisthana*) creative **passion** and **emotional** flow.

The Luminous Trailblazer's Elixir

→ REFER TO **PG 209** FOR ADDITIONAL PRACTICES, POSES, *breathwork, and correspondences related to Blaze Essence.*

4. Suggested Embodiment Shapes / Poses:
- **Warrior II** (*Virabhadrasana II*) – embodies **boldness** and direction
- **Bow Pose** (*Dhanurasana*) – **energizes** creative drive
- **Cobra Pose** (*Bhujangasana*) – awakens resilience and **life** force
- **Chair Pose** (*Utkatasana*) – builds strength and **courage**

5. Dance & Intuitive Movement:
- Move fiercely and fluidly with quick gestures of action followed by fluid-like expansive movements.
- Visualize flames of transformation surrounding and empowering your every move.

Step 4: Astrology & Body Awareness
- Use your *MoonTree Chart* to identify *Ancestral* body correspondences.
- Enhance **connection** through focused **breath**, **movement**, or **visual** attention to these areas.
  Lunar Phase:
- Align the **ritual** with a significant *Lunar* phase or *Ancestral* date (e.g., birthday or passing) to amplify *confidence* and *courage*, or any other *Lunar* phase that feels aligned to you for this **ritual**. Follow your **intuition**.

Step 5: Reflection & Writing
- Meditation / journaling.
- Reflect on *Ancestral* patterns and themes of **leadership** and **courage**.
- Practice automatic writing / receive intuitive messages and guidance on themes around *ambition, renewal,* and *your inner* **Fire**.

Step 6: Ancestral Offering
- Offer flowers or flower *essences* aligned with the **Luminous Trailblazer:**
  - **Peony** (*Fire*) – for **passion** and vibrant energy
  - **St. John's Wort** (*Fire*) – for clarity and **courage**
  - **Amaranth** (*Fire*) – for endurance and **strength**
  - **Hibiscus** – bold **creativity** and expression
  - **Marigold** – personal **transformation**
  - **Rose** – for visionary **love** and leadership
- Light a red **candle** connecting to the **authentic** and **trailblazing** essence of your *lineage*.

Step 7: Closing
- Offer **gratitude** for the *insights* and support received.
- Acknowledge any insights or *energy* shifts.
- Let the **ritual** integrate as you let the *Luminous Trailblazer's* creative **flame** move you forward on your path, burning **brightly** with *Ancestral* purpose.

Closing Reflection

The *Luminous Trailblazer* **ritual** links you to the pioneering **spirit** of your *ancestors*. Even if you are unaware of their life stories, their **bravery** and **drive** are clear within you. Your *MoonTree Chart* reveals an *elemental* **pattern** that mirrors their lineage of daring **initiatives**, **innovative** thinking, and **influential** *leadership*. Embracing these *elements* **empowers** you to *unlock* your complete capabilities – to **lead**, **motivate**, and forge new paths of **transformation**.

△△△

* Fire Safety: *When working with candles and incense, practice caution.*

the INTUITIVE VOYAGER

Elemental Trio: **Air, Air, Water (in any order)**
Keywords:
**Insightful. Expressive. Trailblazing. Traveling (also Astral).
Intuitive.**

THE *INTUITIVE VOYAGER* SEEKS HORIZONS, BOTH PHYSICAL
and spiritual. Blending **Air's** expansiveness with **Water's** depth, they
explore thoughts, emotions, cultures, and unseen realms. A messenger
and guide, they reveal hidden truths, bridging distances between inner,
outer, and ancestral worlds. Adaptable, they navigate life's changes with
grace. Curiosity, insight, and heartfelt communication bring clarity and
inspire transformation, while grounding them in self-awareness.
Whether traveling the globe, exploring astral planes, or guiding others,
the *Intuitive Voyager* embodies wisdom and growth.

ANCESTRAL ESSENCE

The *Intuitive Voyager* follows the footsteps of way-finders, storytellers,
and seekers - those who traversed both physical and **metaphysical**
realms to share messages, knowledge, and wisdom. Their ancestors
served as cultural bridges and spiritual interpreters, weaving significance
into their movements and translating experiences into teachings.
Embodying this archetype involves honoring their legacy by nurturing
curiosity, fostering openness, and conveying truth with clarity and
compassion. The *Intuitive Voyager* carries on their journey marked by
insight, growth, and deep soul connections.

The Intuitive Voyager - Ancestral Elemental Archetype

SHADOW THREAD

THIS ARCHETYPE'S FREEDOM AND EXPANSIVENESS CAN ALSO be challenging. Acknowledging these shadow aspects fosters integration and groundedness:

- **Restlessness**: A constant need for motion can lead to instability and difficulty finding peace.

- **Overthinking:** Excessive analysis may stifle intuition, causing hesitation and disconnection.
- **Emotional Distance:** Over-reliance on intellect can diminish emotional depth and connection.

By recognizing these tendencies, the *Intuitive Voyager* can balance movement and stillness, clarity and feeling, exploration and grounding. A helpful practice is deep breathing: inhale, letting inspiration fill you with ideas, and exhale slowly, allowing emotions to soften and settle.

- Affirmations like "*I explore with presence and connect with depth*" can help harmonize curiosity with connection.

<hr />

JUST LIKE *MIST* RISING AND DANCING WITH THE WIND, THE *Intuitive Voyager* merges **Air** and **Water**, creating an *alchemical* rhythm of **movement**, **expression**, and **depth**. This *essence* inspires heartfelt **communication**, *magical* **exploration**, and **reverence** for *Ancestral* paths along the continuous journey of discovery.

ELEMENTAL ALCHEMY

- **Air + Water** = *Mist Essence* – harmonizes emotional flow with intellectual clarity, fostering adaptability and intuitive understanding.
- **Air + Air** = *Wind Essence* – expands intellectual precision, mobility, and communicative power, creating space for inspired movement and exploration.

This **ritual** unites mental **clarity**, **emotional** flow, and fluid **movement**. It enhances **communication**, supports **adaptability**, and invites **journeys**—whether across landscapes, through memory, or into the **unseen** realms.

Ingredients

- **1 x Mist Essence** - Harmonizes emotional depth and mental clarity.
- **1 x Wind Essence** - Amplifies mental agility, movement, and expressive power.
- **1 x Travel Energy** - Visualize winds lifting you into new experiences—physically or astrally.
- **1 x Clarity** - Envision a wide-open sky readily offering deep insights.

The Intuitive Voyager's Elixir

Intuitive Voyager

Alchemical Elixir Recipe & Ritual

Instructions

Step 1: Prepare the Space

- Arrange symbolic items of **Air & Water**: Feathers, wind chimes, a bowl of water.
- Add a Map, compass, or any other travel token meaningful to you to anchor the energy of exploration.
- Imbue the space with uplifting scents such as **Sandalwood** (*mental clarity*) and **Frankincense** (*energizing/focus*).

Step 2: Set Intention

- Begin with **Anjali Mudra** (*palms at heart*) – honors **connection** and **insight**.
- Transition to **Gyan Mudra** (*thumb + index finger, palms up*) - *opens* the mind and brings **clarity**.
- **Honor your** *ancestors*: Embrace their adaptable **wisdom** and **fluidity** on your journey.

Recite:

"I honor the wisdom and adaptability of my ancestors. With clarity and openness, I embrace the journeys that call to me and express my truth with confidence"

Step 3: Embodiment Practice

1. **Warm Up**
- Begin with gentle movement to awaken breath and energy flow.

2. **Elemental Breath & Movement:**
- Breathe with intention—fluid, expansive, and focused.
- Choose breath practices from the *Elemental Essences* section that align with **Mist & Wind Essences**.

3. **Chakra Focus:**
- Activate **Throat Chakra** (*Vishuddha*) for expression, communication, the **Sacral Chakra** (*Svadhisthana*) for *movement*, *creativity* and *adaptability*, and the **Heart Chakra** (*Anahata*) for *emotional connection*.

→ REFER TO **PGS 200** & **215** FOR PRACTICES, POSES, *breathwork, and correspondences related to Mist & Wind Essences.*

4. Suggested Embodiment Shapes / Poses:
- **Twisted Low Lunge**(Parivrtta Anjaneyasana) – encourages **release** and flexibility
- **Dancer's Pose** (Natarajasana) – expresses transformation and **creative** grace
- **Side Plank** (Vasisthasana) – builds strength and balance in **shifting** currents

5. Dance & Intuitive Movement:
- *Intuitively* shift your movements; blend *flowing* **Water** motions, *powerful* **Fire** bursts, and *expansive*, **Airy** sweeps.
- In your movement, be adaptable–*supple*, *daring*, *liquid*, and *ferocious*, **shapeshift**.

Step 4: Astrology & Body Awareness
- Use your *MoonTree Chart* to identify *Ancestral astrological* body correspondences.
- Use **breath**, **visualization** and focused **movement** to enhance the energetic link.
  Lunar Phase:
- Align the **ritual** with a significant *Lunar* phase or *Ancestral* date (e.g., birthday or passing) to amplify *confidence* and *courage*, or any other *Lunar* phase that feels aligned to you for this **ritual**. Follow your *intuition*.

Step 5: Reflection & Writing
- Meditation / journaling.
- Reflect on *Ancestral* patterns and themes of resilience and **adaptability**.
- Practice automatic writing / receive intuitive messages and guidance on themes around *transformation and* **creativity**.

Step 6: Ancestral Offering
- Offer flowers or flower *essences* aligned with the ***Ethereal Shapeshifter:***
  - **Poppy** (*Water*) – for **visionary** flow
  - **Peony** (*Fire*) – for passionate **resilience**
  - **Dandelion** (*Air*) – for **adaptability** and renewal
  - **Lilac** – for clarity and perspective-**shifting**
  - **Violet** – for intuition and deep emotional **passion**
  - **Carnation** – for inventive **transformation**
- Light a **candle** and say aloud:
  "Thank you for your strength, your adaptability, and your creative fire. I carry your legacy forward with courage and vision."

Step 7: Closing
- Offer **gratitude** for the *insights* and support received.
- Reflect on the *sensations*, *shifts* that arose.
- Let the **ritual** integrate carry the **Fire** of *transformation* and the flow of *resilience* into your daily *movement*, *creation*, and choices.

Closing Reflection

Connect with your *ancestors*' transformative power through the *Ethereal Shapeshifter* **ritual**. Their **courage**, **adaptability**, and **creativity** live on in you, even without knowing their stories. Your *MoonTree Chart's elemental* **pattern** reflects this *Ancestral* **energy**. Embrace these elements to honor their legacy and unleash your potential for **growth**, **creativity**, and **change**.

▽△△

* FIRE SAFETY: WHEN WORKING WITH CANDLES AND incense, practice caution.

the ETHEREAL SHAPESHIFTER

Elemental Trio: **Water, Fire, Air (in any order)**
Keywords:
Transformation. Creativity. Resilience. Intuition. Fluidity.

The Ethereal Shapeshifter - Ancestral Elemental Archetype

THE *ETHEREAL SHAPESHIFTER* EFFORTLESSLY GLIDES between worlds, flowing seamlessly through the realms of form and formlessness, existence and potentiality. Combining Water's fluidity, Fire's passion, and Air's expansiveness, this archetype embodies constant change, creative alchemy, and graceful adaptation. Change isn't feared, but embraced, shaped into possibilities through instinct and imagination. Unbound by norms, the *Ethereal Shapeshifter* thrives in evolution's ever-shifting currents. Their presence reveals new paths, illuminates untapped potential, and celebrates impermanence and metamorphosis.

ANCESTRAL ESSENCE

Mystics, artisans, innovators, and **pioneers**: the *Ethereal Shapeshifter* embodies their fearless legacy of embracing the unknown and courageously reinventing life. These forbears wove new traditions, reshaped beliefs, guided others through change, and saw transformation as *sacred*. To embody this archetype is to honor their gift, navigating life's ever-shifting landscape with trust, creativity, and deep resilience. The *Ethereal Shapeshifter* teaches us to see change not as loss, but as emergence.

SHADOW THREAD

The gift of fluid transformation also brings its challenges. Being aware of these patterns helps with integration and grounding.

- **Scattered Focus:** The vastness of Air and the flow of Water might make it hard to stay focused in one direction.
- **Emotional Intensity:** The combination of Water's emotional depth with Fire's passion can lead to overwhelm or inner turmoil.
- **Resistance to Stability:** A preference for movement could cause avoiding structure, grounding, or long-term commitments.

Acknowledging these tendencies enables the *Ethereal Shapeshifter* to use their gifts purposefully, balancing freedom with focus and transformation with a powerful presence. A helpful practice: take a deep inhale, feeling the changing energies within; exhale slowly, connecting with the wisdom of the present moment.

- Affirmations like *"I embrace change while staying centered"* help align adaptability with inner strength.

JUST AS THE *ETHEREAL SHAPESHIFTER* BLENDS **WATER**, **FIRE**, and **Air** to mold the unseen into form, their *essence* transforms into an *alchemical* practice. This practice embraces impermanence, awakens creative power, and carries the *mystical* wisdom of their *lineage* forward through the ever-spiraling dance of becoming.

ELEMENTAL ALCHEMY

- **Water + Fire** = *Steam Essence* – emotional depth merges with transformative power, igniting resilience and renewal.
- **Fire + Air** = *Aetherflame Essence* – inventive creativity propelled by passion and mental clarity.
- **Water + Air** = *Mist Essence* – intuitive flow harmonized with emotional insight, offering adaptability and gentle wisdom.

This **ritual** awakens your power to **transform**, adapt, and innovate. By embodying the fluidity of **Water**, the ignition of **Fire**, and the expansion of **Air**, you tap into your Ancestral **resilience** and **creative** potential —fusing **courage**, **clarity**, and **flow** into your daily life.

Ingredients

- **1 x Steam Essence** – Ignites resilience and catalyzes transformation.
- **1 x Aetherflame Essence** – Channels inventive thought and visionary creativity.
- **1 x Mist Essence** – Enhances emotional adaptability and intuitive flow.
- **1 x Adaptability** – Visualize flowing Water carrying you gracefully through change.
- **1 x Courage** – Visualize an inner Fire rising from the Solar Plexus to meet transformation with boldness.
- **1 x Ingenuity** – Picture expansive Air sweeping through your mind, sparking new paths and possibilities.

The Ethereal Shapeshifter's Elixir

Ethereal Shapeshifter
Alchemical Elixir Recipe & Ritual

Instructions

Step 1: Prepare the Space
- Place elemental symbols to anchor the ritual. A bowl of **Water**, a lit candle calls in **Fire** and feathers to symbolize **Air**.
- Infuse the space with scents like **Cardamom** (inspiration & inner **Fire**) **Dill** (willpower & boldness) and **Rosemary** (**Air** element and focus)

Step 2: Set Intention
- Begin with **Varuna Mudra** (*little finger + thumb*) – enhances emotional flow and *adaptability*.
- Transition to **Prithvi Mudra** (*ring finger + thumb*) – strengthens *resilience*
- **Honor your *ancestors***: Speak their names aloud or hold their presence in your *heart*.
- Invite their energy into your **ritual** as you anchor your intention.

Recite:
"I honor the courage and adaptability of my ancestors. I welcome their wisdom and strength as I embody my power to transform and create."

Step 3: Embodiment Practice
  1. Warm Up
- Start by gently moving or breathing to awaken your energy and presence.
  2. Elemental Breath & Movement:
- *Weave* breath and movement together to awaken *emotions*, stir *creative* flow & *resilience*.
- Choose a practice from the **Steam, Mist** and **Aetherflame Essence** sections to amplify intention.
3. Chakra Focus:
- Activate **Solar Plexus** (*Manipura*) confidence & courage, **Sacral Chakra** (*Svadhisthana*) for creativity & passion, **Heart Chakra** (*Anahata*) for expansion & connection and **Third Eye Chakra** (*Ajna*) for clarity & intuition

---

→ REFER TO **PGS 215, 221 & 227** FOR ADDITIONAL PRACTICES, poses, & correspondences related to Steam, Aetherflame, & Mist Essences.

4. Suggested Embodiment Shapes / Poses:
- **Twisted Low Lunge** (Parivrtta Anjaneyasana) – encourages **release** and flexibility
- **Dancer's Pose** (Natarajasana) – expresses transformation and **creative** grace
- **Side Plank** (Vasisthasana) – builds strength and balance in **shifting** currents

5. Dance & Intuitive Movement:
- *Intuitively* shift your movements; blend *flowing* **Water** motions, *powerful* **Fire** bursts, and *expansive*, **Airy** sweeps.
- In your movement, be adaptable—*supple, daring, liquid,* and *ferocious,* **shapeshift**.

Step 4: Astrology & Body Awareness
- Use your *MoonTree Chart* to identify *Ancestral astrological* body correspondences.
- Use **breath, visualization** and focused **movement** to enhance the energetic link.
  Lunar Phase:
- Align the **ritual** with a significant *Lunar* phase or *Ancestral* date (e.g., birthday or passing) to amplify *confidence* and *courage,* or any other *Lunar* phase that feels aligned to you for this **ritual**. Follow your ***intuition***.

Step 5: Reflection & Writing
- Meditation / journaling.
- Reflect on *Ancestral* patterns and themes of resilience and **adaptability**.
- Practice automatic writing / receive intuitive messages and guidance on themes around *transformation and **creativity***.

Step 6: Ancestral Offering
- Offer flowers or flower *essences* aligned with the ***Ethereal Shapeshifter:***
  - **Poppy** (*Water*) – for **visionary** flow
  - **Peony** (*Fire*) – for passionate **resilience**
  - **Dandelion** (*Air*) – for **adaptability** and renewal
  - **Lilac** – for clarity and perspective-**shifting**
  - **Violet** – for intuition and deep emotional **passion**
  - **Carnation** – for inventive **transformation**
- Light a **candle** and say aloud:
"Thank you for your strength, your adaptability, and your creative fire. I carry your legacy forward with courage and vision."

Step 7: Closing
- Offer **gratitude** for the *insights* and support received.
- Reflect on the *sensations, shifts* that arose.
- Let the **ritual** integrate carry the **Fire** of *transformation* and the flow of *resilience* into your daily *movement, creation,* and choices.

Closing Reflection

Connect with your *ancestors'* transformative power through the *Ethereal Shapeshifter* **ritual**. Their **courage, adaptability,** and **creativity** live on in you, even without knowing their stories. Your *MoonTree Chart's* elemental **pattern** reflects this *Ancestral* **energy**. Embrace these elements to honor their legacy and unleash your potential for **growth, creativity,** and **change**.

▽△△

* **FIRE SAFETY:** *WHEN WORKING WITH CANDLES AND incense, practice caution.*

the GUARDIAN ALCHEMIST

Elemental Trio: **Earth, Fire, Water (in any order)**
Keywords:
Steady. Compassionate. Radiant. Resilience. Creativity.

The Guardian Alchemist - Ancestral Elemental Archetype

THE *GUARDIAN ALCHEMIST*, A **PROTECTOR** AND **NURTURER**, blends **strength, warmth**, and **adaptability**. This steady force in turbulent times provides both the **Fire** of growth and the soothing **Waters** of renewal. **Mindful** and emotionally *intelligent*, they purposefully *cultivate* change, **care** deeply, and meet challenges with **innovative** quiet **strength**. Their enduring energy is both **steadfast** and **flexible**, gently **nurturing** growth and enabling **healing** with *powerful* calm.

ANCESTRAL ESSENCE

The *Guardian Alchemist* **embodies** the wisdom of **healing, protection**, and **strength**-building *ancestors*, **protectors**, **artisans**, and *wisdom* **keepers** who balanced *softness* and *strength*, they built and repaired, and *cultivated* safety through **presence** and **care**. To *embody* this *archetype* is to walk in their **footsteps**, creating **sanctuaries** where others feel held, **nourished**, and **empowered**. Continuing this legacy, the *Guardian Alchemist* harmonizes **structure** with **flow**, embodying the *sacred* balance of **protection** and *transformation*.

SHADOW THREAD

This *archetype's* **shadow**, while deeply *caring*, presents unique challenges. Understanding these *inclinations* can aid in restoring **balance**.

- **Overextending Energy:** The constant urge to nurture may lead to emotional exhaustion or blurred boundaries.
- **Resistance to change:** Earth's stabilizing energy may hinder needed transformations, reducing adaptability.
- **Emotional Volatility:** The merging of Fire and Water creates a volatile emotional landscape, resulting in inner turmoil or overwhelming feelings.

By recognizing these patterns, the *Guardian Alchemist cultivates* **resilient** flexibility, **strengthens** energetic **boundaries**, and **balances** giving and receiving. Grounding practices, such as *deep*, **Earth**-*connecting* breaths followed by gentle, *releasing* exhales, are *key*.

- Affirmations like *"I nourish myself as I nourish others"* reinforce the *sacred* reciprocity vital to this *archetype's* strength.

As **EARTH**, **FIRE**, AND **WATER** *COMBINE* TO CREATE *FERTILE* ground, so too does the *Guardian Alchemist* transform their *essences* into an *alchemical* **art** of **healing**, **protection**, and lasting **change**. This ensures the **prosperity** and thriving of *individuals* and *communities*, magically *cultivating* **strength**, **radiance**, and **rejuvenation**.

ELEMENTAL ALCHEMY

- **Earth** + **Fire** = *Lava Essence* – he steady force of grounded action, merging resilience with creative passion.
- **Fire** + **Water** = *Steam Essence* – emotional intensity and transformation, igniting renewal and dynamic change.
- **Water** + **Earth** = *Mud Essence* – fertile grounding that nurtures connection, healing, and emotional depth.

This **ritual** activates the radiant **strength**, **nurturing** energy, and emotional **adaptability** inherited from your *lineage*. By merging the **grounding** power of **Earth**, the **transformative** force of **Fire**, and the fluid **renewal** of **Water**, you *cultivate* a **resilient**, **compassionate**, and **centered** *presence*.

Ingredients

- **1 x Lava Essence** – Ignites creative transformation and steady action.
- **1 x Steam Essence** – Channels emotional passion and the energy of renewal.
- **1 x Mud Essence** – Deepens connection and cultivates emotional grounding and adaptability.
- **1 x Stability** – Visualize Earth anchoring you with resilience and grounded presence.
- **1 x Compassion** – Envision warmth flowing gently from your heart, nurturing self and others.
- **1 x Radiance** – Feel the Fire within illuminating clarity and inspired momentum.

The Guardian Alchemist's Elixir

Guardian Alchemist
Alchemical Elixir Recipe & Ritual

Instructions

Step 1: Prepare the Space
- Place elemental symbols to anchor the ritual. A bowl of **Water**, a lit candle calls in **Fire** and stones, crystals or soil to symbolize **Earth**.
- Infuse the space with scents like **Patchouli** (**Earth** element) **Frankincense** (**Fire** element) and **Vanilla** (**Water** element)

Step 2: Set Intention
- Begin with **Hridaya Mudra** – *place hands at heart to invite compassion and connection*
- Transition to **Prithvi Mudra** *(ring finger + thumb)* – grounding energy and inner stability
- **Honor your** *ancestors*: Speak their names aloud or hold their presence in your *heart*.
- Invite their protective, radiant, and nurturing energies into your practice.

Recite:
"I honor the vitality and wisdom of my ancestors. I call upon their strength, passion, and fluid grace to guide me in nurturing growth and cultivating resilience."

Step 3: Embodiment Practice
  1. Warm Up
- Begin with slow movements and breath to center your awareness in the body.

  2. Elemental Breath & Movement:
- *Weave* breath and movement together for grounding, inner **Fire** connection & renewal.
- Choose a practice from the **Lava, Steam** and **Mud Essence** sections to amplify *intention*.

3. Chakra Focus:
- Activate **Solar Plexus** (*Manipura*) strength & action, **Sacral Chakra** (*Svadhisthana*) adaptability, passion & creative flow, **Root Chakra** (*Muladhara*) for grounding & safety.

→ Refer to **pgs 212, 224 & 227** for additional practices, poses, breathwork, & correspondences related to Lava, Steam, & Mud.

4. **Suggested Embodiment Shapes / Poses:**
- **Child's Pose** (*Balasana*) – **grounding** and surrender
- **High Lunge** (*Anjaneyasana*) – builds **Fire**, inspiration & encourages forward **momentum**
- **Seated Forward Fold** (*Paschimottanasana*) – introspection and flow

5. **Dance & Intuitive Movement:**
- Blend *fluid*, *expressive* gestures with a stable, *rooted* posture.
- To **embody** the archetype's steady *warmth* and *nurturing* **adaptability**, alternate between *grounded* stillness and *fluid* expansive movements.

Step 4: Astrology & Body Awareness
- Use your *MoonTree Chart* to identify *Ancestral astrological* body correspondences.
- Use **breath**, **visualization** and focused **movement** to enhance the energetic link.
  Lunar Phase:
- Align the **ritual** with a significant *Lunar* phase or *Ancestral* date (e.g., birthday or passing) to amplify *confidence* and *courage*, or any other *Lunar* phase that feels aligned to you for this **ritual**. Follow your **intuition**.

Step 5: Reflection & Writing
- Meditation / journaling.
- Reflect on *Ancestral* patterns and themes of resilience and **adaptability**.
- Practice automatic writing / receive intuitive messages and guidance on themes around **compassion**, *resilience and nurturing energies.*

Step 6: Ancestral Offering
- Offer flowers or flower *essences* aligned with the ***Guardian Alchemist***:
  - **Comfrey** (*Earth*) – **grounding** and inner resilience
  - **Chrysanthemum** (*Fire*) – longevity, clarity, and **illumination**
  - **Jasmine** (*Water*) – emotional **adaptability** and intuition
  - **St. John's Wort** – energetic **protection** and strength
  - **Rose** – heart-opening compassion and **strength**
  - **Sunflower** – confidence, warmth, and radiant **life force**
- Light a **candle** and say aloud:
"*Thank you for your strength, your care, and your radiant guidance. I honor the protection and renewal you've passed into me.*" and include any personal objects that represent stability, **love** and warmth

Step 7: Closing
- Offer **gratitude** for the *insights* and support received.
- Sit or move in *stillness*, allowing the energies of **Earth**, **Fire**, and **Water** to integrate.
- Let the **ritual** integrate carry the *essence* of the *Guardian Alchemist*, into your daily **life**–as *strength in softness*, and **radiance** in **rootedness**.

Closing Reflection

The *Guardian Alchemist* **ritual** connects you to the **strength**, **brilliance**, and **adaptability** of your *lineage*. Although the specifics of your *ancestors'* lives may be unknown, their **resilience**, **passion**, and **wisdom** are undeniably present within you. This *elemental* **pattern**, representing their energetic heritage, is unveiled by your *MoonTree Chart*. By embracing these *elements*, you *unlock* your **potential** to cultivate **resilience**, **transformation**, and **harmony**.

* ***Fire Safety:*** *When working with candles and incense, practice caution.*

the ELEMENTAL CATALYST

Elemental Trio: **Fire, Earth, Air (in any order)**
Keywords:
Grounded. Expansive. Energetic. Innovative. Wisdom.

The Elemental Catalyst - Ancestral Elemental Archetype

THE *ELEMENTAL CATALYST* IGNITES ACTION, *EMBODYING* **momentum**, **ignition**, and **transformation**. Seeing potential where others see only undeveloped ideas, acting decisively. Drawing on **Earth's** *grounding*, **Air's** expansive *intelligence*, and **Fire's** bold energy, this *archetype* effortlessly **bridges** *inspiration* and execution. They expertly blend **vision** and **structure**, **spark** and **form**. Their presence motivates, sparking action and turning concepts into reality. A bridge between imagination and creation, the *Elemental Catalyst* brings dreams to life with **clarity**, **determination**, and **innovative** boldness.

ANCESTRAL ESSENCE

The *Elemental Catalysts* are revolutionaries, **builders**, and **pioneers** who didn't wait for opportunities but created them with **vision** and **determination**. Their *ancestors* were transformative architects, merging *inspiration* and action to shape the future; these change makers built **momentum**, turning ideas into **lasting** realities. *Embodying* this *essence*, therefore, means embracing both **vision** and **effort**, balancing **creativity** with the strength to see it through, *transforming* insight into **action**, and ultimately, action into *mastery*.

SHADOW THREAD

This *archetype's* powerful *energy* brings with it certain challenges. Recognizing these **patterns** promotes better *equilibrium*.

- **Distraction:** Air's vastness and Fire's intensity can lead to a lack of focus and wasted energy.
- **Burnout:** Constant motion and high energy can lead to exhaustion if rest and grounding aren't prioritized.
- **Resistance to Change:** The rigidity of the Earth's elements may make it difficult to adapt or shift direction when needed.

Through **pattern** recognition, the *Elemental Catalyst* channels intense energy with clarity and consistency. Centering involves a deep **inhale**, building inner **creative** *energy*, followed by a slow **exhale**, directing it with focused *intent*.

- Affirmations such as *"I channel my Fire with purpose"* support alignment between vision and action.

<hr/>

JUST AS **FIRE**, **EARTH**, AND **AIR** COMBINE TO SPARK *transformation*, the *Elemental Catalyst* refines their *essence* into an *alchemical* **rhythm**, transforming *momentum* into *mastery* and **vision** into impact. Their legacy is not merely to **initiate** change, but to uphold it **boldly**, **wisely**, and with **grounded** devotion.

ELEMENTAL ALCHEMY

- **Fire + Earth** = *Lava Essence* – transforms raw passion into steady, actionable momentum; forges resilience and creative endurance.
- **Earth + Air** = *Dust Essence* – grounds expansive thinking with practical wisdom, stabilizing ideas into form.
- **Fire + Air** = *Aetherflame Essence* – sparks visionary breakthroughs and fuels energetic, bold movement.

This **ritual** activates your *Ancestral* inheritance of **grounded** resilience, **creative** passion, and visionary **expansion**. By blending the *elements* of **Earth**, **Fire**, and **Air**, you *harmonize* stability, **clarity**, and **momentum**—awakening your inner force of *transformation* and **purposeful** creation.

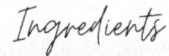

Ingredients

- **1 x Lava Essence** – Transforms passion into grounded, steady action.
- **1 x Dust Essence** – Encourages the development of big ideas and promotes resilience.
- **1 x Aetherflame Essence** – It fuels bold creativity and visionary pursuits.
- **1 x Resilience** – Envision Earth's stabilizing energy strongly grounding you in the present.
- **1 x Expansion** – Let Air open the way for your intellect and imagination to blossom.
- **1 x Momentum** – Feel Fire building within, sparking movement and fueling your drive.

The Elemental Catalyst Elixir

Elemental Catalyst
Alchemical Elixir Recipe & Ritual

Instructions

Step 1: Prepare the Space
- Arrange elemental symbols around ritual space. Feathers or incense for **Air**, a lit candle calls in **Fire** and stones, crystals or soil to symbolize **Earth**.
- Infuse the space with scents like **Sandalwood** (**Earth** element) **Ginger** or **Cinnamon** (**Fire** element) and **Peppermint** (**Air** element)

Step 2: Set Intention
- Begin with **Bhu Mudra** – (fingers touching **Earth**)- *roots you in stability and presence.*
- Transition to **Vajrapradama Mudra** *(hands interlaced at heart)* – for confidence and inner strength.
- **Honor your *ancestors***: Speak their names aloud or hold their presence in your *heart.*
- Invite their **resilience** and **creativity** into your **ritual** space.

Recite:

"I honor the wisdom and momentum of my ancestors. I call upon their strength, clarity, and passion to guide me as I create and transform purposefully."

Step 3: Embodiment Practice
  1. Warm Up
- Begin with slow movements and breath to center your awareness in the body.
  2. Elemental Breath & Movement:
- *Weave* in breath & movement practices from **Lava**, **Dust**, and **Aetherflame** essences for full *elemental* embodiment.

3. Chakra Focus:
- Activate **Solar Plexus** (*Manipura*) confidence & momentum, **Heart Chakra** (*Anahata*) connection & compassion, **Root Chakra** (*Muladhara*) for stability & safety and the **Third Eye Chakra** (*Ajna*) intuition.

→ REFER TO **PAGES 212, 218 & 221** FOR PRACTICES, POSES, *breathwork, & correspondences related to Lava, Dust, & Aetherflame.*

4. Suggested Embodiment Shapes / Poses:
- **Low Lunge** (*Anjaneyasana*) – grounds and promotes **forward** motion.
- **Revolved Triangle** (*Parivrtta Trikonasana*) – **focus** and mental clarity.
- **Camel Pose** (*Ustrasana*) – opens the heart to transformation and **inspiration**.

5. Dance & Intuitive Movement:
- Move **fluidly**, blending measured gestures with *dynamic*, **expressive** movement.
- Let your movement reflect the *connection* between **stillness** and **growth**, *form* and *change*.

Step 4: Astrology & Body Awareness
- Use your *MoonTree Chart* to identify *Ancestral astrological* body correspondences.
- Use **breath**, **visualization** and focused **movement** to enhance the energetic link.
  Lunar Phase:
- Align the **ritual** with a significant *Lunar* phase or *Ancestral* date (e.g., birthday or passing) to amplify *confidence* and *courage*, or any other *Lunar* phase that feels aligned to you for this **ritual**. Follow your **intuition**.

Step 5: Reflection & Writing
- Meditation / journaling.
- Reflect on how your *ancestors* embodied the *alchemy* of **grounded** strength, creative **transformation**, and **unique** insight.
- Practice automatic writing / receive intuitive messages and guidance on themes around **momentum**, *purpose and initiating meaningful change*..

Step 6: Ancestral Offering
- Offer flowers or flower *essences* aligned with the **Elemental Catalyst:**
  - **Vervain** (*Fire*) – for bold **transformation** and creative clarity
  - **Honeysuckle** (*Earth*) – for *Ancestral* grounding and **continuity**
  - **Yarrow** (*Air*) – for *clarity* and *energetic* **protection**
  - **Lavender** – for *calm*, **grounding**, and balance
  - **Rose** – for **heart-led** vision and emotional *expansion*
  - **Rosemary** – for *energetic* vitality and **remembrance**
- Light a **candle** and say aloud:

"*Your strength and clarity inspire me. Your passion resonates with me. I am guided by your wisdom in my creation.*"

Step 7: Closing
- Offer **gratitude** for the *energies* and support received.
- Sit or move in *stillness*, allowing the energies of **Fire**, **Earth**, and **Air** to integrate.
- Let the **ritual** integrate & carry the *essence* of the *Elemental Catalyst,* into your daily **life.**

Closing Reflection

The *Elemental Catalyst* **ritual** links you to the **stability**, **clarity**, and **momentum** of your *lineage*. Even though the specifics of your *ancestors'* lives may be obscure, their **resilience**, **creativity**, and **vitality** resonate within you. By exploring this *Ancestral elemental* blueprint, revealed in your *MoonTree Chart*, you enhance your capacity to **spark** change, *translating* thoughts into **deeds** and **momentum** into significant outcomes.

* FIRE SAFETY: *WHEN WORKING WITH CANDLES AND incense, practice caution.*

the ROOTED DREAMER

Elemental Trio: **Earth, Earth, Air (in any order)**
Keywords:
Grounded. Strategic. Prophetic. Visionary. Resilient.

THE *ROOTED DREAMER ESSENCE* DWELLS ON THE BOUNDARY between the **visible** and **invisible** *realms*, where the timeless wisdom of the **Earth** intersects with the boundless **vision** of the sky. This *archetype* possesses a unique talent: the capacity to envision beyond the **present** while staying firmly connected to reality. Combining the *solidity* of the **Earth** with the vastness of the **Air**, the *Rooted Dreamer* receives **prophetic** *insights* and *magical* perspectives, **grounding** them into *practical*, attainable plans. While others may *disregard* grand **dreams**, the *Rooted Dreamer* recognizes their possibilities and *skillfully* molds them into **enduring** strategies. They serve as a reminder that **imagination**, when *rooted* in **patience** and **purpose**, can leave a lasting *impact*.

ANCESTRAL ESSENCE

The *Rooted Dreamer* **embodies** the legacy of **architects, seers, planners**, and **way-finders**. These *ancestors* looked beyond their era, constructing with foresight for *generations* to come. They established sound **foundations**, envisioned clearly, and created enduring physical and energetic structures. *Embodying* this *archetype* means following their *path* with **patience** and **precision**. The *Rooted Dreamer* serves as a link between **vision** and **creation**, *transforming* **dreams** into lasting *influence* while respecting the *Ancestral* wisdom of turning **vision** into *reality*.

The Rooted Dreamer - Ancestral Elemental Archetype

SHADOW THREAD

HAVING THE GIFT OF *FORESIGHT* REQUIRES **ADAPTABILITY**. *Recognizing* **patterns** improves **integration** and **balance**.

- **Overthinking**: Striving for perfection can stifle creativity and spontaneity.
- **Perfectionism's Grip:** The fear of making mistakes can stifle creativity and exploration.

- **Rigid Thinking:** Earth's grounding force might become too fixed, resisting growth-inducing changes.

By recognizing these **patterns**, the *Rooted Dreamer* can blend structure with **imagination**, **logic** with **intuition**. A helpful practice involves taking deep breaths to connect with **Earth's** stability and expanding awareness into the **Air** around you.

- Affirmations like *"I trust my vision and act confidently"* can help bring ideas into reality gracefully.

JUST AS **EARTH** AND **AIR** COMBINE TO *SCULPT* **MOUNTAINS** from *dreams*, the *Rooted Dreamer* distills their *essence* into an *alchemical* **rhythm**, one that brings **vision** into **reality**, and ensures that what is built not only endures but inspires.

ELEMENTAL ALCHEMY

- **Earth + Earth** = *Mountain Essence* – strength, resilience, and the power of enduring stability.
- **Earth + Air** = *Dust Essence* – grounded clarity that blends visions & intuition with strategic action.

This **ritual** activates the **clarity**, **resilience**, and **expansive** thinking *woven* through your *lineage*. It helps you **root** visionary insight into **practical** reality– harmonizing **stability** with **innovation** so your dreams can take *form* and **thrive**.

Ingredients

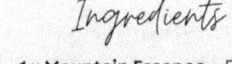

- **1 x Mountain Essence** – Embodies deep-rooted strength & unshakable resilience.
- **1 x Dust Essence** – Grounds vision with structure and practicality.
- **1 x Grounded Vision** – Visualize Earth's steady energy anchoring your ideas with purpose and focus.
- **1 x Strategic Insight** – Visualize Air expanding your mind and sharpening your thoughts with clarity.

Rooted Dreamer
Alchemical Elixir Recipe & Ritual

Instructions

Step 1: Prepare the Space

- Place symbolic items representing **Earth** (a bowl of *soil*, *potted plant* or even *grounding gemtones* like **Tiger's Eye** or **Jasper**) and *incense* for the **Air** *element*.
- Imbue the space with *scents* like **Sandalwood** (**Earth** element) and **Thyme** or **Peppermint** (**Air** element)

Step 2: Set Intention

- Begin with **Prithvi Mudra** – (ring finger + thumb)- *promotes grounding and stability*.
- Transition to **Hakini Mudra** *(all fingertips touching)* – stimulates insight and mental alignment.
- **Honor your** *ancestors*: Speak their names aloud or hold their presence in your *heart*.
- Invite their **strategic** *wisdom* and **foresight** into your **ritual** space.

Recite:

"I honor the resilience and vision of my ancestors. I call upon their wisdom to guide my dreams, grounding them in reality and purpose."

Step 3: Embodiment Practice

   1. Warm Up

- Begin with slow movements and breath to center your awareness in the body.

   2. Elemental Breath & Movement:

- *Weave* in breath & movement practices from the **Mountain and Dust essences** sections for full *elemental embodiment*.

3. Chakra Focus:

- Activate the **Heart Chakra** (*Anahata*) for love and grounded *connection*, **Root Chakra** (*Muladhara*) for resilience and stability and the **Crown Chakra** (*Sahasrara*) *foreseeing* insight and *intuitive* guidance.

→ REFER TO **PGS 203** & **218** FOR MORE PRACTICES, POSES, *breathwork*, & *correspondences related to Mountain* & *Dust Essences.*

4. Suggested Embodiment Shapes / Poses:
- **Child's Pose** (*Balasana*) – grounds and **connects** to the **Earth's** support.
- **Bridge Pose** (*Setu Bandhasana*) – *strengthens* and opens the **heart** space, and *supports* energetic *flow*.
- **Mountain Pose with Arms Overhead** (*Urdhva Hastasana*) – *aligns* **body** and **spirit** allowing for **energy** to *flow*.

5. Dance & Intuitive Movement:
- *Inspire* your movements to alternate between firm, **planted** stances and expansive, *flowing* actions.
- Strive for a blend of **structure** and **imagination**. Tap into your *psychic* **roots**.

Step 4: Astrology & Body Awareness
- Use your *MoonTree Chart* to identify *Ancestral astrological* body correspondences and *imprints*.
- Use **breath**, **visualization** and focused **movement** to enhance the energetic link.
  Lunar Phase:
- Align the **ritual** with a significant *Lunar* phase or *Ancestral* date (e.g., birthday or passing) to amplify *confidence* and *courage*, or any other *Lunar* phase that feels aligned to you for this **ritual**. Follow your ***intuition***.

Step 5: Reflection & Writing
- Meditation / journaling.
- Reflect on how your *ancestors* embodied the *alchemy* of **grounded** *wisdom*, and expansive **vision**.
- Practice automatic writing / receive *intuitive* messages and guidance on themes around **stability**, grounding **psychic** visions and **resilience**.

Step 6: Ancestral Offering
- Offer flowers or flower *essences* aligned with the ***Rooted Dreamer:***
  - **Vervain** (*Earth*) – for creative **structure** and discipline
  - **Honeysuckle** (*Earth*) – for deep *Ancestral* **connection**
  - **Yarrow** (*Air*) – for *clarity* and energetic **protection**
  - **Chamomile** – **grounded** and calming
  - **Geranium** – for *aligned*, heart-led **action**
  - **Lilac** – for **visions**, dreaming and insight
- Light a **candle** and say aloud:
  "Thank you for the clarity, strength, and vision passed through me. I root your wisdom into my actions and build from your dreams."

Step 7: Closing
- Offer **gratitude** for the *energies* and support received.
- Sit or move in *stillness*, allowing the energies of **Earth** and **Air** to integrate.
- Let the **ritual** integrate & carry the *essence* of the *Rooted Dreamer*, into your daily **life**.

Closing Reflection

The *Rooted Dreamer* **ritual** connects you to the grounded **stability** and **prophetic** dreams passed down through your *lineage*. Even though the details of your *ancestors'* lives may be a **mystery**, their **resilience** and **foresight** are *present* within you. Embracing these qualities allows you to pay tribute to their legacy and *unlocks* your ability to blend **dreaming** with **action**, nurturing **intuition**, and balanced *decision-making*.

---

* Fire Safety: When working with candles and incense, practice caution.

the AERIAL FIREWEAVER

Elemental Trio: **Air, Air, Fire – (in any order)**
Keywords:
Clairvoyant. Creative. Dynamic. Passionate. Insightful.

The Aerial Fireweaver - Ancestral Elemental Archetype

THE *AERIAL FIREWEAVER EMBODIES* THE POWER OF **inspiration**, a *mystical* dance of **intellect** and **passion**. Fueled by dual **Air** and **Fire** *elements*, this *archetype* channels **innovation** and change, shaping fresh ideas with **precision** and *vigor*. At the intersection of **curiosity** and **creativity**, they transform abstract possibilities into *tangible* outcomes with **clarity** and **determination**. Drawing on *Ancestral* wisdom, the *Aerial Fireweaver* balances boundless potential with purposeful action, aiming for a lasting, rather than *fleeting*, **impact**.

ANCESTRAL ESSENCE

The *Aerial Fireweaver essence* is the legacy of *visionary* minds, **thinkers**, **creators**, **inventors**, and **truth-seekers** who fused **intellect** and **passion** to ignite *transformation*. These *ancestors* sparked **revolutions**, shared *paradigm-shifting* **stories**, and turned dreams into reality; their brilliance lay not only in their vision, but in their decisive action. *Embodying* this *archetype* means following in their footsteps, blending mental *insight* with the **Fire** of *creation* to shape ideas into **action** *rooted* in *Ancestral* wisdom.

SHADOW THREAD

The dynamic combination of **Air** and **Fire** is invigorating yet can *overwhelm* if not **balanced**. Recognizing these **patterns** promotes *integration* and sustainability. Challenges may include:

- **Scattered Focus:** where Air's expansiveness may lead to unfinished ideas or a lack of direction.
- **Impulsiveness:** Fire's urgency can cause hasty decisions without considering long-term consequences.
- **Burnout:** where constant mental activity and fiery energy can lead to exhaustion without proper rest.

Awareness of these **patterns** enables the *Aerial Fireweaver archetype* to *cultivate* **clarity**, **direction**, and **sustainable** *energy*. A centering practice involves deep inhales to draw in *inspiration*, followed by slow exhalation to focus that *energy* on a single point.

- Affirmations such as *"I direct my energy with purpose"* reinforce the significance of intentional action and creative discernment.

JUST AS **AIR** FUELS **FIRE'S** *TRANSFORMATIVE* POWER, THE *Aerial Fireweaver* harnesses this alchemy as a *sacred* practice – where **insight** drives **action**, **movement** carries **meaning**, and *Ancestral wisdom* is passed down through the *currents* of **flame** and **thought**.

ELEMENTAL ALCHEMY

- **Air** + **Air** = *Wind Essence* – intellectual clarity and the expansive power of inspired thought.
- **Air** + **Fire** = *Aetherflame Essence* – visionary creativity merged with dynamic energy, offering clarity, insight, and transformative action.

This **ritual** awakens the *Ancestral* gifts of **Clairvoyance** and **creativity**. By working with the *elements* of **Air** and **Fire**, you ignite your *capacity* for intuitive **innovation** and articulate **transformation**– uniting **thought** with **action**, and **inspiration** with **impact**.

Ingredients

- **1 x Wind Essence** – Elevates intellectual clarity and expansive vision.
- **1 x Aetherflame Essence** – Sparks transformative creativity and dynamic insight.
- **1 x Vision** – Visualize sweeping winds crystallizing inspired ideas into vivid focus.
- **1 x Harmony** – Feel Air's clarity and Fire's intensity merging in balance–steady yet dynamic.

Aerial Fireweaver
Alchemical Elixir Recipe & Ritual

Instructions

Step 1: Prepare the Space
- Gather symbolic items representing **Air** (*Feathers, Wind chimes or incense*) and Candles, *Bloodstone or Smoky Quartz* for the **Fire** *element*.
- *Imbue* the space with *scents* that *inspire* and *energize* like **Jasmine** (**Earth** element) and **Ginger** or **Vanilla** (**Air** element)

Step 2: Set Intention
- Begin with **Vayu Mudra** – (fold the index finger to the base of the thumb)- *cultivates* **Air** *balance* and mental *clarity*.
- Transition to **Agni Mudra** (*press ring finger to base of thumb*) – *activates* inner **Fire** and creative *transformation*.
- **Honor your** *ancestors*: Speak their names aloud or hold their presence in your *heart*.
- Invite their **insight** and **creativity** into your **ritual** space.

Recite:
"*I honor the clarity and creativity of my ancestors. With insight and passion, I embrace the power to innovate, create, and transform.*"

Step 3: Embodiment Practice
  1. **Warm Up**
- Begin with breath and slow intuitive movement to connect to your body.
  2. **Elemental Breath & Movement:**
- *Weave* in breath & movement practices from the **Wind and Aetherflame essences** to *embody* mental focus & *fiery* inspiration.
3. **Chakra Focus:**
- Activate the **Third Eye Chakra** (*Ajna*) clairvoyance and inner sight, **Throat Chakra** (*Vishuddha*) *expression*, clarity, *insight* & **Solar Plexus Chakra** (*Manipura*) confidence, energy *dynamic* action.

→ REFER TO **PGS 200** & **221** FOR MORE PRACTICES, POSES, *breathwork, & correspondences related to Wind & Aetherflame essences.*

4. Suggested Embodiment Shapes / Poses:
- **Half Moon Pose** (*Ardha Chandrasana*) – balance and *strengthens* **vision**
- **Chair Pose** (*Utkatasana*) – grounds **Fire's** power and **will**
- **Triangle Pose** (*Trikonasana*) – aligns **breath** and vision

5. Dance & Intuitive Movement:
- *Blend light, Airy gestures with* **powerful**, *focused* **Fire** *expressions.*
- Flow between *softness* and *intensity*–let your body channel *insight* and **imagination** into *creative* form. Invite *visions* or messages to surface as you move with *Ancestral* rhythm.

Step 4: Astrology & Body Awareness
- Use your *MoonTree Chart* to identify *Ancestral astrological* body correspondences and *imprints.*
- Use **breath**, **visualization** and focused **movement** to enhance the energetic link.
  Lunar Phase:
- Align the **ritual** with a significant *Lunar* phase or *Ancestral* date (e.g. birthday or passing) to to align your **ritual** with *clarity* and *transformational* flow.

Step 5: Reflection & Writing
- Meditation / journaling.
- Reflect on how your *ancestors* embodied the *alchemy* of **clairvoyance**, **creativity** and passionate **insight**.
- Practice automatic writing / receive *intuitive* messages around the **themes** and *essence* of this *Ancestral Elemental Archetype.*

Step 6: Ancestral Offering
- Offer flowers or flower *essences* aligned with the ***Aerial Fireweaver:***
  - **Violet** (*Air*) – enhances **psychic** clarity and inner vision
  - **Clover** (*Air*) – supports **intellectual** abundance and creativity
  - **Holy Basil** (*Fire*) – activates dynamic energy and **passion**
  - **Mugwort** – strengthens **clairvoyance** and dreamwork
  - **Lavender** – **calms** the mind and fosters inspired *expression*
  - **Dandelion** – supports resilience and **expression** through change
- Light a **candle** and say aloud:
"Thank you for your gifts of insight, vision, and transformation. I carry your wisdom into the world with creative Fire and clear Air inspired intention."

Step 7: Closing
- Offer **gratitude** for the *energies* and support received.
- Sit or move in *stillness*, allowing the energies of **Air** and **Fire** to integrate.
- Reflect on your *embodiment* journey and how **clarity** and **creativity** now move through you.
- Let the **ritual** integrate & carry the *essence* of the *Aerial Fireweaver*, into your daily **life.**

Closing Reflection

The *Aerial Fireweaver* **ritual** links you to the **dynamic, vibrant** and **intuitive** energy of your *lineage*. Even though the specifics of your *ancestors'* lives might be shrouded in *mystery*, their **clarity** and **creativity** *flow* within you. *Embracing* these aspects allows you to **venerate** your *lineage* and awaken your capacity to blend **thought** and **action**, sparking impactful personal development.

* **FIRE SAFETY:** WHEN WORKING WITH CANDLES AND *incense, practice caution.*

the
PHOENIX
INTUITIVE

Elemental Trio: **Fire, Fire, Water (in any order)**
Keywords:
Passionate. Resilient. Transformative. Rebirth. Courageous.

THE *PHOENIX INTUITIVE* EMBODIES A POWERFUL FORCE OF *transformation*, where the *elements* of **Fire** and **Water** converge. It is a realm where passion delves into the depths and where endings serve as fertile soil for new beginnings. This archetype combines the primal energy of **Fire** with the emotional depth of **Water**, welcoming change not as a burden but as a sacred journey. The *Phoenix Intuitive* navigates through cycles of destruction and rebirth with bravery, resilience, and elegance. Like the legendary phoenix, they repeatedly rise from the ashes, carrying the flame of wisdom through the waters of rejuvenation. Drawing from ancestral wisdom, they teach us that even the most intense changes harbor the potential for renewal. By embracing surrender, we emerge as our truest selves.

ANCESTRAL ESSENCE

The *Phoenix Intuitive* embodies the legacy of ancestors who faced change with grace and turned pain into power. They walked through fire and emerged renewed, not afraid of transformation, but embracing it as a catalyst for growth. Embodying this archetype means inheriting their ability to turn pain into purpose, trusting the process of shedding and renewal, and inspiring others to rise from their challenges with strength and clarity.

The Phoenix Intuitive - Ancestral Elemental Archetype

SHADOW THREAD

DEEP TRANSFORMATION BRINGS PROFOUND INTENSITY. Being aware of these patterns enables grounded integration.

- **Emotional Intensity:** The combination of Fire and Water can trigger overwhelming emotional waves without awareness.
- **Burnout:** Striving for growth can cause exhaustion without a balance of rest and stillness.

- **Impulsiveness:** Making quick decisions can overlook the wisdom found in pause and reflection.

Recognizing these tendencies empowers the Phoenix Intuitive to develop emotional regulation, sustainable energy, and focused transformation. A centering practice: Inhale deeply, sensing the warmth of transformation rising within; exhale slowly, allowing the waters of renewal to flow through you.

- Affirmations like *"I honor the cycle of release and renewal"* reinforce trust in the sacred rhythm of rebirth.

JUST AS FIRE AND WATER BLEND TO FORM STEAM, THE Phoenix Intuitive refines this elemental alchemy into a purposeful transformation practice, where passion drives healing, and growth becomes a deliberate act of creation. Their essence reminds us we rise, not despite our endings, but because of them.

ELEMENTAL ALCHEMY

- **Fire + Fire** = *Blaze Essence* – amplifies transformative passion and creative intensity.
- **Fire + Water** = *Steam Essence* – embodies emotional resilience, blending fiery drive with compassionate flow.

This **ritual** honors the *fiery passion* and emotional **resilience** within your *Ancestral* line. It invites you to embody **transformation**, soothe emotional **intensity**, and **rise** *renewed*. By harmonizing **Fire** and **Water**, you awaken the *sacred* balance between **courage** and **adaptability**, **action** and **renewal**.

Ingredients

- **2 x Blaze Essence** – Fuels passion, creative drive, and inner Fire.
- **1 x Steam Essence** – Balances fiery transformation with emotional flow.
- **1 x Passion** – Visualize vibrant flames fueling your courage, creativity, and purpose.
- **1 x Rebirth / Renewal** – Visualize Water cooling and restoring your spirit, building resilience.

The Phoenix Intuitive Elixir

Phoenix Intuitive
Alchemical Elixir Recipe & Ritual

Instructions

Step 1: Prepare the Space

- Place symbolic items representing **Water** (*Bowl of Water, Seashells or Moonstone*) and *Candles, red/orange fabric or Smoky Quartz* for the **Fire** *element*.
- *Imbue* the space with *scents* like **Allspice** (**Fire** element) and **Vanilla** (**Water** element)

Step 2: Set Intention

- Begin with **Surya Mudra** – (*ring finger to thumb*)- *connects* with inner **Fire** and drive
- Transition to **Shakti Mudra** (*join the ring & little fingers of both hands, fold the middle & index fingers under the thumbs.*) – *Encourages* emotional *adaptability* and **fluid** *strength*.
- **Honor your** *ancestors*: Speak their names aloud or hold their presence in your *heart*.
- Invite their **presence** and **suppoprt** into your **ritual** space.

Recite:

"I honor the transformative power of my ancestors.With fiery passion and emotional wisdom, I embrace renewal and rebirth."

Step 3: Embodiment Practice

1. Warm Up

- Begin with breath and slow intuitive movement to connect to your body.

2. Elemental Breath & Movement:

- *Choose* breath & movement practices from the **Blaze** and **Steam essences** to *awaken* energy and flow.

3. Chakra Focus:

- Activate the **Solar Plexus Chakra** (*Manipura*) *empowerment* and inner **Fire**, **Sacral Chakra** (*Svadhisthana*) emotional adaptability and *creative* flow & **Heart Chakra** (*Anahata*) connection, compassion, and emotional healing.

→ *Refer to* **pgs 209** *&* **227** *for additional practices, poses, breathwork, and correspondences related to Blaze & Steam Essences.*

4. Suggested Embodiment Shapes / Poses:
- **Warrior III** (Virabhadrasana III) – *strengthens* focus and **balance**
- **Camel Pose** (Ustrasana) – opens the *heart* and **releases** emotional blocks
- ***Dancer Pose*** *(Natarajasana) – integrates grace, strength, and* **transformation**

5. Dance & Intuitive Movement:
- *Move freely, shifting between bold, fiery* ***expressions*** *and gentle, wave-like gestures.*
- Embody to *rise*, to *release*, and renewal–mirroring the *phoenix's* journey of **rebirth**.

Step 4: Astrology & Body Awareness
- Use your *MoonTree Chart* to identify *Ancestral astrological* body correspondences and *imprints.*
- Use **breath**, **visualization** and focused **movement** to enhance the energetic link.
  Lunar Phase*:*
- Align the **ritual** with a significant *Lunar* phase or *Ancestral* date (e.g. birthday or passing) to connect with energies of *renewal*, **passion**, *courage* and *transformational* flow.

Step 5: Reflection & Writing
- Meditation / journaling.
- Reflect on how your *ancestors* met **life's** *challenges* and *transformations.*
- Practice automatic writing / receive *intuitive* messages around the **themes** of *resilience*, **renewal**, *passion*, and *creative* courage.

Step 6: Ancestral Offering
- Offer flowers or flower *essences* aligned with the ***Phoenix Intuitive:***
  - **Carnation** (*Fire*) – fuels **creative** passion
  - **Mullein** (*Fire*) – strengthens **emotional** resilience
  - **Rose** (*Water*) – supports heart-opening and **healing**
  - **Passionflower** – nurtures emotional **balance** and depth
  - **Sunflower** – **radiates** strength and joy
  - **Marigold** – symbolizes growth through **transformation**

- Light a **candle** and say aloud:
"I honor the legacy of resilience and rebirth passed through my lineage. May your flame guide me and your Waters renew me."

Step 7: Closing
- Offer **gratitude** for the *energies* and support received.
- Sit or move in *stillness*, allowing the energies of **Water** and **Fire** to integrate.
- Reflect on your *embodiment* journey and how **renewal** and **passion** can now move through you.
- Let the **ritual** integrate & carry the *essence* of the *Phoenix Intuitive*, into your daily **life.**

Closing Reflection

The *Phoenix Intuitive* **ritual** connects you to the *transformative* **cycles** inherited from your *lineage*. Even if the specifics of your *ancestors'* lives remain a **mystery**, their **resilience** and deep emotions continue to *resonate* within you, a **pattern** reflected in your *MoonTree Chart's elemental* display of their *energetic* influence. Embracing these *elements unlocks* your potential for **creative passion**, emotional intelligence, and meaningful **rejuvenation**.

△ △▽

*** FIRE SAFETY:*** *WHEN WORKING WITH CANDLES AND incense, practice caution.*

the FIERY MINDSCAPER

Elemental Trio: **Fire, Fire, Air (in any order)**
Keywords:
Passionate. Resilient. Intensity. Rebirth. Courageous.

The Fiery Mindscaper - Ancestral Elemental Archetype

THE *FIERY MINDSCAPER* IS PURE **CREATIVE** *MOMENTUM*, A fusion of **Fire's passionate** drive and **Air's expansive** intellect. This *archetype* is a *visionary* capable of *bold* **innovation** and *rapid* **transformation**. Ideas spark like **wildfire**, carried by the *winds* of **curiosity**, igniting *possibilities* others may not yet see. With **eloquence** and **precision**, the *Fiery Mindscaper* bridges the gap between abstract **inspiration** and **tangible** *reality*, forging new paths while staying **rooted** in *Ancestral wisdom*. Their **gift** is the ability to turn **thought** into **movement** and **passion** into **progress** when *focus* and *clarity* guide the **flame**.

ANCESTRAL ESSENCE

The *Fiery Mindscaper* carries the *lineage* of **thinkers**, **inventors**, and **storytellers**, those whose ideas shaped *history*, blending *intellectual* **brilliance** with **passionate** *action*. These *ancestors* moved with the **Fire** of *inspiration*, carried by the *winds* of **change**, bringing forth new ways of *thinking*, *creating*, and *leading*. To **embody** this *archetype* is to honor the **inspired** *minds* that came before, those who dared to **dream** *beyond* their time. The *Fiery Mindscaper's* journey is about *cultivating* the *delicate* **balance** between **ambition** and *execution*, ensuring that **ideas** are **envisioned** and *realized*.

SHADOW THREAD

With great **creative** force comes the challenge of harnessing it *effectively*. Awareness of these **patterns** allows for deeper **integration**:

- **Overextension:** The boundless energy of Fire combined with the rapid expansion of Air can lead to burnout if not paced mindfully.
- **Challenges in Materializing Ideas:** A flood of visionary concepts can feel exhilarating, but they may remain intangible without structure.
- **Impulsiveness:** The rush to act can sometimes bypass

moments of refinement, leading to missed opportunities for more profound insight or better execution.

Bringing awareness to these tendencies allows the *Fiery Mindscaper* to balance **inspiration** and **action**. A simple centering practice, inhale deeply, envisioning a steady **flame** held within the hands, exhale, directing its energy with purpose, can help channel their **Fire** without losing focus.

- Affirmations such as *"I honor my vision by giving it form"* reinforce the harmony between ideation and manifestation.

Just as the *Fiery Mindscaper* blends **Fire** and **Air** to ignite *transformation*, their *essence* can be **distilled** into an *alchemical* practice that channels **passion** into **precision**, ensuring ideas take *root* and grow into lasting **creations**.

ELEMENTAL ALCHEMY

- **Fire + Fire = Blaze Essence** – amplifies transformative passion and creative intensity.
- **Fire + Water = Steam Essence** – embodies emotional resilience, blending fiery drive with compassionate flow.

This **ritual** ignites your inner **Fire** while sharpening *mental clarity*, *connecting* you to the **wisdom** and **innovation** of your *lineage*. By blending the **passion** of **Fire** and the brilliance of **Air**, you *awaken* the power to **create**, **express**, and **act** with your *purpose*.

Ingredients

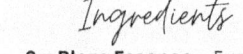

- **2 x Blaze Essence** – Fuels transformative passion and creative innovation.
- **1 x Aetherflame Essence** – Merges Fire with dynamic insight.
- **1 x Focus** – Visualize vibrant flames channeling ideas into tangible outcomes.
- **1 x Clarity** – Imagine winds sweeping away mental fog, illuminating clear direction.

The Fiery Mindcsaper Elixir

Fiery Mindscaper
Alchemical Elixir Recipe & Ritual

Instructions

Step 1: Prepare the Space
- Place symbolic items representing **Fire** (*Candles & gemstones like Carnelian*) and Feathers, *wind chimes or incense* for the **Air** element.
- *Imbue* the space with *scents* like **Rosemary**, **Peppermint** and **Ginger** for *clarity* and *energy*.

Step 2: Set Intention
- Begin with **Surya Mudra** – (*ring finger to thumb*)- *connects* with inner **Fire.**
- Transition to **Jnana Mudra** (*index finger to thumb, palms up.*) – **Air's** clarity and *wisdom*.
- **Honor your *ancestors*:** Speak their names aloud or hold their presence in your ***heart***.
- Invite their **presence** and **suppoprt** into your **ritual** space.

Recite:
"I honor the visionary wisdom and creative spark of my ancestors. With focus and clarity, I channel my passion into meaningful innovation."

Step 3: Embodiment Practice
  1. Warm Up
- Begin with breath and slow intuitive movement to *connect* to your body & *intention*.

  2. Elemental Breath & Movement:
- *Choose* breath & *movement* practices from the **Blaze** and **Aetherflame essences** to *encourage clarity, focus and fiery momentum*.

  3. Chakra Focus:
- Activate the **Solar Plexus Chakra** (*Manipura*) *confidence &* ***creative*** *power*, **Throat Chakra** (*Vishuddha*) expression & communication and the **Third Eye Chakra** (*Ajna*) vision and insight.

→ *Refer to **pgs 209** & **221** for more practices, poses, breathwork, & correspondences related to Blaze & Aetherflame essences.*

4. Suggested Embodiment Shapes / Poses:
- **Warrior II** (*Virabhadrasana II*) – builds strength, focus, and **presence.**
- **Standing Forward Fold** (*Uttanasana*) – grounds energy and promotes inner clarity.
- *Eagle Pose (Garudasana) – enhances focus, balance, and integration of passion & vision.*

5. Dance & Intuitive Movement:
- *Move intuitively with a blend of sharp,* **fiery** *gestures and* **airy**, *sweeping* **expressions**.
- Allow your body to channel **inspiration**, *balancing* the bold *spark* of **Fire** with the *expansive* reach of **Air**.

Step 4: Astrology & Body Awareness
- Use your *MoonTree Chart* to explore *Ancestral astrological* body correspondences and *imprints.*
- Use **breath**, **visualization** and focused **movement** to enhance the energetic link.
  Lunar Phase:
- Align the **ritual** with a significant *Lunar* phase or *Ancestral* date (e.g. birthday or passing) to **amplify** clarity and *creative* energies.

Step 5: Reflection & Writing
- Meditation / journaling.
- Reflect on your *ancestors'* **creativity**, **clarity**, and ability to bring visions to **life**.
- Practice automatic writing / receive *intuitive* messages around the **themes** of *focus*, *action*, *innovation*, and **expression**.

Step 6: Ancestral Offering
- Offer flowers or flower *essences* aligned with the ***Fiery Mindscaper:***
  - **Hibiscus** (*Fire*) – for passion and vitality
  - **Marigold** (*Fire*) – for bold vision and transformation
  - **Bergamot** (*Air*) – for uplifting expression
  - **Lavender** – for calming clarity and communication
  - **Chamomile** – for mental peace and soft insight
  - **Jasmine** – for visionary imagination and alignment
- Light a **candle** and say aloud:

"*I honor the legacy of creativity and clarity passed through my lineage.*
May your Fire fuel my purpose, and your vision guide my path."

Step 7: Closing
- Offer **gratitude** for the *energies* and support received.
- Sit *in stillness*, allowing the energies of **Air** and **Fire** to integrate.
- Reflect on your *embodiment* journey and how **courage** and **resilience** can now move through you.
- Let the **ritual** integrate & carry the *essence* of the *Fiery Mindscaper*, into your daily **life.**

Closing Reflection

The *Fiery Mindscaper* **ritual** connects you to the **creative** and **intellectual** *energies* inherited from your *ancestors*. Although the *specifics* of their lives may be unknown, their **passion** for **innovation** and clear **thinking** *continues* to influence you, a legacy *showcased* in your *MoonTree Chart's* elemental **pattern**. Aligning with these *elements* awakens your ability to **innovate**, articulate your **vision** clearly, and transform **imagination** into **reality.**

△ △△

* FIRE SAFETY: *When working with candles and incense, practice caution*

the NURTURING HARMONIZER

Elemental Trio: **Earth, Water, Air (in any order)**
Keywords:
**Grounded. Intuitive. Compassionate. Harmonizing.
Communication**

The Nurturing Harmonizer - Ancestral Elemental Archetype

THE *NURTURING HARMONIZER* EMBODIES **STABILITY**, emotional **intuition**, and clear **communication**, moving *gracefully* through **life's** complexities and *offering* **balance, empathy,** and deep **connection.** *Rooted* in the *wisdom* of the **past**, this *archetype* embodies **harmony.** Their innate ability to bring **warmth** to difficult **moments** and **clarity** to tangled **emotions** *transforms* **discord** into **unity,** guided by the *elements.*

ANCESTRAL ESSENCE

This *archetype* reflects a *lineage* of **caretakers, healers,** and **communicators** who *nurtured* **stability** and **understanding** within their *families* and *communities.* Their *wisdom* embodies the balance between emotional depth and **intellectual** clarity, listening and expressing, holding space and standing firm. Honoring these *ancestors*, who wove connection through **presence** and **care,** means **aligning** with this *essence.* Thus, the *Nurturing Harmonizer* carries their legacy forward, *cultivating* meaningful **relationships** and creating spaces of healing in their own *lives* and **beyond.**

SHADOW THREAD

Like all gifts, the strengths of the *Nurturing Harmonizer* can also cast a shadow. Awareness of these **patterns** allows for deeper **integration**:

- **Empathetic burnout:** Excessive empathy can lead to emotional exhaustion by absorbing others' feelings.
- **Communication Overload:** Complex emotions and insights can be overwhelming, hindering clear self-expression.
- **Instability:** The conflicting demands of thoughts, emotions, and relationships can lead to a feeling of being stretched too thin.

Recognizing these tendencies is the first step to balance. A simple grounding practice - **inhale** deeply, envisioning *roots* **anchoring** you into stability; **exhale**, releasing emotional weight, can help *restore* **equi-librium**.

- Affirmations such as *"I nurture myself as I nurture others"* reinforce healthy boundaries, ensuring that care flows in both directions.

JUST AS THE *NURTURING HARMONIZER* BLENDS **EARTH**, **Water**, and **Air** to create balance, its *essence* can be **distilled** into an *alchemical* practice that *weaves* the *elements* into a **ritual** of **connection**, **healing**, and **harmony**.

ELEMENTAL ALCHEMY

- **Earth + Water** = *Mud Essence:* Provides grounding stability while nurturing emotional connection, cultivating growth, and adaptability.
- **Earth + Air** = *Dust Essence:* Harmonizes intellectual clarity with grounded insight, enabling effective and practical communication.
- **Water + Air** = *Mist Essence:* This essence combines emotional intuition with the lightness of clarity, allowing for adaptive and compassionate expression.

This **ritual** is a *sacred* **invocation** of *Ancestral wisdom*–connecting you to the deep **emotional strength**, **resilience**, and **clarity** passed down through your *lineage*. You are invited to move with grounded *intention*, express with **compassion**, and **communicate** with clarity– *embodying* the **harmonized** *essence* of **Earth**, **Water**, and **Air**.

Ingredients

- **1 x Mud Essence** – Grounds emotional connection and nourishes with depth and care.
- **1 x Dust Essence** – Combines intellectual acuity and *down-to-earth* solidity.
- **1 x Mist Essence** - Softens communication and enhances intuitive, flowing expression.
- **1 x Stability** - Visualize Earth's energy anchoring your body and relationships.
- **1 x Empathy** - Imagine waves of compassion opening channels for heart-centered connection.
- **1 x Clarity** - Picture Air's movement sweeping insight and gentle truth through your interactions.

Nurturing Harmonizer
Alchemical Elixir Recipe & Ritual

Instructions

Step 1: Prepare the Space
- Place symbolic items representing **Earth** (*Soil or stones like Hematite*) a bowl of **Water** as a *conduit* and for the **Air** element (*feathers / incense*)
- *Infuse* the space with *scents* like **Lavender**, **Chamomile** and **Sage** for *calm*, emotional clarity and sacred protection.

Step 2: Set Intention
- Begin with **Anjali Mudra** – (hands at heart)- to center yourself in love.
- Transition to **Jnana Mudra** (*index finger to thumb, palms up.*) – Inviting *clarity* and peace.
- **Honor your ancestors**: Speak their names aloud or hold their presence in your *heart*.
- Invite their **strength** and **compassion** into your **ritual** space.

Recite:
"I honor the wisdom and compassion of my ancestors. Through their guidance, I embody balance, empathy, and harmony in all my connections."

Step 3: Embodiment Practice
1. **Warm Up**
- *Awaken* the body with gentle *movements* and breath to prepare for *integration*.
2. **Elemental Breath & Movement:**
- *Choose* breath & *movement* practices from the **Mud, Dust** and **Mist essences** to *connect with the nurturing, grounding, & intuitive energies from your lineage.*
3. **Chakra Focus:**
- Activate the **Root Chakra** (*Muladhara*) grounding & safety, **Heart Chakra** (*Anahata*) emotional connection & empathy and the **Throat Chakra** (*Vishuddha*) honest, compassionate expression.

→ *Refer to* **pgs 215, 218 & 224** *for more practices, poses, breathwork, & correspondences related to Mud, Dust, & Mist.*

4. Suggested Embodiment Shapes / Poses:
- **Child's Pose** (*Balasana*) – for **grounding** and *surrender*.
- **Seated Forward Fold** (*Paschimottanasana*) – emotional **reflection**.
- **Bridge Pose** (*Setu Bandhasana*) – for **heart-opening** and *balanced flow*.

5. Dance & Intuitive Movement:
- *Begin with rooted, steady movements embodying* **Earth**
- Transition into *flowing*, wave-like gestures to *mirror* **Water**.
- Moving to **Air** *inspired* expressive motions to invite **clarity** and *Ancestral* wisdom.

Step 4: Astrology & Body Awareness
- Use your *MoonTree Chart* to explore *Ancestral astrological* body correspondences and *imprints*.
- Use **breath**, **visualization** and focused **movement** to enhance the energetic link.
  Lunar Phase:
- Align the **ritual** with a significant *Lunar* phase or *Ancestral* date (e.g. birthday or passing) to *align* with **nurturing** harmony, *Ancestral* **connection** and **intuition**.

Step 5: Reflection & Writing
- Meditation / journaling.
- Reflect on how your *ancestors* embodied **resilience**, **balance**, and **love** in *relationships*.
- Practice automatic writing, receive *intuitive* messages around theses archetypal **themes**.

Step 6: Ancestral Offering
- Offer flowers or flower *essences* aligned with the ***Nurturing Harmonizer:***
  - **Jasmine** (*Earth*) – for grounding and *sacred* **connection**
  - **Daisy** (*Water*) – for emotional **renewal**
  - **Violet** (*Air*) – for **intuitive** clarity
  - **Rose** – for *Ancestral* **compassion**
  - **Honeysuckle** – for **memory** and *sweetness*
  - **Geranium** – for **balance** and emotional regulation
- Light a **candle** and say aloud:
"*I honor the strength and grace of those before me. May their compassion guide my connections and their stability root my actions in love.*"

Step 7: Closing
- Offer **gratitude** for the *energies* and support received.
- Feel/sense the balance of **Earth**, **Water**, and **Air** *harmonizing* within your being.
- Let the **ritual** integrate & carry the *essence* of the *Nurturing Harmonizer*, into your daily **life**.

Closing Reflection

The *Nurturing Harmonizer* **ritual** connects you with the **grounding** stability, emotional **depth**, and **compassionate** clarity inherited from your *ancestors*. Their **nurturing** *wisdom* **flows** through you, even if the specifics of their lives remain unknown. This *elemental* **pattern**, *decoded* and revealed in your *MoonTree Chart*, represents their **energetic** legacy. *Aligning* with these *elements* enhances your ability to **harmonize** relationships, foster **balance**, and cultivate a grounded, **empathetic** *presence*.

---

* ***Fire Safety:*** *When working with candles and incense, practice caution*

the
HEARTHSTONE
SHAPER

Elemental Trio: **Earth-Earth-Fire (in any order)**
Keywords:
Grounded. Creative. Resilient. Visionary. Leadership

THE *HEARTHSTONE SHAPER EMBODIES* THE UNWAVERING strength of **Earth** and the *transformative* spark of **Fire**, *rooted* in **stability** and driven by a *vision* of **creation**. Like the *Ancestral* architects who laid *foundations* for future *generations*, transforming *raw* **potential** into lasting, meaningful works. This extends beyond *physical* structures to *encompass* traditions, knowledge, and **enduring** influence. Guided by *Ancestral wisdom*, they *cultivate* **resilience, resourcefulness**, and *dynamic* **leadership**, shaping both **literal** and **symbolic** spaces that foster *growth*, *stability*, and **inspiration**. The *key* to their **success** lies in *balance*, knowing when to forge ahead and when to pause, ensuring the **sustainability** of their *endeavors*.

ANCESTRAL ESSENCE

This *archetype* reflects the legacy of **builders** and **caretakers**, who laid the **groundwork** for strong *communities*. Their *wisdom* teaches the *power* of **resilience, action,** and **creativity**, showing that **authentic** *leadership* is not just about constructing something new but also about *maintaining* and *honoring* what has come before. To *embody* the *Hearthstone Shaper* is to carry forward this *Ancestral* **gift**, blending **innovation** with **deep-rooted** tradition. The *alchemist* steps into this role *purposefully*, shaping a life of *meaning* and **impact**, just as the *ancestors* once shaped the *world* around them.

The Hearthstone Shaper - Ancestral Elemental Archetype

SHADOW THREAD

LIKE ALL FORCES OF **CREATION**, THE GIFTS OF THE *Hearthstone Shaper* come with challenges. Awareness of these **patterns** allows for deeper **integration**:

- **Resistance to Change:** A deep connection to tradition sometimes makes adaptability difficult. Honoring the past while welcoming innovation is encouraged.

- **Risk of Burnout:** The drive to build, create, and sustain can lead to exhaustion, but even mountains are shaped by time and rest. Learning when to pause is part of the journey.
- **Overextension:** Taking on too much responsibility can drain energy reserves. Knowing where to invest effort ensures lasting strength.

Recognizing these tendencies helps the *Hearthstone Shaper* cultivate **balance**, **adaptability**, and **sustainable** *success*. A simple grounding practice, inhale deeply, *visualizing* the steady **presence** of a *mountain*; exhale, releasing tension and allowing space for *renewal*, can help restore **equilibrium**.

- Affirmations such as *"I honor my limits and trust my path"* reinforce the wisdom that strength is found in action and stillness.

JUST AS THE *HEARTHSTONE SHAPER* BLENDS **EARTH** AND **FIRE** to *create* something **enduring**, their *essence* can be **distilled** into an *alchemical* practice that grounds **ambition**, fuels **creativity**, and honors the *wisdom* of what has already been *built*.

ELEMENTAL ALCHEMY

- **Earth + Earth** = *Mountain Essence:* Symbolizing lasting strength, steadfastness, and resilience, it forms a strong base for ambitious endeavors.
- **Earth + Fire** = *Lava Essence:* Practicality meets passion, igniting transformation and innovation. It teaches that creation and destruction renew each other.

This **ritual** invites you into the rhythm of **building** and **reimagining**–*mirroring* the hands of your *ancestors* who shaped and sustained worlds. By **grounding** into Earth's *resilience* and channeling **Fire's** *transformative* **momentum**, you **activate** your *Ancestral* power to **create** with **strength** and enduring **purpose**.

Hearthstone Shaper
Alchemical Elixir Recipe & Ritual

Instructions

Step 1: Prepare the Space

- Place symbolic items representing **Earth** (*Soil and crystals like Obsidian & Jasper*) and for the **Fire** element (*candles, red/orange fabrics, gemstones like Carnelian*)
- *Infuse* the space with *scents* like **Clove, Cinnamon** and **Ginger** for *warmth*, rooting & *grounding*, and *motivation*.

Ingredients

- **2 x Mountain Essence** – Enhances resilience, sharpens vision, and creates a firm foundation.
- **1 x Lava Essence** – Channels creative Fire and dynamic transformation; reshapes with passionate flow.
- **1 x Determination** - Visualize Earth's solid presence anchoring your intention, like rock that never falters.
- **1 x Ambition** – Visualize Fire's radiant energy fueling your action with intensity, purpose, and enduring momentum.

Step 2: Set Intention

- Begin with **Dhyana Mudra** - (*hands in your lap with palms facing up, rest the right hand on top of the left, with thumbs touching*) - cultivates grounded stillness and inward clarity.
- Transition to **Anjali Mudra** (*Hands at heart*) – Invoke reverence & *Ancestral* creativity.
- **Honor your *ancestors***: Speak their names aloud or hold their presence in your ***heart***.
- Invite their **strength** and **purpose** into your **ritual** space.

Recite:
"I honor the strength and passion of my ancestors. With their guidance, I embrace my power to create, transform, and build a lasting legacy."

Step 3: Embodiment Practice

1. **Warm Up**
- *Awaken the **spine**, **feet**, and **hips**–for rooting in, grounding and activation.*
2. **Elemental Breath & Movement:**
- *Choose* breath & *movement* practices from the **Lava** and **Mountain essences** for transformation & steadiness - building **Fire** through **grounded** presence.
3. **Chakra Focus:**
- Activate the **Root Chakra** (*Muladhara*) stability & **Earth** *connection*, **Sacral Chakra** (*Svadhithana*) creative expression & emotional flow, and the **Solar Plexus Chakra** (*Manipura*) courage, confidence & action.

The Hearthstone Shaper Elixir

→ *Refer to **pgs 203** & **212** for more practices, poses, breathwork, & correspondences related to Mountain & Lava Essences.*

4. Suggested Embodiment Shapes / Poses:
- **Warrior II** (Virabhadrasana II) – for **resilience** and powerful vision.
- **Goddess Pose** (Utkata Konasana) – activate **Fire** and **Earth** elements.
- **Mountain Pose** (Tadasana) – Embody the **Earth**, Root in and Rise.

5. Dance & Intuitive Movement:
- Begin with slow rooted "stomping" bringing energy up from the **Earth**.
- Add dynamic **expressive** movements for Lava, fluid **Fire**.
- Let this dance reflect the **creative** cycles of your lineage.

Step 4: Astrology & Body Awareness
- Use your MoonTree Chart to explore Ancestral astrological body correspondences and imprints.
- Use **breath**, **visualization** and focused **movement** to enhance the energetic link.
  Lunar Phase:
- Align the **ritual** with a significant Lunar phase or Ancestral date (e.g. birthday or passing) to align with **grounding, creation, innovation** and **building** energies of your lineage.

Step 5: Reflection & Writing
- Meditation / journaling.
- Reflect on how your ancestors embodied the **Earth** and **Fire** elemental energies.
- Practice automatic writing, receive intuitive messages around themes of **foundations** and **strength**.

Step 6: Ancestral Offering
- Offer flowers or flower essences aligned with the **Hearthstone Shaper:**
  - **Mugwort** (Earth) – Dreamwork and **ancient** knowing
  - **Poppy** (Water) – Deep Ancestral **feeling**
  - **Dandelion** (Air) – Expression and **resilience**
  - **Carnation** (Fire) – **Creativity** and passion
  - **St. John's Wort** (Fire) – Protection and **boldness**
  - **Red Clover** (Earth) – For grounding and **foundation**
- Light a **candle** and say aloud:

"This flame honors your Fire, and this Earth. May my vision be guided by your resilience and creative purpose."

Step 7: Closing
- Offer **gratitude** for the energies and support received.
- Feel / Sense the resonance of **stability** and **ambition** within.
- Let the **ritual** integrate & carry the essence of the Hearthstone Shaper, into your daily **life**.

Closing Reflection

The Hearthstone Shaper **ritual** links you to the **grounded** strength and **dynamic** energy of your lineage. By connecting with these elements, you unlock the power to transform your **visions** into tangible **realities**. This practice respects the wisdom of your ancestors and empowers you to carve out a path of **innovation** and **purpose**, even if the details of their lives are unknown. The elemental **pattern**, uncovered in your MoonTree Chart, symbolizes their **enduring** energetic essences.

* **FIRE SAFETY:** WHEN WORKING WITH CANDLES AND incense, practice caution

the SACRED WELLKEEPER

Elemental Trio: **Water, Water, Earth (in any order)**
Keywords:
Nurturing. Steady. Compassionate. Intuitive. Renewal

THE *SACRED WELLKEEPER* SERVES AS THE GUARDIAN OF *wisdom* found within the body, **heart**, and **land**, *embodying* the *fluidity* of **Water** and the **grounding** presence of **Earth**. This creates a *nurturing* space for **healing, understanding**, and emotional **bonding**, similar to the **ancient wells** that sustained *generations*. They offer **care** and **nourishment**, emphasizing the importance of mutual support, with an *intuitive* understanding of **life's** natural **rhythms** of **birth**, **death**, and **renewal**. The *Sacred Wellkeeper* respects nature's *cycles* and the knowledge passed down through *generations*. Their unique ability lies in **holding** space, active **listening**, and encouraging peace within themselves and their *communities*.

ANCESTRAL ESSENCE

The *Sacred Wellkeeper* reflects the *lineage* of **healers, nurturers**, and **wise** *individuals* who prioritized the **well-being** of their **communities**, blending physical and emotional care. They were the **midwives, herbalists**, and **storytellers** who integrated teachings into daily life, drawing strength from the *land* and **resilience** from passing time. Embodying this *archetype* involves honoring their *gifts*, acknowledging that **compassion** requires **nurturing**, understanding that **healing** is an *ongoing* process, and realizing that **stability** is found in *adaptability* and *balance*.

The Sacred Wellkeeper - Ancestral Elemental Archetype

SHADOW THREAD:

THE *SACRED WELLKEEPER'S* DEPTH OF **CARE** AND EMOTIONAL **presence** can sometimes lead to *challenges*. Awareness of these **patterns** allows for deeper *integration*:

- **Exhaustion from over-giving:** Always giving can lead to emotional *drain* and *imbalance*.

- **Boundary Struggles:** Difficulty setting clear limits may result in *depletion*, *resentment*, or *absorbing* too much from others.
- **Emotional Stagnation:** The weight of **Water** and **Earth** can create inertia, making it difficult to *adapt*, *release*, or move forward.

Recognizing these **patterns** allows the *Sacred Wellkeeper* to balance their giving nature with **self-care**, establish healthier **boundaries**, and *transform* **emotional** stagnation into **intuitive** *flow* and **renewal**. A simple *grounding* practice, **inhale** deeply, feeling the *steadiness* of the **Earth** beneath you; **exhale**, allowing the **Waters** within to move freely without *overwhelming* the shore, can help restore *equilibrium*.

- Affirmations such as *"I give from a well that is full"* reinforce the *sacred* balance of *nurturing* both self and others.

Just as the *Sacred Wellkeeper* blends **Water** and **Earth** to sustain **life**, their *essence* can be **distilled** into an **alchemical** practice, one that honors the *wisdom* of *cycles*, **replenishes** energy, and *cultivates* deep emotional *connection*.

ELEMENTAL ALCHEMY

- **Water + Water** = *Ocean Essence:* A deep connection to emotional clarity and intuitive flow, offering renewal and depth.
- **Water + Earth** = *Mud Essence:* The stabilizing blend of sensitivity and strength, nurturing growth, healing, and resilience.

This **ritual** connects you to the **nurturing**, **intuitive**, and **grounding** *energies* of your *lineage*. It helps **balance** emotional flow and stability while *cultivating* **self-care**, *Ancestral connection*, and deepened **intuition**. By integrating the fluidity of **Water** and the *solidness* of **Earth** a *sacred* **wellspring** of emotional *wisdom* and **grounded** presence is *created*.

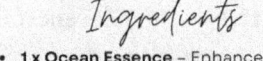

Ingredients

- **1 x Ocean Essence** – Enhances emotional clarity and intuitive flow.
- **1 x Mud Essence** – Grounds emotional energy and nurtures growth.
- **1 x Nurturing** energy - Visualize a flowing, supportive energy enveloping and nourishng you.
- **1 x Compassion** - Envision a gentle, radiant warmth connecting you to your emotional depth and empathy.
- **1 x Intuition** - Feel a subtle yet powerful current of inner knowing guiding your emotions and decisions.

Sacred Wellkeeper
Alchemical Elixir Recipe & Ritual

Instructions

Step 1: Prepare the Space
- Place *symbolic* items representing **Earth** (*Soil and gemstones like Quartz & Malachite*) *and for* **Water,** a bowl of **Water** or even an image of **Water**, like the *Ocean*.
- *Infuse* the space with *scents* like **Clove** and **Frankincense** for *grounding and balance*.

Step 2: Set Intention
- Begin with **Anjali Mudra** – (*palms together at the heart*) - to ground & center, and honor ancestral wisdom.
- Transition to **Jala Mudra** (*Gesture of Water - little finger to the thumb*) – Enhance *fluidity, adaptability*, and emotional receptivity.
- **Honor your** *ancestors*: Speak their names aloud or hold their presence in your ***heart***.
- Invite their **intuitive, nurturing** and **stabilizing** *essences* into your **ritual** space.

Recite:
"I honor the nurturing wisdom, deep intuition, and grounding strength of my ancestors. I call upon their guidance as I create balance, harmony, and clarity within myself and my life."

Step 3: Embodiment Practice
  1. **Warm Up**
- *Awaken the body with gentle movements and breath to prepare for integration.*
  2. **Elemental Breath & Movement:**
- *Choose* breath & *movement* practices from the **Ocean** and **Mud essences** to deepen connection.
  3. **Chakra Focus:**
- Activate the **Root Chakra** (*Muladhara*) *stability* & **Earth** *connection*, **Sacral Chakra** (*Svadhithana*) *creative expression & emotional adaptability*, and the **Heart Chakra** (*Anahata*) for *openess and connection.*

→ REFER TO **PGS 206 AND 224** FOR ADDITIONAL PRACTICES, *poses, breathwork, and correspondences related to Ocean & Mud Essences.*

4. Suggested Embodiment Shapes / Poses:
- **Butterfly Pose** (Baddha Konasana) – Encourages emotional **openness** and relaxation.
- **Wide-Legged Forward Fold** (*Prasarita Padottanasana*) – **Grounds** energy while allowing *introspection* and emotional *release*.
- **Half Pigeon Pose** (Eka Pada Rajakapotasana) – *Opens the hips and sacral area, releasing stored emotions and cultivating deep* **connection**.

5. Dance & Intuitive Movement:
- *Move intuitively, flowing between gentle, fluid movements and deep, grounded stances.* **Embody** *the qualities of* **Water's** *adaptability and* **Earth's** *stability.*
- Explore movements that mimic the rolling of **waves** or the stillness of deep **Waters**, allowing your body to express the **rhythm** of *wisdom* and *resilience*.

Step 4: Astrology & Body Awareness
- Use your *MoonTree Chart* to explore *Ancestral astrological* body correspondences and *imprints.*
- Use **breath**, **visualization** and focused **movement** to enhance the energetic link.
  Lunar Phase:
- Align the **ritual** with a significant *Lunar* phase or *Ancestral* date (e.g. birthday or passing) to *align* with **grounding**, **intuition**, **self-care** and **connection** energies of your *lineage.*

Step 5: Reflection & Writing
- Meditation / journaling.
- Reflect on how your *ancestors* embodied the **Earth** and **Water** *elemental* energies.
- Practice automatic writing, receive *intuitive* messages around these *elemental* themes.

Step 6: Ancestral Offering
- Offer flowers or flower *essences* aligned with the **Sacred Wellkeeper:**
  - **Yarrow** (*Water*) – Supports emotional healing and **intuition**
  - **Lady's Mantle**(*Water*) – Encourages **protection** and deep emotional wisdom
  - **Primrose** (*Earth*) – Grounds and **nurtures** resilience
  - **Angelica** – Compassion and spiritual **connection**
  - **Chamomile** – Provides grounding, **soothing** energy
  - **Lavender** – Enhances **intuition** and inner peace
- Light a **candle** to honor the *nurturing* and *intuitive* strength of your *lineage*:
"*This flame honors the Ancestral Waters, and the Earth holding memories. I invite your guidance, nurturing care and grounded, intuitive essences*"

Step 7: Closing
- Offer **gratitude** for the *energies* and support received.
- Feel / Sense the *resonance* of **Water** and **Earth** within.
- Let the **ritual** integrate & carry the *essence* of the *Sacred Wellkeeper*, into your daily **life.**

Closing Reflection

The *Sacred Wellkeeper* **ritual** connects you to the **nurturing**, **intuitive**, and **grounding** energies that flow through your *lineage*. Although the specific details of your *ancestors*' lives may be unknown, their **care**, **resilience**, and profound *wisdom* reside within you. The *elemental* **pattern** revealed through your *MoonTree Chart* illustrates their energetic legacy. By aligning with these *elements*, you honor their memory and awaken your capacity for **balance**, **compassion**, and **intuitive** *wisdom*.

▽ ▽ ▽

---

* FIRE SAFETY: *WHEN WORKING WITH CANDLES AND incense, practice caution*

Part Five

WE ARE THE ANCESTORS OF THE FUTURE

THE RESPONSIBILITY OF LINEAGE

Beyond the
MoonTree Chart

*A*s future *ancestors*, we hold the *sacred* responsibility of shaping a *lineage* that will echo through time. Every choice we make *plants* **seeds**, **stories**, **values**, and **energies** that will take *root* in those who come after us. We are not only **recipients** of what has been, but **stewards** of what is, and **architects** of what will be. *Lineage* is not bound solely to blood. It is a **living elixir** crafted from our lived *experiences*, the *wisdom* we **distill**, and the *transformations* we **embody**. It flows through the choices we make, the **rituals** we tend, and the **healing** we allow. We are shaped not only by the *ancestors* of our bloodline, but also by the land we inhabit. The **Ancestors of Place**, those who **lived**, **loved**, and **cared** upon these lands long before us, those who continue to whisper through the **rivers**, **trees**, and **stones**. The **Earth** itself holds **sediments** of **memory**, **ritual**, and **resilience**. Beneath our feet are layers of **story** waiting to be *acknowledged*.

To walk with reverence is to honor these **UNSEEN** *forces* to recognize that the **elixir** of becoming is already **infused** with their *presence*. Every step is part of the **alchemical** process. Every breath is a chance to **remember**.

Living as
Future Ancestors

Creating a meaningful legacy begins with *cultivating* **love** and *transformation*, the *sacred* **alchemical** process of turning inherited **sediments** into something **life-giving**. By confronting *Ancestral* wounds, dissolving *cycles* of suffering, and *nurturing* **resilience**, we refine the **raw**

ingredients of the **past** into an **elixir** that *nourishes* what lies ahead. This journey is not about *perfection*, it is about **intention**. It is about living the values we wish to pass on. Every **story** we tell, every **healing** we invite, and every act of **love** we choose contribute to this **alchemy**. The **elixirs** we **craft** are not just for our direct *descendants*, but for **all** who will walk this **Earth** after us. Through **empathy, kindness,** and **connection,** our *essence* weaves itself into the greater **human story,** both within our *lineage* and in the **collective** field of existence. A true inheritance is not held in objects or accolades. It lives in the *energies* we transmute, the wounds we **heal,** the **love** we **embody.** The treasures we pass down are *subtle* yet **powerful:** the *courage* to feel deeply, the grace to **forgive,** the *wisdom* to live with *reverence.* To offer a *lineage* **infused** with **resilience, creativity,** and **compassion** is to gift the world with a living elixir—one **potent** enough to dissolve the griefs of the **past** and *seed* new *possibilities.*

To live as a future ancestor is to walk this alchemical path with *open* **eyes** and *open* **heart.** We take the **sediments,** the **grief,** the **stories,** the **unspoken** wounds, and through **presence, practice,** and **purpose,** we *transmute* them into something **medicinal** and **magical.**

Something Whole.
Something Beautiful.
Something that Lasts.

THIS IMPORTANT TASK **URGES** US TO ACT THOUGHTFULLY, TO craft the *legacy* we will eventually pass on:

- **Healing Cycles** – Acknowledge the **residue** of pain, trauma, and silence in your family. With focused *presence* and *intention*, turn them into sources of *strength, wisdom,* and *renewal.*
- **Nurturing Wisdom** – Pass down the **distilled** *essence* of your lived experience, *stories, rituals,* and *insights—*so future *generations* inherit the *ingredients* they need to craft their *elixirs* of *resilience.*
- **Embodying Values** – Live the principles you long to see *flourish.* Let your *integrity, compassion, creativity,* and *courage* become *potent* **infusions** in the legacy you are weaving.
- **Cultivating Connection** – Shape an **elixir** that nourishes the threads between *humanity,* **Earth,** and *Spirit,* leaving the collective field more whole.
- **Honoring the Ancestors of Place** – Acknowledge the land as a *sacred alchemical* **vessel,** alive with memory. By tending to it with reverence, you participate in the great work of *balance, reciprocity,* and *rooted* stewardship.

Reflections

TAKE TIME TO REFLECT ON YOUR ROLE AS A FUTURE ancestor. Breathe into the awareness that you are already crafting the elixir that will be passed down through memory, energy, and action.

ASK YOURSELF

1. **What ingredients will you offer** to the elixir of future generations? What values, stories, and energies will infuse your legacy?

2. **What sediments**, old *patterns*, inherited wounds, or burdens are ready to be transmuted into *wisdom*, strength, and healing?

3. **How can you honor the land beneath you**, recognizing its *Ancestral* memory and energetic presence as part of your extended *lineage*?

4. **What conscious choices can you make today** to *cultivate* a legacy that *nourishes*, *heals*, and *inspires* those who will one day walk in your footsteps?

A Sacred Opportunity

Each moment offers us the chance to refine the *elixir* of our *legacy*. By living with *intention*, *presence*, and **heart**, we step into the *sacred* responsibility of becoming **future ancestors**, not just in *name*, but in *energy*, *action*, and **remembrance**. Participating in the great alchemy of existence. To contribute to a future shaped by *wisdom*, nourished by **love**, and *transformed* by **conscious** care. Let us move forward with **grace**, **gratitude**, and **devotion**, crafting a heritage that reflects the *interwoven* beauty of our *presence*. A legacy poured into our relationship with *land*, *lineage*, the *unseen*, and the *ever-unfolding* **story** of **life** itself.

Through this *sacred* **alchemy**, we *weave* a **future** where our *essence* continues to **ripple** outward, an *elixir* of **light** carried through **time**, whispering: *"We were here, and we walked with love."*

Our legacy does not only encompass the stories we lived or the wisdom we gathered-but the healing we embraced. the beauty we shared. and the love we infused into the world

INTEGRATION & EMBODIMENT

Living the Ancestral Alchemical Path

*I*ntegration is the *sacred* act of weaving *Ancestral mysticism* into the fabric of our daily lives. **Embodiment** transforms this *connection* from concept into lived experience, allowing the guidance of our *lineage* to shape how we move, feel, choose, and create. This alchemy of remembrance becomes a rhythm: subtle, potent, and deeply personal. But our lineage extends beyond bloodlines. We are also shaped by the *Ancestors of Place*, the spirits of the land, the beings who once tended and lived upon it, and the **Earth** herself. The land holds memory. It speaks through stones, rivers, trees, and wind. Honoring these subtle voices is part of the *elixir*, helping us walk with **reverence**, **reciprocity**, and right **relationship**. Each step becomes an act of **alchemy**, blending the *mystical* with the *practical*, and the unseen with the embodied. Through daily *rituals*, *movement*, and *creative* expression, we attune to the *sacred* frequencies of our *lineage* and the living **Earth**.

Alchemy in Motion:
Daily Practices for Integration

Every relationship with ancestral healing is unique. These practices are not prescriptions, but invitations, tools to explore, refine, and infuse your own sacred rhythm.

HERE ARE THE WAYS I RETURN TO THE ELIXIR:

- **Ancestral Connection** - Begin each day with a gesture of acknowledgment: light a candle, whisper a name, breathe with an object tied to your lineage or the land. Let it be a thread of continuity.

- **Breathwork & Movement** - Use intentional breath, ecstatic dance, Kundalini yoga, or somatic flows to awaken and move ancestral energy through the body.
- **Cooking with Intention** - Prepare ancestral recipes or intuitively crafted meals. Stir gratitude into each bite. Before eating, offer thanks to the Earth, your ancestors, and the spirits of place.
- **Honoring the Land** - Learn about the original stewards of the land you live on. Offer Water, herbs, or prayer. Listen to the land's stories.
- **Gratitude as Ritual** - Let gratitude become a daily ceremony. Thank the seen and unseen forces shaping your journey, gifts, lessons, and experiences.
- **Journaling & Storytelling** - Record dreams, patterns, messages. Write family stories or letters to ancestors. Bring the hidden into the light.
- **Seasonal & Lunar Attunement** - Align with the Moon, solstices, and equinoxes to deepen your ancestral timing. These cycles once guided your ancestors, and they still speak.
- **Flower Essences & Plant Allies** - Work with flowers that mirror the elemental signatures in your lineage. Let their spirits support gentle, emotional, and energetic shifts.

RITUALS FOR CONNECTION & GROWTH

Rituals are vessels of alchemy, containers for integration, transformation, and sacred witnessing. They help us bring the ineffable into form.

BELOW ARE SOME EXAMPLES

- **Seasonal Celebrations** - Create altars and offerings for the turning of the year. Let nature's rhythms guide your own.
- **Lunar & Solar Work** - Moon circles, Solstices and Equinoxes.
- **Rites of Passage** - Birthdays, anniversaries, deaths, and rebirths, honor them as sacred thresholds in your lineage.

- **Creating a Sacred Altar** - Build a space that pulses with Ancestral presence. Include candles, elements, symbols, and offerings. Let this be a touchstone for your daily devotion.
- **Healing Through Story** - Speak the names. Tell the tales. Reclaim silence. Each story is a thread in your lineage's evolving myth.
- **Time in Nature** - Walk slowly. Listen to the wind. Sit by the Water. Let the land remember you as you remember it.
- **Plant Spirit Work** - Choose flowers aligned with your lineage's elemental makeup, let them soften, support, and stir the sacred within.

WALKING THE PATH OF *ANCESTRAL EXPLORATION* MEANS *embodying* the *elixir*, blending **Earth** and *cosmos*, **ritual** and *rhythm*, **shadow** and *light*. It is a **life** of *sacred* **weaving**, where we tend to inherit stories and **choose** what **grows** next. Through these practices, we become the *bridge*: honoring what **was**, healing what **is**, and dreaming what will **be**. We **align** with the *rhythms* of our *ancestors* and of the **Earth**, letting both our **rootedness** and our *curiosity* guide us forward.

This is the work of the Alchemist.
It is Creative.
It is Embodied.
It is Life.

ENRICHING THE ANCESTRAL ELIXIR

Integrating Planetary Energies and Numerology

*E*xploring *ancestry* is both about **remembering** and about **resonating**. A living *pulse* within *cosmic* **patterns, numbers,** and *subtle* **vibrational** *threads* of time. These *imprints* speak of **destiny, transformation,** and inherited *essence*. **Planetary** *energies* and *numerology* **unlock** a deeper understanding of recurring themes, *spirit* agreements, and *energetic* **codes,** both *personal* and *Ancestral*. These tools **refine** our **Ancestral Elemental Elixir,** the unique *wisdom, healing,* and *creative* power we **embody** and share.

PLANETARY ENERGIES IN THE LINEAGE

Each **planet** *embodies* unique themes, lessons, gifts, and challenges woven into your family's history. When examining your *Moon Tree Chart*, observe recurring planetary patterns and how they resonate with your ancestors.

Here are some core planetary *essences* to explore:

PLANET	KEYWORDS	ESSENCE
☿ Mercury	Communication, intellect, adaptability	A lineage of public speakers, writers, quick-witted thinkers, or nervous systems in need of calm.
♂ Mars	Courage, survival, ambition, resilience	A pattern of warriors, survivors, protectors—or deep Ancestral rage seeking resolution.
♃ Jupiter	Expansion, wisdom, abundance, spiritual evolution	The lineage of teachers, seekers, abundance cycles, or spiritual inheritance.
♄ Saturn	Responsibility, discipline, endurance, karmic cycles	Ancestral burdens, long-held vows, or structures passed down through time.

Each planet adds nuance to your *Moon Tree Chart* and *Ancestral elemental* **blueprint**.

NUMEROLOGY & ANCESTRAL PATTERNS

More than mere **symbols**, *numbers* vibrate with meaning. In *Ancestral* work, *numerology* **unveils** hidden *cycles*, **recurring** lessons, and *karmic* **patterns** spanning *generations*. **Decoding** your *Life Path Number* and those of your *ancestors* reveals more **shared** *essences* flowing through your **family** history.

You might find that multiple ancestors share the same Life Path number, or see your own echoed in the past. These shared numbers point to **recurring lessons, sacred callings, and karmic loops** imprinted in your lineage.

HOW TO CALCULATE A LIFE PATH NUMBER

1. Write the full birthdate in **MM/DD/YYYY** format.
2. Reduce each section (month, day, year) to a **single digit** by adding the numbers together.
3. Add those digits together. If the result is **11, 22, or 33**, stop there; these are *Master Numbers*.

EXAMPLE

- Birthdate: **December 25, 1990**
- Month: **12** → **1 + 2 = 3**
- Day: **25** → **2 + 5 = 7**
- Year: **1990** → **1 + 9 + 9 + 0 = 19** → **1 + 9 = 10** → **1 + 0 = 1**
- Final Sum: **3 + 7 + 1 = 11** (Master Number)

NUMBER	ESSENCE
1 (One)	Leadership, innovation, independence
2 (Two)	Diplomacy, sensitivity, balance
3 (Three)	Creativity, joy, self-expression
4 (Four)	Structure, stability, endurance
5 (Five)	Change, adaptability, freedom
6 (Six)	Responsibility, healing, nurturance
7 (Seven)	Spiritual seeking, introspection, wisdom
8 (Eight)	Manifestation, power, resilience
9 (Nine)	Service, transformation, compassion
11 (Eleven)	Intuition, spiritual vision, illumination
22 (Twenty Two)	Sacred architecture, legacy building, grounded transformation
33 (Thirty Three)	Teacher of teachers, embodied healing, divine guidance

Life Path Number Meanings

**Enriching the Ancestral Elixir,
adding layers. To heal, to transform—
across time, space, and Ancestral memory.**

CLOSING REFLECTION

Final Distillation

*R*emembering *That We Are the Elixir.*

The journey into our ancestral roots is a sacred return to the energetic, elemental, and cosmic threads that live within, held by Earth, shaped by stardust, and woven by time. To honor our ancestors is to attune to the celestial patterns imprinted across generations, signatures formed by planetary rhythms, elemental essences, and the memory held in breath and bone. In doing so, we remember that we are the bridge between the cosmos and the Earth, the past and future, the seen and unseen. We are not separate from—we are embodiment embodied. We are alchemists in motion, shaping and being shaped by what we inherit, and by how we choose to meet it. This living alchemy is formed through hearth, heart, ceremony, movement, grief, choice, and change. We become vessels through which memory transforms into meaning. Each breath we take is part of the elemental dance of existence. When we gaze into the mirror of our ancestry, we find medicine. *Encoded within us are the gifts we've inherited, the wisdom we're here to embody, and the patterns we've come to transmute. This is a path of reclamation. Not to erase what was, but to* illuminate *it. To offer healing that extends in all directions, past, present, and future. We are the keepers of flame and memory. Those who collect the broken pieces and create beauty from them. Alchemists of the ordinary. Tenders of the sacred. This is the heart of **Ancestral Alchemology**. A reminder that we are the elixir. And a devotion that shapes a more beautiful world,* within and beyond.

FURTHER EXPLORATION

SUGGESTED READINGS

Books and Online Resources

1. **Parker's Astrology:** The Definitive Guide to Using Astrology in Every Aspect of Your Life – *Julia and Derek Parker*
2. **Astrology for the Soul** – *Jan Spiller*
3. **Astrology and the Authentic Self:** Integrating Traditional and Modern Astrology to Uncover the Essence of the Birth Chart – *Demetra George*
4. **New Moon Astrology:** The Secret of Astrological Timing to Make All Your Dreams Come True – *Jan Spiller*
5. **The Lunation Cycle:** A Key to the Understanding of Personality – *Dane Rudhyar*
6. **The Complete Guide to Lunar Living:** Working with the Magic of the Moon Cycles – *Kirsty Gallagher*
7. **The Moon Book:** Lunar Magic to Change Your Life – *Sarah Faith Gottesdiener*
8. **Honoring Your Ancestors:** A Guide to Ancestral Veneration – *Mallorie Vaudoise*
9. **Astrology and Destiny** – *Liz Greene*
10. **Soul-Centered Astrology** – *Alan Oken*
11. **The Complete Herbal** – *Nicholas Culpeper*
12. **Healing Ancestral Karma:** Free Yourself from Unhealthy Family Patterns – *Dr. Steven Farmer*
13. **It Didn't Start with You:** How Inherited Family Trauma Shapes Who We Are and How to End the Cycle – *Mark Wolynn*
14. **The Wild Edge of Sorrow:** Rituals of Renewal and the Sacred Work of Grief – *Francis Weller*
15. **The Body Keeps the Score:** Brain, Mind, and Body in the Healing of Trauma – *Bessel van der Kolk*
16. **Waking the Tiger:** Healing Trauma – *Peter A. Levine*
17. **Braiding Sweetgrass:** Indigenous Wisdom, Scientific Knowledge, and the Teachings of Plants – *Robin Wall Kimmerer*

18. **Wheels of Life:** An Alchemist's Guide to the Chakra System – *Anodea Judith*
19. **Eastern Body, Western Mind:** Psychology and the Chakra System as a Path to the Self – *Anodea Judith*
20. **The Sevenfold Journey:** Reclaiming Mind, Body, and Spirit through the Chakras – *Anodea Judith & Selene Vega*
21. **Kundalini Dance:** A Manual for Ecstatic Awakening – *Leyolah Antara*
22. **Maps to Ecstasy:** The Healing Power of Movement – *Gabrielle Roth*
23. **The Subtle Body:** An Encyclopedia of Your Energetic Anatomy – *Cyndi Dale*
24. **Llewellyn's Complete Book of Correspondences:** A Comprehensive & Cross-Referenced Resource for Pagans & Wiccans – *Sandra Kynes*
25. **Mudras for Healing and Transformation** – *Gertrud Hirschi*
26. **Sun Signs** (1968) – *Linda Goodman*
27. **Love Signs** (1978) – *Linda Goodman*
28. **Star Signs** (1987) – *Linda Goodman*
29. **Relationship Signs** (1998, posthumously completed by Crystal Bush) – *Linda Goodman*

Online Resources:

Genealogy & Ancestral Research
Ancestry.com
FamilySearch.org

Astrology & Lunar Cycles
Astro-seek.com
Moongiant.com
Astrograph.com

GLOSSARY OF TERMS

A

Alchemical Elixir
A metaphorical blend of ancestral wisdom, elemental energies, and personal practices designed to inspire healing, transformation, and spiritual alignment.

Ancestral Aura
The energetic field carrying the imprints of your lineage's experiences, wisdom, and vibrational patterns. This aura connects past, present, and future energies, supporting healing and resilience.

Aura
A radiant energy field surrounding the body that reflects our physical, emotional, and spiritual well-being. It acts as both shield and mirror.

Ancestral Alchemology
A transformative practice combining genealogy, astrology, and the elements (Fire, Water, Earth, Air) to uncover patterns in family histories, strengthen connection to lineage, and promote healing.

Air
One of the four fundamental elements representing creativity, clarity, and inspiration. Fosters freedom in thought and expression.

Alchemy (Ancestral)
The ancient and spiritual art of transformation—symbolically turning inherited patterns into sacred strengths.

Ancestral Alchemical Potion / Elixir
A symbolic formula created through elemental and astrological energies from the MoonTree Chart. Used to support personal growth and insight.

Astrology
The study of celestial influence on life. In this context, it reveals ancestral and emotional patterns via the Sun, Moon, and Venus.

Ancestor
A person from whom one is descended, whose life and energy influence your own.

Amniotic Sac (Mermaid Birth)
A rare birth in which a baby is born en caul, still enclosed in the unbroken amniotic sac.

Ancestral Healing
The practice of transforming inherited trauma into pathways of growth, strength, and connection.

Ancestral Trauma
Unresolved survival strategies and pain passed through generations, often held in the nervous system.

Ancestral Elemental Archetype
A symbolic blend of inherited strengths and lessons derived from the triple elemental combination of Sun, Moon, and Venus placements.

Ancestral Lens
A way of seeing and interpreting patterns, traits, and zodiac energies through the inherited ancestral line.

B

Body Magic
The sacred integration of astrology, somatics, and embodiment–aligning cosmic wisdom and ancestral energy through movement.

Breathwork
Intentional breathing techniques used to release tension and harmonize prana or life force energy.

Body Awareness
Becoming present to the sensations and stories within the body, where ancestral and elemental imprints may reside.

Birth Chart
A snapshot of the sky at the moment of birth, mapping the positions of planets and their ancestral influence.

Birth Dates
Key temporal markers used to trace patterns and traits in genealogy and astrology.

Brewing (Potion)
The sacred act of combining intention, ritual, and energetic ingredients to form an Ancestral Elixir.

Body Memories
Imprints stored in the body from lived and inherited experience, revealed through somatic exploration.

Birth Locations
The geographical origin of an ancestor, essential for casting their astrological chart.

Body Potion
A SPELLidance™ embodiment journey created with elemental, planetary, or astrological intention. Combines movement, somatics, and ritual into a transformational experience.

C

Chakras
Seven primary energy centers aligned with the spine. Each holds ancestral imprints, offering portals for healing.

Cosmic Parents
The Sun and Moon–celestial guides influencing our rhythm, growth, and internal polarity.

Carl Jung
A psychoanalyst whose work with archetypes and alchemy helped lay the foundation for mystical psychology.

Cosmic Map
A metaphorical guide that links your physical and spiritual self to celestial patterns.

Celestial Archetypes
Sun = vitality and identity, Moon = emotions and cycles, Venus = harmony and heart. These form the foundation of your MoonTree Chart.

Cycles of Life
The repeating seasons of growth, loss, and renewal reflected in both Nature and astrology.

Cosmic Rhythms
The movement of celestial bodies–Sun, Moon, and planets–as they influence ancestral and personal energies.

Cancer (Astrological Sign)
A Water sign linked with emotion, family, protection, and ancestral memory–deeply tied to lineage.

Connection
A core principle of Ancestral Alchemology–bridging self, lineage, nature, and the unseen.

Creativity
A sacred tool of transmutation–turning emotional or ancestral energies into movement, sound, or art.

Core Essence
The life force radiating from the Sun sign–representing the original light within an ancestor.

Cosmic Anchor
The stabilizing energy of the Sun, around which the rest of our chart orbits–offering presence and vitality.

Cosmic Heart Space
Venus's realm of universal love, relationships, and the harmonic resonance of ancestral beauty.

Cosmically Coded
A phrase describing the energetic blueprint passed down through the stars and your lineage–infused in your birth chart and elemental makeup.

D

DNA Testing
A tool for discovering ancestral connections and biological lineage through genetic analysis.

Dual Elemental Combinations
Blends of two elements (e.g., Fire + Water = Steam) used in Ancestral Alchemology to represent hybrid essences and ancestral dynamics.

E

Elemental Energies
The foundational forces–Earth, Water, Air, and Fire–each symbolizing qualities like grounding, flow, clarity, and transformation within the Ancestral line.

Earth
An element representing stability, groundedness, and physical lineage. It governs the body, traditions, and long-lasting structures.

Elemental Archetypes
Ancestral expressions formed through elemental combinations in your MoonTree Chart, reflecting traits, gifts, and lessons.

Elemental Essence
A refined energetic signature formed from two elemental forces (e.g., Lava, Mist), representing an alchemical blend of ancestral influence.

Elemental Magic
The use of natural forces–Earth, Water, Air, Fire–in ritual, movement, and healing to align with ancestral and cosmic energies.

Epigenetics
The study of how environment and experience influence gene expression–central to understanding inherited ancestral trauma and resilience.

F

Flower Essences
Vibrational remedies made from flowers that support emotional balance and energetic healing across ancestral lines.

Family Tree
A diagram representing ancestral relationships, often explored in genealogy to reveal patterns and connections.

Fire Energy
Ancestral boldness, creativity, and resilience–passed down as passion and drive.

Fire
An element of transformation, courage, and purification. It activates passion and ancestral strength.

G

Genealogy
The study of familial lineage used in Ancestral Alchemology to map traits, stories, and elemental patterns.

Grief
A sacred teacher and portal for transformation–connecting us to loss, love, and ancestral remembrance.

Generational Trauma
Patterns of inherited pain passed through family lines, often rooted in survival, silence, or separation.

Gene Activity
How genes express themselves over time–shaped by ancestral experience and environment.

Generational Patterns
Recurring emotional, physical, or spiritual themes within a family system, revealed through MoonTree Chart and rituals.

GeneaLunacy
The mapping of Moon signs across the family tree to reveal ancestral emotional patterns and lunar wisdom.

H

Healing Ancestral Wounds
The act of turning inherited pain into insight through ritual, embodiment, and remembrance.

Heritage
The collection of traditions, beliefs, and energies passed down through your lineage.

I

Inherited Patterns
Tendencies or behaviors passed through generations, forming both challenges and gifts.

Intention
The focused energy behind every ritual and healing practice–activating transformation in your lineage.

Intergenerational Trauma
The compounding effect of trauma passed through multiple generations.

L

Lunar
Connected to the Moon–ruling intuition, cycles, emotional memory, and maternal lineage.

Lineage
The living web of ancestors, energies, and stories you descend from.

Legacy
The energetic and emotional inheritance passed on–both consciously and unconsciously.

Linda Goodman
A foundational figure in modern astrology whose work inspired parts of the MoonTree Chart framework.

Lunar Phases
The Moon's shape in the sky at any time–each phase carries specific ancestral and energetic teachings.

Lineage Archetypes
Symbolic energies that repeat across a family line–seen through zodiac signs and elemental combinations.

M

MoonTree Chart
A unique chart in Ancestral Alchemology using Sun, Moon, and Venus signs across family generations to uncover elemental and archetypal patterns.

Moon Sign
The zodiac sign the Moon occupied at the time of one's birth–reveals inherited emotional traits and rhythms.

Moon (The)
A celestial archetype tied to intuition, emotion, cycles, and ancestral remembering.

Mutable Signs
Gemini, Virgo, Sagittarius, Pisces–flexible signs linked to adaptability and transformation in lineage work.

N

Natal Chart
The astrological snapshot of the heavens at one's birth. A foundational tool for understanding ancestral and personal energy.

Nadis
The subtle energy channels in the body through which life force (prana) flows—Ida and Pingala being the primary lunar and solar pathways.

Near-Death Experience
A threshold moment that inspired the author's connection to Water and deepened the work of Ancestral Alchemology.

Neurotransmitters
Brain chemicals influencing emotion and memory, often impacted by generational trauma.

Non-Biological Connections
Chosen family and adoptive ties that influence your energy and are included in your MoonTree Chart.

Narrative (Family)
The story passed down—shaped by shared beliefs, silence, survival, and love.

P

Pranayama
Breathwork practices that regulate prana, balance energy, and connect to cosmic and ancestral rhythms.

R

Ritual Cleansing
The use of water, herbs, or sound to release stagnant energy and make space for transformation.

Rituals
Sacred acts of intention used to connect with ancestors, realign with nature, and embody healing.

Reincarnation
The belief in the cyclical return of spirit—suggesting ancestral bonds stretch across lifetimes.

S

Somatics
Body-based awareness practices that uncover and release stored ancestral emotion and memory.

Sediment (Ancestral)
In Ancestral Alchemology, refers to the emotional debris or residue left from generational patterns, often stored in the body.

Solar
Related to the Sun—symbol of vitality, purpose, and outward identity.

Sun Sign
The zodiac sign the Sun was in at birth—represents the core essence of both you and your ancestors.

Sun (The)
A celestial archetype embodying light, confidence, and expression. Seen as the life-force or vital fire.

Spiritual Wildcrafting
The art of harvesting wisdom from experience—gathering insight from both shadow and light.

T

Transformation
The sacred alchemical act of turning inherited pain into empowerment, grief into wisdom, and memory into magic.

Triple Elemental Combination
The unique blend of Sun, Moon, and Venus elements forming your archetypal lineage elixir.

W

Wildcrafting
The ritual of gathering what life offers—whether herbs, memories, or emotions—and turning it into healing.

Z

Zodiac (The)
The twelve-sign astrological wheel, each sign offering specific energies that weave into your ancestral and personal chart.

ACKNOWLEDGMENTS

I poured my heart into this book. As author, editor, formatter, illustrator, and publisher of **ELIXIR**, I've undertaken a deeply personal and sacred journey.

With that said, I did not walk it alone.

Kam Bains, thank you for the amazing cover design and your patience with my process. **Gen**, thank you for calming my doubts and believing in my ability to finish. **Family**, your love, support, and patience throughout this long journey mean the world. **Ancestors**, known and unknown, named and unnamed, thank you for flowing through me. This book echoes your rhythm, resilience, and mystery. **Earth, Moon**, and **Stars**, thank you for guiding me through each cycle, teaching me to trust timing and quiet. And to you, **dear reader**, thank you for joining me on this path of remembrance. May **ELIXIR** and the exploration of *Ancestral Alchemology* find you exactly where you are.
With all my heart,
Stay **Magical**,

Gisella Rose

Gisella Rose is an *artist, sacred embodiment practitioner, ritualist*, and guide whose work explores the intersection of *movement, memory*, and the *unseen*, using the body as a *vessel* for healing, connection, and transformation. Drawing on her background in professional *genealogy, sacred* and *mystical arts,* and somatic exploration, she developed *Ancestral Alchemology*, a unique method that weaves together astrology, genealogy, ritual, and embodiment into a grounded practice of *Ancestral* connection and healing. This approach invites individuals to explore *lineage* patterns, work with *elemental* energies, and tap into the wisdom that resides within their *bodies*. Her journey began with *dance* at the age of four, progressing through the Royal Academy of Dance curriculum and culminating in over a decade as a *Circus Sideshow* and *Body Artist*. Blending this experience with yoga and dance, her embodiment work evolved into *SPELLidance* and *SOMAmagical*, unique *Body Potion* practices guiding others through *mystical* embodiment using *somatic* exploration, *astrology*, and the rhythms of the *Moon, Earth*, and *Stars*. This embodied research, *Ancestral* study, and creative practice culminated in **ELIXIR**, her debut book, a deeply personal work, yet also a shared resource for exploring *lineage, memory*, and *transformation*. Through her online platform, **SOMAmagical**, *Gisella* offers classes, workshops, and immersive experiences supporting others in reclaiming *Ancestral* wisdom and reconnecting to their *elemental* nature, inviting them to **"wildcraft their mystery and Wake Their Magic."**

If you enjoyed this book, or have any questions:

LEAVE A REVIEW   ALL MY LINKS   WORK WITH ME   INSTAGRAM

www.somamagical.com